Ministry with Youth in Crisis

Ministry with Youth in Crisis

Harley Atkinson

Religious Education Press
Birmingham, Alabama

The paper in this book meets the guidelines for permanence and durability of the Committee on Production Guidelines of the Council on Library Resources.

Library of Congress Cataloging-in-Publication Data

Atkinson, Harley.
Ministry with youth in crisis / Harley Atkinson.
    Includes bibliographical references and indexes.
    ISBN 0-89135-099-3 (pbk. : alk. paper)
    1. Church work with teenagers. 2. Teenagers—United States.
I. Title
BV4447.A85   1997   96-45209
269'.23–dc21   CIP

Religious Education Press
5316 Meadow Brook Road
Birmingham, Alabama 35242-3315
10 9 8 7 6 5 4 3 2

Religious Education Press publishes books exclusively in religious education and in areas closely related to religious education. It is committed to enhancing and professionalizing religious education through the publication of serious, significant, and scholarly works.

PUBLISHER TO THE PROFESSION

Contents

Tables and Figures

Preface

In the early 1980s, I was a youth pastor in a mid-sized church in Western Canada. The teenagers that I came in contact with over the few years I was there struggled with typical adolescent issues: career choice, difficulties with parents, peer pressure, indifference to the church, and so forth. Yes, we had our moments, like the time a couple of the boys came to a youth function with alcohol on their breath. But, for the most part, the teenagers I encountered were interested in spiritual matters, were cooperative, and were reasonably well-behaved.

A decade later, I did volunteer youth work in a small congregation and the issues I encountered were much different: open rebellion and insolence, severe family dysfunction, sexual molestation, and trouble with the law. I am not so naive as to think that these things did not occur prior to the 1990s, nor do I believe that all youth today are engaging in at-risk behaviors or encountering crises that threaten their well-being. But the two contrasting experiences do illustrate the fact, in my mind at least, that life is considerably more difficult, dangerous, and complex for teenagers today than it ever has been.

The stress, struggles, and crises that characterize the lives of contemporary youth make the task of the youth religious educator much more difficult as well. This book is designed to be a source of help for the youth worker who is working with teenagers in crisis. It is both descriptive and prescriptive. It is descriptive in that it seeks to portray the problems and critical issues facing contemporary youth. It is prescriptive in that it endeavors to provide strategies and procedures for providing religious education to youth in crisis.

I am grateful to a number of individuals who have made the writing of this book a possibility. James Michael Lee, my publisher and editor, in his meticulous and thorough critique of my rather rough original manuscript has taught me much about writing.

Appreciation is offered to Jon Harris and Don Ratcliff, my colleagues at Toccoa Falls College, for their insights and suggestions for improvement. I am especially grateful to Suzanne Rich for her careful editing of the manuscript. I want to express my deepest gratitude to my wife, Shirley, and my daughters, Sarah and Hannah, for allowing me to spend many hours at my computer and in my office, even to the point of agreeing to shorten a summer trip.

Finally, I am indebted to a man who was my first adult youth leader. In the days when full-time professional youth ministers were rare, Bob Davidson took it upon himself to shepherd the teenagers in our small church in Vernon, British Columbia. Without any formal training in youth ministry and with little understanding of adolescent development, theories of learning, or strategizing for long-term effectiveness, he positively impacted the lives of many teenagers. With an obvious love for youth, a sincere desire to serve God, and a down-to-earth ability to relate to teenagers like Dennis, Joe, Walter, Janice, Jim, June, Doug, Jake, and me, Bob assisted us through the turbulent years of adolescence and helped prepare us for adulthood. To Bob Davidson and countless other volunteer youth workers who often receive little recognition for their labors, I dedicate this book.

1

Youth in Crisis

Jeremy is 16 years old and will be graduating in another year. For some time, he has been considering his future and what he will do upon finishing high school. His parents want him to go to medical school and become a doctor like his father, but Jeremy has a strong desire to go to Bible college. Jeremy has always been a good kid and has never given his parents any serious problems. But recently, discussions have become heated over this issue, and relations have been strained between Jeremy and his parents.

• • •

James is 17 years old and dropped out of school when he was 15. Although he has a good mind, school always bored him, and he was a constant source of trouble and concern to his teachers. Over the past year, James has run away from home twice, been kicked out once, and most recently had a minor run-in with the law. James is from a good Christian home, and his parents are left wondering what went wrong.

• • •

It was a year ago today that Brandon's father took a .22 rifle, went out to the barn, and took his own life. Brandon comes from a family with a long history of farming, but in recent years farming has not been good to them. After three straight years of failed crops and significant financial losses his father could take no more. For several days now Brandon has been in a state of depression as he is reminded of his father's suicide and the possibility that his

1

family could lose their farm. As he stares at the closet where his own gun is stored, he wonders if suicide is not the best alternative for him as well.

• • •

By age 11 Joni was already talking about her weight and looks. As she moved into her early teen years, she became increasingly conscious of her appearance and desired to have the body and looks of the models in the teen magazines she so admired. While family and friends insisted she was not overweight, perhaps even a little thin, she felt she was fat and ugly. In the past year her dieting has become more intense. Her weight has dropped far below normal, and her mother cannot get her to eat on a regular basis.

• • •

Brad is 13 years old and has just begun junior high school. He had been excited, though slightly nervous, about moving up to junior high and his parents had anticipated no major problems with this significant change in his life. But after three days of classes, Brad was dragging his feet and showing resistance to going to school. Finally, the issue came to a confrontation, and Brad ran to his room crying, insisting he would never go back to that school. Sensitive and insightful probing by his father revealed that Brad was in a P.E. class that required the boys to shower after class. Changing and sharing the shower with twenty other boys frightened and intimidated the shy and body sensitive boy. The fact that some of the bolder and more aggressive boys teased the others and made crude jokes about the body made it especially difficult for Brad.

What is common to the above scenarios? In each case, the teenager is experiencing a crisis or a crisis situation. It might be something as common as a confrontation with a parent or as serious as an attempted suicide. There is no limit to the number of crises adolescents can experience: separation or divorce of parents, failing a class at school, getting kicked out of school, witnessing a drive-by shooting, deciding on a career, experiencing an unwanted pregnancy, undergoing an abortion, losing a part-time job, or moving to a new town and school. The list can go on and on. And all the research and statistics indicate that in every area of life, adolescents and their families are experiencing more crises in their lives than did any previous generation. Youth religious education in the 1990s and into the next millennium will mean, more than ever before, working with adolescents who are experiencing crises of various sorts. Unfortunately, many youth workers, whether volunteer or professional, are ill-equipped to deal with the critical issues today's adolescents are faced with. This book is designed to help prepare the religious educator of youth to better assist members of a troubled generation to successfully survive the turbulent and stressful years of adolescence.

WHAT IS A CRISIS?

The notion of crisis became especially apparent in popular developmental literature of the 1970s. Gail Sheehy's best-seller *Passages* created tremendous public interest in its description of developmental crises or passages through predictable life events.[1] Shortly after, Roger Gould likewise described the predictable crises and changes in adult life in his popular book *Transformations.*[2] Perhaps the most definitive book related to developmental crises across the life cycle was Daniel Levinson's *Seasons of a Man's Life.* In this research publication Levinson made popular the phrase *male mid-life crisis* and suggested that a man experiences a crisis when he finds his current life structure intolerable, yet seems unable to construct a better one. In a severe crisis life itself is threatened, and he experiences the danger of chaos and dissolution, and the loss of hope for the future.[3]

The popular works of the 1970s, however, were preceded by the theoretical study of life-cycle development by Erik Erikson. Erikson proposed eight stages of life, each presenting a new challenge or crisis. His theory assumed that each stage of life is characterized by turning points or crises.

Erikson's concept of *identity crisis* is considered critical to the understanding of adolescent development. He originally used the term to describe the breakdown of inner controls of psychiatric patients. The phrase was eventually used by other psychologists to describe adolescents when similar characteristics were found in young people

---

1. Gail Sheehy, *Passages* (New York: Bantam, 1974).
2. Roger Gould, *Transformations* (New York: Simon & Schuster, 1978).
3. Daniel J. Levinson et al., *The Seasons of a Man's Life* (New York: Ballantine, 1978), 58.

who suffered disturbances and conflict. For Erikson, a crisis does not mean catastrophe or complete breakdown, but rather a critical period when the individual must move one way or another, and when one's view of himself or herself is no longer appropriate to the life changing setting.[4]

James Fowler is a widely regarded researcher in the psychology of religion and is best known for his theory of faith development. Building on the works of Jean Piaget, Erikson, and Lawrence Kohlberg, he describes life crises as challenges and disruptions that bring disequilibrium or imbalance to one's life, and therefore require changes in the ways of seeing and being. These crises can result in growth and development, as change of some sort is required.[5]

For developmentalists, a crisis is a turning point, the result of a struggle or threat to one's emotional security or physical safety. But it can bring opportunity for growth or change, as well as danger or destruction. Norman Wright says when doctors talk about a crisis, they are referring to the point in the course of a disease when a change for better or worse occurs. When counselors talk about a marital crisis, they are speaking of turning points when the marriage can go either way.[6] Thus an individual experiencing a crisis can never assume to remain static. Gary Collins gives a simple and straightforward definition of "crisis" as any event or series of circumstances which endanger a person's well-being and hinder his or her daily routine of living.[7]

Crises that teenagers experience might be considered as one of two types: situational or developmental. *Situational crises* are precipitated by traumatic events that have a significant impact on the teenager's life: the loss of a loved one, the breakup of a relationship, parents' divorce, moving to a new city and school, becoming pregnant, getting raped, or being involved in an accident. Usually crises of this nature occur with little or no warning, catching the adolescent totally off guard. The chief characteristics of situational life crises may be summarized as follows:
• *Sudden onset:* they seem to strike from nowhere.
• *Unexpectedness:* few adolescents prepare for or believe that these crises will happen to them.

---

4. Erik H. Erikson, *Identity, Youth and Crisis* (New York: W. W. Norton, 1968).
5. James W. Fowler, *Stages of Life* (San Francisco: Harper & Row, 1981), 100–101.
6. H. Norman Wright, *Crisis Counseling* (Ventura, Calif.: Regal, 1993), 20.
7. Gary R. Collins, *How to Be A People Helper* (Santa Ana, Calif.: Vision House, 1976), 71.

• *Emergency quality:* many situational crises threaten physical or psychological well-being.
• *Danger and opportunity:* while danger may be the watchword of situational crises, some sort of reorganization or recovery must eventually begin. Since these events call for coping and resolve to overcome the adversity, it is possible for an individual to emerge from the crises better equipped to face life in the future.[8]

Developmental crises tend to be a natural or expected part of growing, or going through transitions: gaining independence from parents, developing peer relationships, dating, undergoing pubescent changes, and entering high school.[9] In each case the teenager reaches a stress point where the demands push the individual close to or beyond the limit of being able to cope effectively. However, developmental crises often cause less pain and anxiety than situational crises because they are generally predictable. In some cases or for some adolescents, the coping mechanisms continue to function well during developmental crises; in other cases special support and help are necessary. The common theme in developmental crises is that the precipitating events are strongly embedded in the life maturation process.[10]

Again, there is a positive side to experiencing crises. The Chinese word for crisis involves two characters or meanings: danger and opportunity. In a similar manner, the Greeks' word for crisis means a decision-making time that could turn out for better or for worse. A crisis is dangerous because an individual may not be able to cope effectively with the situation in a positive manner. It is an opportunity because in crisis situations people are given an occasion, or are even forced, to grow and change. The youth religious educator is in an ideal position to help adolescents turn crises, or what appear to be negative situations, into opportunities for transformation and spiritual growth.

UNDERSTANDING ADOLESCENCE

Before any effort is made to address the critical issues that adolescents encounter, a discussion of the psychology of adolescence is in order. Adolescence is a transitional stage of life where the individual is considered to be neither child nor adult. Unfortunately, the boundaries

---

8. Karl A. Slaikeu, *Crisis Intervention* (Boston: Allyn and Bacon, 1990), 64–93.
9. G. Keith Olson, *Counseling Teenagers* (Loveland, Colo.: Group, 1984), 282–283.
10. Slaikeu, *Crisis Intervention,* 42.

for adolescence are unclear, and in contemporary Western culture there is no single rite of passage that defines entry into this phase, nor are there identifiable criteria that clearly signal an exit from adolescence.

The term adolescence is derived from the Latin word *adolescere,* meaning to grow into maturity. It is a critical period of human development lying between childhood and adulthood, ranging anywhere from age 12 to 20 or 21. The beginning of adolescence is often identified with the onset of puberty, which for a girl begins with her first menstruation and for a boy, his first ejaculation. The average age of menarche (first menstrual period) is about 12.5; boys reach puberty approximately two years later.

When adolescence ends is not so easily determined. A number of criteria or elements, however, help signal termination.

• *Legally:* reaching the age of majority. In the United States this is 18 years of age.

• *Biologically:* when physical maturity is achieved; when the teenager is finished growing.

• *Socially:* when the teenager has successfully passed through certain social institutions. Finishing high school and gaining economic and emotional independence from parents are two examples of key social transformations.

• *Psychologically:* completing certain developmental tasks such as achieving identity and gaining skills for coping with demands of society.

Unfortunately, the existence of multiple criteria makes it difficult to come to a consensus on the completion of adolescence. For example, while a young person may be 18 (the legal age for adulthood), he may live with his parents, have his mother wash his clothes, and not yet have his own bank account. Some observers speak of an extended adolescence where young Americans remain adolescents well into their twenties—not yet willing to make full commitments to the primary social institutions such as vocation, marriage, and family.[11]

Other terms used to describe this transition period are improperly used as synonyms for adolescence. While describing the approximate age group and capturing certain aspects of the concept of adolescence, they sometimes exclude essential qualities or include peripheral connotations. The term *juvenile* is often used for this age span but should

---

11. Hans Sebald, *Adolescence: A Social Psychological Analysis* (Englewood Cliffs, N.J.: Prentice-Hall, 1984), 9.

be limited to matters of law violations and enforcement, for example, juvenile court or juvenile delinquency.[12]

The term *teenager* is perhaps the most popular word used in referring to young people in Canada and the United States. While it refers to a specific age bracket (13 to 19), its connotation suggests a stereotypical behavior that is immature and less valued by the adult population. Sociologist Hans Sebald suggests that the terms *teenager* and *adolescent* are closely related, yet slightly different. Referring to a person as an "adolescent" means that we emphasize the particular time of life between childhood and adulthood. On the other hand, referring to a person as a "teenager" calls attention to age and the tendency to associate with peers and subcultural activities.[13]

The term *youth* is generally used in a broader and nonspecific manner. It refers to the younger generation, including children, teenagers, and young adults.[14] In religious education, however, *youth* ministry generally refers to work done with young people in secondary school.

In this book the three terms *adolescent, teenager,* and *youth* will be used interchangeably, even though each carries with it a slightly different connotation. Unless otherwise noted, each term will refer to young people approximating the ages of 13 to 18.

Developmental Changes

Teenagers are especially vulnerable to crises in that during the adolescent years rapid and dramatic change occurs in so many areas of life. An awareness of these developmental changes can help the youth worker in understanding what adolescence is all about. In turn, the religious educator of youth is better prepared to nurture teenagers through these critical and tumultuous years.

Physical Change: The physical development that an adolescent experiences is second only to that which occurs in the earliest years of life. But while infants are unable to ponder the metamorphosis they are going through, the adolescent has the intellectual capacity to reflect on the changes that are occurring. This awareness of what is happening to the body is often a major cause of anxiety, frustration, and, at times, embarrassment.

---

12. Ibid., 8.
13. Ibid., 10.
14. Ibid., 8.

For both boys and girls, a rapid growth spurt characterizes the preadolescent and early adolescent years, with girls maturing about two years
earlier than boys. For girls their first menstruation, or menarche, marks
the beginning of puberty. Along with menarche, the development of
pubic hair, enlargement of breasts, and widening of hips are among
the physical changes taking place. This rapid growth period for boys is
marked by the emergence of facial and pubic hair, voice deepening, and
the enlargement of the testes and penis.

Physical development can be the source of much worry, anxiety, and
frustration to teenagers, especially if there is delayed development or
unusual spurts of growth. Problems such as clumsiness, body odor, acne,
and voice "cracks" are also related to puberty, and are additional sources
of consternation. As the body takes on new shapes and characteristics the
teenager suddenly becomes aware of his or her sexuality. New thoughts,
feelings, and experiences related to sexual maturation often confuse,
frustrate and concern the young adolescent.[15]

Social Change: Coinciding with physical changes are dramatic social
changes. The strong, dependent relationship the preadolescent had with
his or her family begins to change. While still physically dependent
on parents, there is a gradual movement towards peers for emotional
dependence. Parents are still the main source of guidance and support
for moral decisions, but even this pattern shifts, as adolescents assume
more and more personal responsibility for decision making.

Peer relationships will change over the adolescent years as well.
Initially, same-sex relationships will predominate, but gradually interest
in the opposite sex will precipitate more boy-girl relationships. As a
general rule, casual dating and going steady will become increasingly
important but will not totally replace peer group relationships and
friendships. Without proper instruction and supervision, heterosexual
relationships can be the source of sexual crises when temptations and
feelings are allowed to get out of control.

Significant social change also takes place in the school environment. Sixth-graders move from the safe haven of a smaller elementary
school to the much larger and impersonal junior high. Likewise, eighth-

---

15. For additional insights on physical development the reader is referred to Richard M.
Lerner and Nancy L. Galambos, eds., *Experiencing Adolescents* (New York: Garland,
1984), ch. 2; Olson, *Counseling Teenagers,* 24–27.

or ninth-grade students move into the even more threatening senior high school.

Intellectual Change: Cognitive skills are changing as well. Young adolescents move into a stage of life where their thinking capacity becomes more abstract and less concrete. Teenagers can engage in debate with others because their advanced thinking skills allow them to anticipate the arguments of their opponents and prepare in advance to counter them.[16] Abstract thinking skills allow adolescents to imagine the ideal and to compare reality with the imagined world. Usually, reality does not meet the standards of fantasized perfection. As a result adolescents may question or challenge their parents, and may become skeptical of religious beliefs and practices such as prayer or church attendance.

Schoolteachers may also come under the critical eye of the teenager. While children may not like a teacher, they are rarely critical of his or her teaching skills. The adolescent, on the other hand, may be very disparaging of the teacher's competence and knowledge. Toward the middle adolescent years, youth become a little less critical of parents and teachers, and turn their critical eye on government, the church, and other social institutions. They become more concerned with social issues and may criticize other countries and societies as well.[17]

At times the newly discovered thinking skills cause adolescents to challenge almost everything that they previously believed or were taught. They may doubt the existence of God, question the teachings of their church, or reject, or at least seriously challenge, the values and mores they have been brought up with. Such relativistic thinking often creates conflict and interpersonal problems between teenagers and their parents.[18]

A Tumultuous Stage of Life

Many psychologists and researchers have characterized adolescence as an extremely difficult and tumultuous period of one's life. For

---

16. David Elkind, *A Sympathetic Understanding of the Child,* 3rd ed. (Boston: Allyn and Bacon, 1994), 220.

17. Ibid., 224.

18. For an extensive study of adolescents and religious development see Kenneth E. Hyde, *Religion in Childhood and Adolescence* (Birmingham, Ala.: Religious Education Press, 1990).

example, Norm Wright says that for some "adolescence is a time of continual crisis with a few respites in between. For others, their development is a bit smoother. But overall, adolescence is one of the most difficult transitions of life. It is a roller-coaster experience, a time of stress and storm."[19] In reference to this stage of life, psychology professor Ronald Koteskey says Western culture has created a monster and is now having trouble controlling it.[20] At the turn of the twentieth century, American psychologist G. Stanley Hall, the first to write on the psychology of adolescence, characterized these years as *Sturm und Drang*—storm and stress.[21]

The phase of life we now identify as adolescence has always been considered somewhat turbulent. Socrates and Aristotle described youth and young men as having contempt for authority, disrespect for elders and teachers, having strong passions, and thinking they know everything. However, even in the recent past most teenagers were expected to successfully ride out the turbulence of youth relatively unscathed. Certainly there were those who stumbled and fell or in some way became casualties, but they were the exception. Now each generation of adolescents seems to face an increasingly complex, stressful, and confusing world.

Many of the experts who work with youth or those who study and research adolescence and youth culture are concerned about the difficulty many contemporary teenagers are experiencing in getting through this phase of life. One source says, "Unfortunately, too many of our young people are not doing well. Too many are falling by the wayside. In fact, so many are falling away—so many are at risk—that we might conclude that our society itself is at risk."[22] Peter Benson, of Search Institute, an organization that conducts extensive empirical research on adolescents, says, "It is not clear whether growing up now is riskier business than it once was, or whether we are simply doing a better job of naming and counting the problems that have existed before. It does not really

---

19. Wright, *Crisis Counseling,* 228.
20. Ronald L. Koteskey, *Understanding Adolescence* (Wheaton, Ill.: Victor, 1987), 16.
21. G. Stanley Hall, *Adolescence: Its Psychology and Its Relations to Physiology, Anthropology, Sex, Crime, Religion and Education,* vol. 1 (New York: Appleton, 1904).
22. J. Jeffries McWhirter et al., *At-Risk Youth: A Comprehensive Response* (Pacific Grove, Calif.: Brooks/Cole, 1993), 4.

matter. What does matter is that there are too many casualties, too many wounded, too many close calls."[23]

Growing up is clearly a risky business today. Issues such as sexuality, dating, self-image, peer pressure, vocational decisions, school, and parents still typify the worries of teenagers. But a host of new concerns frighten and bring anxiety to many adolescents. The quality of family life is negatively impacting this generation of young people, as a majority of them are growing up in broken homes or dysfunctional families. Child abuse, date rape, AIDS, drive-by shootings, crime, suicide, and substance abuse are a few of the additional issues many of today's youth are confronted with. Furthermore, teenagers are burdened by broader domestic and worldwide issues such as nuclear war, homelessness, and pollution.

Seminary professor Wade Rowatt says, "Perhaps as many as 30 to 50 percent of the current teen population will experience a major crisis before reaching the age of eighteen. They will be hospitalized, appear in court, have major parental conflicts, attempt suicide, abuse alcohol or drugs, drop out of school, get pregnant, pay for or have an abortion, or something else of this magnitude. Many will experience multiple crises!"[24]

A youth pastor in North Carolina also observes that the severity and frequency of youth crises are increasing in this generation. He says the youth "I work with are becoming more sophisticated at an earlier age, so they are dealing with more sophisticated and complex problems. Their crises are dramatic—and often fatal. In my ministry I continually confront crises of teen depression, preoccupation with death, suicidal impulses and families in which a teen suicide has occurred."[25]

Indeed, in a world that is experiencing change and transformation at a breathtaking rate, teenagers are suffering the stressful and often damaging consequences. David Elkind says that contemporary American society has struck teenagers a double blow. It has rendered them

---

23. Peter Benson, Dorothy Williams, and Arthur Johnson, *The Troubled Journey* (Minneapolis, Minn.: Search Institute, 1993), 1.

24. G. Wade Rowatt, *Pastoral Care With Adolescents in Crisis* (Louisville, Ky.: Westminster/John Knox, 1989), 20.

25. These are the words of Tim Condor, a youth pastor at the Chapel Hill Bible Church in North Carolina. He is quoted in Kevin Ford, *Jesus For a New Generation* (Downers Grove, Ill.: InterVarsity, 1995), 18.

more vulnerable to stress, while at the same time exposing them to new and more powerful stresses than were ever faced by youth in previous generations.[26] The same could be said for teenagers in most Western societies around the world.

An Invention of Culture

The transition from childhood to adulthood, argues David Elkind, always takes place in a particular historical and sociocultural context. In many cultures past and present where puberty was or is regarded as a sign of adulthood, adolescence as Western culture understands it, does not exist.[27] Adolescence, the transition between childhood and adulthood, is essentially a cultural invention, more specifically an invention of postindustrial civilization. Prior to the Industrial Revolution, a rapid transformation from childhood to adulthood took place, with no evidence of a stage of life separating the two. Hans Sebald reminds us that teenagers of the Middle Ages often made history at an age when today's adolescents are still going to high school. Edward, the Black Prince, was 16 when he triumphed at the Battle of Crecy in 1346, and Joan of Arc was 17 when she captured Orleans from the English in 1429. Ivan the Terrible was also 17 when he began to make his name as the "Terrible" and had himself crowned czar of Russia in 1547.[28]

With the Industrial Revolution, however, came increasing urbanization and industrialization. With increasing technology there emerged a growing concern and need for formal education and occupational training, which in turn gave rise to new educational institutions. Furthermore, the fact that children were no longer needed in the labor force, coupled with a more humanitarian attitude towards them, led to a series of child labor laws. By 1914, in the United States, almost every state had laws prohibiting the employment of young people below a certain age. In most cases, this age was 14.[29] Individuals who engaged in education and training found themselves in a phase of life that was neither childhood or adulthood.[30]

---

26. David Elkind, *All Grown Up and No Place to Go* (Reading, Mass.: Addison-Wesley, 1984), 6.
27. Elkind, *A Sympathetic Understanding of the Child,* 203.
28. Sebald, *Adolescence,* 12.
29. Elkind, *All Grown Up and No Place to Go,* 20.
30. Sebald, *Adolescence,* 12.

There was at least one more contributing factor to the emergence of the adolescent stage of life. Throughout history, men and women married at much earlier ages, generally around the age of puberty. As recently as two hundred years ago in the United States, men could legally marry at age 14 and women at 12. However, in the last two centuries, while laws increasing the minimal age for marriage to 18 were enacted, the age of puberty was dropping significantly.[31]

So while the age of puberty was decreasing, the minimal legal age for marrying was increased; there was a growing emphasis on education, and labor laws lowered the legal age for working. This was the creation of adolescence—an invention of culture.

A GENERATION AT RISK

Teenagers today are part of a troubled generation—a generation at risk. Consider the statistics below. While they will be expanded on in subsequent chapters, at the moment they serve as a stark reminder of the pressing concerns and critical issues confronting contemporary youth.

• According to the Centers for Disease Control, approximately 54 percent of the students in grades 9–12 have had sexual intercourse. One in four girls is having sex by age 15. The average age for first having sex is 15 for girls and 14 for boys.

• Approximately 1.1 million teenage girls become pregnant each year; about half carry the pregnancy to term. Of girls under the age of 15, 125,000 become pregnant each year.

• Over 2.5 million teenagers contract sexually transmitted diseases (STDs) each year, and rates among adolescents are escalating. Teenagers have more STDs than any other age group.

• While estimates of physical abuse fluctuate wildly, some estimate there are as many as 1.5 million cases per year. Some researchers believe that the incidence of sexual abuse of children of all ages is even greater.

• One of the most disturbing trends in the adolescent subculture is sexual abuse of children by other children, especially teenagers. More than 50 percent of young boys and 20 percent of girls who are sexually abused are molested by teenagers.

---

31. Koteskey, *Understanding Adolescence*, 14–15.

• The rate of suicide for adolescents has quadrupled since 1950. Between 4,000 and 6,000 teenagers a year take their own lives, making it the third leading cause of death for this age group behind accidents and homicides.
• One source cites a figure in excess of 1.5 million runaway and homeless youth annually. Most of these young people get involved with drugs and prostitution.
• Estimates of latchkey children, children who stay at home alone, range from 2 million to 15 million, or 7 to 45 percent of all elementary school children.
• An increasing number of teenage girls suffer from eating disorders. Nearly 5 percent of young women experience anorexia nervosa, while 15 percent have bulimia, the habit of bingeing and purging.
• Young people are experimenting with alcohol, drugs, and tobacco at increasingly early ages. Alcohol is the drug of choice for teenagers. Use of illegal drugs such as marijuana and cocaine has recently declined, but there are indications this trend has either plateaued or is on the rise again.
• School violence is on the rise, not only in inner cities, but the suburbs as well. Nine percent of eighth-grade students carry a gun, knife, or club to school; more than 3 million crimes a year are committed in or near United States schools. Schools are adding "drive-by-shooting" drills, installing metal detectors, and conducting locker searches.

This alarming index of problems tells us the current generation of youth indeed is in crisis, and there is no indication that things will get better. And we might add to this list a number of less dramatic, yet significant issues such as loneliness, depression, hopelessness, boredom, school problems, and family conflict that might be considered normal as one progresses through adolescence.

The term *at risk* emerged in literature in the 1980s in a number of fields such as education, psychology, and medicine. Some have used the term to describe many of today's youth. One source uses *at risk* to denote a set of cause-and-effect dynamics that place the individual child or adolescent in danger of negative *future* events. For example, young people who use tobacco are at risk for alcohol use; teenagers who use alcohol are at risk for illicit drug use.[32] Many of our teenagers—including churched youth—are at risk. That is, they are involved in activity or in situations

---

32. McWhirter et al., *At-Risk Youth,* 6.

that may lead to more destructive behaviors or activities. And many more have already reached the point where their activities and behaviors are harmful in a number of ways.

Factors Contributing To A Generation At Risk

Today the enormity of adolescents' problems and critical issues causes us to question why today's teenagers are experiencing such a difficult time coping with life. Some possibilities are the breakdown of the family, a diminishing role of the church and religion, the education system, and a growing negative influence by the media.

Breakdown of the Family: The family in North America has undergone significant and critical changes in the twentieth century, especially in the last three decades. In the first half of the century the extended family—a familial network of parents, children, grandparents, and perhaps an aunt or uncle—was replaced by the nuclear family. The nuclear family normally consisted of one adult of each sex and five or six children.

Since the 1960s, however, radical changes have taken place in the family structure. Skyrocketing rates of divorce, separation, remarriage, out-of-wedlock births, and single parenting have all contributed to the restructuring and breakdown of the "traditional" American family. Today many teenagers are growing up without the support, nurturance, guidance, and role modeling of parents and other relatives. In fact, empirical studies have estimated that the probability that a child will live with only one parent at some time before he or she reaches the age of eighteen is between 40 and 60 percent.[33]

The quality or lack of quality in family life today is a key contributor to the critical condition of our current youth generation. Children and adolescents need the discipline, security, and affection exhibited in strong families, and when these characteristics are not present, loneliness, alienation, stress, and frustration are likely to emerge. Indeed virtually every risky or destructive behavior including suicide, running away, substance abuse, sexual promiscuity, and violence, can be linked to some degree to the dysfunctional or broken home.

Diminishing Role of Religion: Paralleling the breakdown of the family is the diminishing role of religion and religious institutions in the

---

33. Ibid., 42.

lives of North American adolescents. While teenagers still affirm a belief in God and admit that they have spiritual needs, their involvement in churches and other religious organizations has deteriorated. According to one report, more and more young people are leaving organized religion, and for those that remain, only a small minority experience a life-transforming faith characterized by a strong relationship with God.[34] Another concludes that while the church seems to have garnered a place in the life of teens, it does not play a dominant or even significant role.[35] Kevin Ford, in his analysis of the current generation of young people, observes that youth today tend to be skeptical of institutional religion.[36]

Most young people today are shaping their values and beliefs in the absence of systematic religious instruction in formal settings. Without such religious instruction, they unconsciously embrace attitudes, principles, practices, and ethics that are appealing to self and friends, and those which are proclaimed through music, television, and movies, and modeled by parents or other adults such as teachers. Because religion is no longer one of the dominant guidance systems for developing consciences with convictions, other less positive sources of influence have often come to assume that role.[37]

A Crumbling Public Education System: In addition to the family and church, it has fallen to the school to contribute to the development of the young person. Since the 1960s, however, the public education system has come under fire from many who believe that it is in shambles and is in many ways failing our young people. Numerous studies compare the standardized test scores of American students with those of other countries, with the scores consistently favoring others. While some might charge that these standardized tests are inaccurate measurements of true learning, most would argue that the education taking place in United States schools is far from what it should be, and that the quality has taken a dramatic downswing since the 1960s.[38]

---

34. Eugene C. Roehlkepartain and Peter L. Benson, *Youth in Protestant Churches* (Minneapolis, Minn.: Search Institute, 1993), 5, 7.

35. *Today's Teens: A Generation in Crisis* (Glendale, Calif.: The Barna Research Group, 1991), 12.

36. Ford, *Jesus for a New Generation,* 134.

37. Reginald W. Bibby and Donald C. Posterski, *Teen Trends: A Nation in Motion* (Toronto, Ont.: Stoddart, 1992), 251.

38. See the National Commission on Educational Excellence, *A Nation at Risk* (Washington, D.C.: U.S. Government Printing Office, 1983), 5–6.

Crime is also of concern on the campuses of American high schools. According to a report by *U.S. News and World Report,* about 9 percent of eighth-grade students carry a firearm, knife, or club to school at least once a month, and more than 3 million crimes a year are committed near or in the 85,000 public schools.[39] Students have come to accept the fact that guns, violence, and crime are all part of going to school.

Increasing Influence of Television and Other Mass Media: It would be inaccurate and unfair to suggest that the institutions of the family, church, and public school system have no positive impact on attitudes, values, thought patterns, and behaviors of teenagers. Nonetheless, it is true that the positive influences of these institutions have in many ways been eroded. At the same time, teenagers are increasingly influenced by the mass media, especially television. Sociologist Tony Campolo argues that television dominates the consciousness of young people.[40] Children have watched 5,000 hours by the time they finish the first grade and 19,000 hours by the time they complete high school. By this time the average student will have witnessed 200,000 acts of violence, 40,000 of which are murders.[41] While there is still debate as to the effect of TV on actions and thoughts of viewers, researchers are finally admitting that violence does indeed have an impact on behavior. For example, evidence demonstrates that depicted violence can lead to a short-term rise in aggressive behavior such as getting into fights and disrupting the play of others.[42]

Campolo suggests that television has also rendered real life uninteresting. Its ability to create an environment that is much more exciting than reality makes it difficult for parents to involve their children in family activities. Creating family activities that can compete with television techniques often proves to be a monumental task for parents and youth workers alike.[43]

---

39. Thomas Toch, "Violence in Schools," in *U.S. News and World Report,* Nov. 8, 1993, 31.

40. Anthony Campolo, *Growing Up in America* (Grand Rapids, Mich.: Zondervan, 1989), 74.

41. Cited in an editorial by Mortermer Zuckerman, "The Victims of TV Violence," in *U.S. News and World Report,* Aug. 2, 1993, 64.

42. William Allman, "Science Looks at TV Violence," in *U.S. News and World Report,* July 12, 1993, and Mortermer Zuckerman, "The Victims of TV Violence," 64.

43. Campolo, *Growing Up in America,* 74.

Mass media—television, movies, music—are designed with the intent of shaping and influencing attitudes, values, thinking, and behavior. Adolescents today are exposed, as never before, to varieties of ideologies, values, life-styles, and worldviews, most of which are antithetical to Christian standards. Adolescents who no longer inherit a consistent value system from family, church, and school are, as Peter Benson puts it, cast adrift to make hit-and-miss choices from among a variety of known values and sources.[44]

CONCLUSION

As an invention of a postindustrial, Western culture, adolescence is often a tumultuous and critical period of life. Delaying marriage and career creates a span of life between puberty and adulthood given to preparing for the adult years. While always considered a difficult time of life, adolescence seems to be an increasingly troublesome age span, as teenagers encounter a more complex, stressful, and confusing world. Sociologists and others who work with adolescents speak of a generation in crisis. Many of today's adolescents are in some way at risk, and there is a growing concern in the United States and many other countries about the future status of today's youth.

The institutions that have traditionally contributed to the development and well being of the teenager—family, church, and school—have in many ways failed in recent decades. On the other hand, mass media, especially television, have played a greater role in shaping the values of children and teenagers. Unfortunately, the ideologies and beliefs that young people are receiving challenge traditional values and the teachings of a Judeo-Christian heritage.

The purpose of this book is to assist the youth religious educator in the difficult tasks of ministering to and doing religious education with adolescents in crisis. Each chapter will deal with a specific area of need that contemporary youth encounter.

---

44. Peter L. Benson, "Kids Aren't the Way They Used to Be: Values of America's Adolescents," in Reynolds R. Ekstrom, ed., *Media and Culture* (New Rochelle, N.Y.: Don Bosco, 1992), 116.

2

Who Am I? The Adolescent
Search for Identity

One of the most urgent yet arduous challenges of adolescence is discovering who one is, the task of what psychologists call identity formation. During the formative teenage years young people face the crises of discovering how they fit into society and what roles they will play in life. Identity formation includes the evaluation of the goals, values, and beliefs acquired from one's family, church, school, peers, and other elements of society. It also necessitates the asking of questions such as Who am I? Where did I come from? and Where am I going? with the goals of achieving self-certainty, coming to terms with sexuality and gender roles, developing a system of beliefs and attitudes, and choosing an occupation.

Achieving a sense of personal identity is no doubt a more formidable task for today's teenagers than it has ever been. Until the nineteenth century, technological and societal changes came very slowly, and one's occupation and place in society were often predetermined by class structure or family pursuits. Gender roles were well defined. Men were given the economic responsibilities while homemaking duties fell to the women. This pattern is no longer characteristic of most American families since many wives are in the work force before and after marriage, and after the birth of children. The impact of changing gender roles has affected men as well. In many modern families in which both the husband and wife work, men have come to assume a greater role in child care and other household responsibilities.

Many teenagers experience confusion or uncertainty in regard to sexuality and sexual orientation. Adolescence is the stage of life when sexual changes are most pronounced, and teenagers often experience anxiety over these physical transformations. There may also be some uncertainty with regard to appropriate sexual behavior.

The issue of deciding on and preparing for life vocation represents one of the major developmental tasks of the teenage years. What one does for a living is a public statement of personal identity and a primary source of information in regard to who one is.

Finally, identity development is reflected in the normal course of religious faith development. Adolescence provides a rich and fruitful setting for faith formation as teenagers move from a conformist type of faith that seeks to fulfill the expectations of significant others to one that is entrenched in personal commitments.

This chapter will explore the critical issues and problems related to the adolescent developmental task of identity achievement. It begins by defining and describing identity and identity formation and then addresses the various dimensions related to the achievement of identity such as sexuality, gender roles, vocation, and a faith system.

IDENTITY FORMATION—WHAT IS IT?

The concept of identity as used in current developmental literature and research originates in the work of developmental psychologist Erik Erikson, who proposed eight psychosocial stages of humankind.[1] Erikson's theoretical structure is based on the notion that an individual's personality is shaped by a co-influence of psychological or intrinsic forces (psycho), and societal or extrinsic elements (social) such as parenting and educational opportunities.

His stages begin with the first contacts after birth that lead to trust or mistrust, to the final struggles for integrity or the assuming of responsibility for what one's life is and was. The critical stage of adolescence is characterized by the crisis of identity achievement versus identity diffusion, whereby the individual becomes concerned with self-esteem, as well as societal roles and responsibilities. Simply put, the adolescent

---

1. Erikson's view of the life cycle is presented in Erik H. Erikson, *Identity: Youth and Crisis* (New York: Norton, 1968); *Identity and the Life Cycle* (New York: Norton, 1980); *The Life Cycle Completed* (New York: Norton, 1982).

seeks to understand who he or she is in relationship to the surrounding world.

Erikson suggests that the young person seeking an identity does not go around asking the question Who am I? Nor does the person with a secure sense of identity usually stop to think or to brag about the fact that he or she has achieved it and of what it consists. Rather, it is a more subtle harmonizing of inner resources, traditional values, and opportunities of action. It is derived from a fusing of intrinsic personality processes and extrinsic environmental forces.[2]

The term *identity*, as used in this book, refers to a clearly defined definition of self, a self-definition comprised of beliefs, values, and goals that the adolescent finds personally worthy and to which he or she is unquestionably committed. These commitments are chosen because the goals, values, and beliefs are regarded as meritorious and virtuous of providing direction, purpose, and meaning to life.[3]

In the search for identity most adolescents are apt to go through a crisis or some sort of struggle that includes emotional and mental stress, or a point of challenge that includes the possibility of turmoil.[4] Crisis is essential if an adolescent is going to arrive at a wholesome, integrated sense of identity.

Four Types of Identity Formation

While there have been a considerable number of efforts to study personal identity by means of questionnaires, the most productive effort was done by James Marcia. To further categorize identity formation, Marcia developed an interview technique whereby he was able to identify and describe four identity types of adolescents.[5] These types, or *statuses*, as Marcia calls them, are *identity diffused, identity moratorium,*

---

2. Erik H. Erikson, "Youth and the Life Cycle," in Rolf E. Muuss, ed., *Adolescent Behavior and Society* (New York: Random House, 1971), 259.

3. Adapted from Alan S. Waterman, "Identity in the Context of Adolescent Psychology," in Alan S. Waterman, ed., *Identity in Adolescence: Process and Contents* (San Francisco: Jossey-Bass, 1985), 6.

4. See Les Steele, "Identity Formation Theory and Youth Ministry," in *Christian Education Journal* 9, (Autumn 1988), 91.

5. For a more complete description of Marcia's identity theory see James E. Marcia, "Identity in Adolescence," in Joseph Adelson, ed., *Handbook of Adolescent Psychology* (New York: Wiley, 1980); James E. Marcia, "Development and Validation of Ego Identity Status," in Rolf E. Muuss, ed., *Adolescent Behavior and Society* (New York: Random House, 1971).

identity foreclosed, and *identity achieved.* Each status describes where an adolescent might possibly be in regards to identity formation. According to Marcia, two criteria are necessary for the achievement of a mature identity in youth: *crisis* and *commitment.* The four identity statuses are defined by their positions on these two conceptual dimensions. Crisis has already been described as the struggle or emotional turmoil one goes through in making choices, while commitment refers to the amount of personal investment an individual exhibits in a choice.

Identity-Diffused Youth: In terms of the two criteria, crisis and commitment, the identity-diffused youth are characterized as not experiencing crises and as making no or few commitments. In other words, these adolescents have not thought seriously about goals, values, or beliefs, nor have they made any decisions in those areas. These teenagers, for example, have not chosen an occupation or career, and are little concerned about it. Simply put, identity-diffused adolescents are relatively aimless and uncommitted to any set of goals, values, and beliefs.

Identity-diffused adolescents use a variety of psychological defenses to ward off anxiety caused by an undefined identity. They may engage in intense, immediate experiences such as parties, drugs, and thrills, to provide a "right-now" sensation and enable them to ignore or put off the responsibilities of making commitments and important decisions. Some move from peer group to peer group trying to establish a sense of

Figure 2.1
Types of Identity Formation

IDENTITY DIFFUSION	FORECLOSURE
• Lack of Crisis	• Lack of Crisis
• Lack of Commitment	• Commitment
MORATORIUM	IDENTITY ACHIEVEMENT
• Crisis	• Crisis
• Lack of Commitment	• Commitment

belonging, while others engage in extreme fad behavior to escape the anxiety of meaninglessness. Identity-diffused adolescents are further characterized by a sense of inferiority and alienation, as well as by poor self-concepts. These adolescents are generally less mature than expected or desired in the areas of cognitive skills and emotional development.[6]

How can youth workers help adolescents who are the identity-diffused type? Religious education ministry to these individuals begins by understanding why they tend to be aimless and uncommitted. Identity-diffused youth often come from families that are more rejecting and detached. Often the father is absent through separation or divorce, and the fathers who are at home may not be very encouraging to their teenage children and may show signs of negativity.[7] Consequently, these young people need to be given the opportunity to observe adult youth workers and role models who are, by contrast, accepting, warm, and encouraging.

In looking for religious education procedures that touch teenagers as whole individuals, that shape emotions, perceptions, values, and behaviors in an integrated manner, the youth worker must consider the importance of modeling and learning by imitation.[8] Psychologists note that most of the behaviors, values, and attitudes that people display have been learned, either intentionally or unintentionally, through modeling.[9] However modeling will be especially effective with identity-diffused youth because this type of adolescent may be averse to formal instruction and, again, are in special need of good role models, especially males.

Spontaneous modeling is not planned; rather, it simply happens. In the context of youth ministry, it is the youth religious educator living his or her life before adolescents.[10] Modeling is the youth worker

----

6. See Gerald R. Adams and Thomas Gullotta, *Adolescent Life Experiences,* 2nd ed. (Pacific Grove, Calif.: Brooks/Coles Publishing, 1989), 241.

7. Ibid., 251.

8. Lawrence O. Richards, *A Theology of Christian Education* (Grand Rapids, Mich.: Zondervan, 1975), 80–82.

9. Morris Bigge, *Learning Theories for Teachers,* 4th ed. (New York: Harper & Row, 1982), 163–64; Robert F. Mager, *Developing Attitudes Toward Learning* (Belmont, Calif.: Fearon, 1968), 61–65; Robert F. Biehler, *Psychology Applied to Teaching,* 5th ed. (Boston: Houghton Mifflin, 1986), 317. The acknowledged spokesman for observational learning is Albert Bandura, who presents this theory of learning in *Social Learning Theory* (Englewood Cliffs, N.J.: Prentice-Hall, 1977).

10. Klaus Issler and Ron Habermas, *How We Learn* (Grand Rapids, Mich.: Baker, 1994), 85.

demonstrating to the adolescent how he or she might behave or live.[11] It is how the youth worker reacts to having a flat tire, to being abruptly cut off in traffic, or to displaying enthusiasm over prayer or personal study of the Bible. In essence, modeling is demonstrating the validity of what it means to be "Christian" through intimate relationships with God and others. Consequently, it is critical that the youth religious educator is with youth outside the formal instructional setting, in daily life.[12]

A beneficial summary of effective modeling principles has been compiled by Lawrence Richards.[13] A modification of his seven points provides the youth religious educator with the kind of direction he or she needs in modeling a life-style that might positively influence the behavior of identity-diffused youth as well as other adolescents.

• Adolescents need frequent, long-term contact with models.
• Adolescents need to experience warm, loving relationships with models.
• Adolescents need to be exposed to the inner values and emotions of models.
• Models need to be observed in a variety of life situations and settings.
• Models must exhibit clarity and consistency in attitudes, values, and behaviors.
• There must be a compatibility between the behavior of the models and the standards and beliefs of the larger community.
• There need to be explanations of the life-style of the models, along with accompanying demonstrations of life.[14]

Identity-diffused adolescents need to be given recognition and offered approval for the things they do well. Youth workers should enable them to see their strengths in personality, performance, knowledge, skills, and attitudes. There are a number of simple activities that can be effective in affirming and encouraging adolescents who struggle with feelings of rejection and failure. For example, people can encourage one another (not just identity-diffused youth, but all members) by pinning a piece of paper on each person's back. Have group members then circulate

---

11. James Michael Lee, *The Flow of Religious Instruction* (Birmingham, Ala.: Religious Education Press, 1973), 166.

12. Richards, *A Theology of Christian Education,* 85.

13. Ibid., 84–85.

14. Issler and Habermas, *How We Learn,* 85, adapt Richards' principles for youth ministry.

and write on the paper one positive attribute or quality they see in each person. Allow time for each person to read his or her list.[15]

Identity-diffused adolescents also need special help in focusing on an occupation or career, or selection of a college. The student who is unable to decide what steps to take toward reaching such significant goals will not continue to mature until the issue is resolved. Most likely such an individual will drift in and out of college, shift from one major to another, and achieve less than desirable grades. The youth worker should help these students develop abilities to assess possibilities, evaluate these possibilities, and make valid and meaningful choices based on the values placed on each.

Finally, using identity-diffused teenagers as summer camp workers or involving them in work or service projects can help them develop a sense of purpose and direction. Often such ministries and projects can lead young people into a deeper commitment to Jesus Christ, instill in them or trigger a desire to serve God in a particular capacity, and challenge them to have an impact on the lives of others. Some ideas for service projects that teenagers can be involved in include working in an orphanage or school, repairing a run-down church, assisting the elderly in home maintenance or upkeep, and helping in food distribution programs.[16]

Identity-Foreclosed Youth: Foreclosure-type adolescents are characterized by not having experienced crises, yet having expressed commitments to goals, values, or beliefs. These teenagers, however, assume a commitment that is handed to them by significant others, most notably their parents, rather than through personal searching and exploring. Identity-foreclosed teenagers can tell you what they want to be but cannot clearly express why, or they indicate that this is what their parents desire. In terms of values and faith, identity-foreclosed adolescents accept what others (such as parents, religious educators, teachers, and youth workers) tell them to believe, with little reflection and appropriation. These youth might say something like, "If it is right for my parents, it must be good enough for me!"

---

15. Wayne Rice, *Up Close and Personal* (Grand Rapids, Mich.: Zondervan, 1989), 45.
16. Two helpful sources on mission and service projects are Anthony Campolo, ed., *Ideas for Social Action* (El Cajon, Calif.: Youth Specialties, 1983) and Tony Campolo, 101 *Ways Your Church Can Change the World* (Ventura, Calif.: Regal, 1993).

Identity-foreclosed adolescents tend to pursue quiet, orderly, and in-dustrious life-styles and endorse authoritarian values such as obedience, strong leadership, and respect for authority.[17] Foreclosure-type youth often come from strongly child-centered families, where the parents may be possessive and intrusive with their children.[18] While parents appear to be highly encouraging and supportive, there is some evidence of strong pressures to conform to family attitudes, values, and beliefs.

To parents and youth workers, identity-foreclosed youth often appear attractive and are generally compliant and easy to work with. However, these adolescents may remain cautious and overly dependent on others, and are unlikely to provide creative leadership or direction.[19] When parents or church leaders are not present these individuals lack an individualized value system that can guide decisions. In terms of faith, they simply believe what significant others have told them, with little or no serious personal reflection on those faith-related beliefs, values, and attitudes.[20]

In moving adolescents beyond the identity-foreclosed status, wise and sensitive youth workers will avoid a preachy, authoritarian type of religious education and strive to create an atmosphere that encourages questioning and exploration. Adolescents should be equipped to dis-cover truth for themselves. They should be encouraged to ask questions, given the freedom to doubt, and taught to do independent and critical thinking. Through small group discussions, role-playing, moral and faith dilemmas, discovery learning, playing the devil's advocate, and by simply challenging them to search for answers, youth workers can help facilitate identity formation in identity-foreclosed teenagers.

Wayne Rice and Mike Yaconelli of Youth Specialties, have compiled a collection of what they call "tension getters." Tension getters are real-life situations or issues designed to get young people to think through alternatives and consequences before arriving at a moral or ethical deci-sion. They are designed to create tension in the cognitive and affective domains of the adolescent by introducing conflicting or overlapping

---

17. See Adams and Gullotta, *Adolescent Life Experiences,* 242.
18. Ibid., 252.
19. Ibid., 242.
20. See Les Steele, "Identity Formation Theory and Youth Ministry," in *Christian Education Journal* 9, (Autumn 1988), 93, for additional comments.

values that make a simple black-and-white answer impossible. Consider, for example the following case study:

Judy is twenty-nine years old and the mother of four children. Very recently she has learned that she is pregnant once again. Her husband does not want another child and is extremely upset. He insists that Judy abort the baby. Judy understands that they cannnot afford another child, yet the thought of getting an abortion frightens her and goes against everything she believes. She is torn in several directions: loyalty to her husband whom she loves very much, responsibility for the care of her other children, and her personal belief that abortion is wrong.
- *What would you do if you were Judy?*
- *What would you do if you were Judy and you only had one other child?*
- *What if preliminary tests showed that the baby would be born mentally retarded?*
- *What if Judy found out that her husband was having an affair?*[21]

Part of the identity-formation task is helping adolescents sort out values that are personal from those that are fixed and absolute. Values pertaining to clothing, hairstyle, occupation, and music are generally individualistic, and freedom of expression should be encouraged. In contrast, premarital sex, lying, cheating, and disobeying parents are examples of absolute values and are not matters of personal choice. It is important that religious educators of youth model the ability to differentiate between personal values and absolutes. If adults who do religious education ministry with youth are as judgmental of teenage males wearing earrings as they are of adolescents using drugs, suggests Bonnidell Clouse, they can hardly expect these young people to discriminate between behaviors they have a right to choose for themselves and behaviors that must be accepted as a given.[22]

Unfortunately, many of our parenting and educational strategies encourage a foreclosure type of identity formation. Parents and religious education teachers become uncomfortable and defensive if adolescents

---

21. Adapted from Wayne Rice and Mike Yaconelli, eds., *Tension Getters Two* (Grand Rapids, Mich.: Zondervan, 1985), 58.
22. See Bonnidell Clouse, "Adolescent Moral Development and Sexuality," in Donald Ratcliff and James A. Davies, eds., *Handbook of Youth Ministry* (Birmingham, Ala.: Religious Education Press, 1991), 193–94.

ask too many difficult questions about their faith and belief system. However, it is by this very process of questioning and intellectual exploration that teenagers internalize values and beliefs, and develop a faith they can call their own.

Identity-Moratorium Youth: Like the identity-diffused youth, moratorium adolescents are rather vague about commitments. They are distinguished, however, by the appearance of an active struggle to make commitments. This youth is one who is experiencing crisis and actively searching for alternatives but has not yet made any commitments. This is the teenager who is going to be an astronaut today and a missionary tomorrow. These are not flippant choices or changes, however, but seriously considered options.[23]

These adolescents are the most anxious of the identity types, yet are able to maintain a stable sense of self-esteem. They tend to be extreme in their views, independent, competitive, and unpredictable.[24] The homes of these young people are generally active ones, and autonomy, self-expression, and individual differences in areas such as dress and hairstyle appear to be encouraged.

Identity-moratorium might be considered the most normal approach to achieving identity. In fact, our culture treats the whole decade of adolescence as a moratorium during which the individual gradually assumes more and more adult responsibilities and characteristics, yet without being fully accountable as an adult.[25] Adolescents should be encouraged to involve themselves in honest and active struggles to find answers to unsolved questions and to explore or try out various roles.

The trauma of moratorium may not be a pleasant experience, but adolescents should not cut it off too quickly or before an adequate exploration of alternatives has been accomplished. Adolescents may, for example, hastily marry immediately after high school graduation rather than explore the possibility of singleness. Others may choose a career predetermined by their parents, without searching out viable options. Youth workers can reassure young people that late adolescence does indeed involve a certain amount of anguish and trauma as they make life choices and form attitudes, values, and ethical opinions. Adolescents

---

23. Steele, "Identity Formation Theory and Youth Ministry," 92–93.
24. Clouse, "Adolescent Moral Development and Sexuality," 192.
25. Howard Newsom, "Why Teens Need to Establish Their Own Identity," in Jay Kesler, ed., *Parents and Teenagers* (Wheaton, Ill.: Victor, 1984), 162.

should be encouraged to do research on issues they are struggling with, to talk to others, to challenge assumptions, and to be able to support their decisions.

Perhaps parents need as much support as the adolescents themselves. Mothers and fathers surely do not enjoy watching their children suffer emotional distress and psychological pain. Parents will often actively discourage a moratorium status because they do not feel comfortable with uncertainties and lack of commitments.[26] As painful as it may be, parents should be encouraged to allow and enable their adolescent children to go through the healthy process of exploring and searching for answers and options to life's questions and possibilities. For example, rather than forcing or insisting a teenage son or daughter pursue a particular career or occupation, parents might help the child explore valid choices by setting forth the strengths and drawbacks of each option.

Identity-Achieved Youth: Identity-achieved adolescents have not only experienced crisis but are committed to decisions made in regard to critical life issues. This status is the ideal type of identity formation. James Marcia describes these individuals as those who have seriously considered, for example, a number of occupational choices and have come to decisions on their own terms, even though their ultimate decisions may be a variation of their parents' desires. In regard to a faith or belief system, these identity-achieved youth have reevaluated past beliefs and have now achieved a resolution whereby they have internalized and appropriated these beliefs and values. In other words, their faith is their own. In general, it does not appear that these adolescents would be overwhelmed by sudden environmental shifts or unexpected responsibilities.[27]

Identity-achieved youth tend to be more developed in moral reasoning and have a clearer sense of ethics and empathy.[28] They are more stable and mature, consistent in behavior and attitudes, and effective in social relationships.[29] There is also a relationship between faith development and identity achievement. As teenagers mature in faith, they also develop

---

26. Ibid., 162.
27. Marcia, "Development and Validation of Ego Identity Status," 278.
28. Hans Sebald, *Adolescence: A Social Psychological Model,* 3d ed. (Englewood Cliffs, N.J.: Prentice-Hall, 1984), 56.
29. Clouse, "Adolescent Moral Development and Sexuality," 191.

in identity, and vice versa.[30] In general, these adolescents have achieved identity and are ready to assume the roles and responsibilities that adulthood brings to them.

The achievement of identity is one of the adolescent's most important developmental accomplishments, and marks the completion of adolescence and the onset of adulthood.[31] For these reasons it is imperative that youth workers carefully nurture adolescents in such a way that these youth are moving towards the goal of identity achievement. Teenagers who achieve identity or are well on their way to identity achievement will most likely emerge as key leaders in their youth groups and in school. These youth should be encouraged to carry out ministry, not simply perform menial tasks. For example, some of them will be capable of leading small group Bible studies or heading up service projects. Identity-achieved youth should be involved in the planning and carrying out of the overall youth program and related ministries.

Identity Types as Stages of Development

Some psychologists have described identity as a developmental progression.[32] The basic pattern of development is thought to begin with identity diffusion (a state of noncommitment), moving progressively through foreclosure (making choices and commitments without experiencing crisis), moratorium (experiencing crisis and exploring alternatives), and eventually identity achievement (a period of crisis and development of firm commitments). Identity development may begin as early as age 10, and continue into the college-age years.[33]

Based on solid research and theory, one would expect those in preadolescence and early teenage years to be in the diffusion stage. At this juncture of their identity development, young people expend little or no effort in making serious commitments concerning critical life issues such as career, higher education, or marriage. This is not to say that identity formation is not taking place at all. During the preadolescent

---

30. Steele, "Identity Formation Theory and Youth Ministry," 95. For an extensive description of faith development see James W. Fowler, *Stages of Faith* (San Francisco: Harper & Row, 1981).

31. Sharon Parks, *The Critical Years* (San Francisco: HarperSanFrancisco,1986), 76.

32. Steele, "Identity Formation Theory and Youth Ministry," 91–99; Alan S. Waterman, ed., *Identity in Adolescence: Process and Contents,* 14–16.

33. See Hershel D. Thornburg, *Development in Adolescence,* 2nd ed.(Monterey, Calif.: Brooks/Cole, 1982), 522.

years identity is being shaped by the influence of others, their personal life experiences, and the value system in which they live. Preadolescents and young teens are trying out new behaviors and roles, attempting to fashion a coherent faith system. Peers become increasingly important in early adolescent life and preadolescence is the time when the shift from dominant parental influence to dominant peer influence takes place.[34]

As teenagers move into middle adolescence, they are forced to make decisions, such as selection of school courses, that will affect their future. At this point they will be highly dependent on their parents in the decision-making process and their faith system will be highly influenced by significant others. This is the foreclosure phase of identity achievement.

By the time healthy and developmentally mature individuals reach late adolescence, they should be actively exploring and choosing life alternatives with maximum support and advice from parents but with relatively little interference (the moratorium phase of development). Finally, identity achievement, the securing of independence, establishment of roles, and appropriation of beliefs and values, should normally be completed in late adolescence or perhaps in the early twenties.

DIMENSIONS OF IDENTITY FORMATION

The struggle adolescents go through in their search for identity, of finding out who they are, what their roles in society will be, and how they fit into the larger world, is a multifaceted task. As mentioned earlier, much of the task of adolescent identity formation is centered on a variety of critical life issues such as autonomy from parental control, vocation, sexuality, gender roles, religious faith, and self-esteem. While these issues will now be explored in the context of identity formation, most of them will be addressed more fully in subsequent chapters.

The Influence of Parents and Peers

Adolescents live in two worlds—one of parents and the other of peers. As an adolescent grows older, peers and friends become increasingly important, while there is somewhat of a distancing from parents. This shift is critical to the achievement of identity and in the individuation

---

34. Thornburg, *Development in Adolescence,* 523.

process whereby a teenager becomes a unique and separate individual, with his or her own interests, values, attitudes, personality. In order for the adolescent to develop a healthy concept of self, the need for acceptance from peers increases with each year. By the time an individual reaches the teenage years, acceptance and approval are all important.[35]

Empirical research studies indicate that adolescents spend more time with friends than with family or parents. For example, the Barna Research Group found teenagers spent 15.3 hours per week with friends, compared to 13.7 hours with family,[36] while another study estimates adolescents spent 23 percent of their time with classmates, and 29 percent with friends, as compared to 19 percent with family.[37] Studies also indicate adolescents place friends or friendships at the top, or very close to the top, of the list of what they value in life.[38]

As can be expected then, peers and friends have a profound influence in shaping the lives of young people,[39] although parents maintain more impact than they might realize. The Search Institute found that in the fifth to ninth grades the influence of peers increased while the influence of parents decreased, although in no grade was peer influence greater.[40] Whether parents or peers carry more weight often depends on the situation. On issues related to fashion or dress, school-related problems, social activities, and day-to-day concerns, when they seek to establish an immediate sense of identity or status, peer influence is stronger. On significant long-range issues such as career, basic values, and beliefs, adolescents lean toward their parents.[41] Contrary to what many might expect, most adolescents are likely to choose peer groups with values and

---

35. Louise Guerney and Joyce Arthur, "Adolescent Social Relationships," in Richard M. Lerner and Nancy L. Galambos, eds., *Experiencing Adolescents* (New York: Garland, 1984), 91.

36. *Today's Teens: A Generation in Transition* (Glendale, Calif.: The Barna Research Group, 1991), 11.

37. Mihaly Csikszentmihalyi and Reed Larson, *Being Adolescent* (New York: Basic Books, 1984), 71.

38. These include Peter Benson, Dorothy Williams, and Arthur Johnson,*The Quicksilver Years* (San Francisco: Harper & Row,1987), 92; Reginald W. Bibby and Donald C. Posterski, *The Emerging Generation* (Toronto, Ont.: Irwin, 1985), 17; *Today's Teens* (The Barna Research Group, 1991), 20.

39. Bibby and Posterski, *The Emerging Generation*, 102.

40. Benson, Williams, and Johnson, *The Quicksilver Years*, 27.

41. See Diane E. Papalia and Wally Olds, *A Child's World*, 5th ed. (New York: McGraw-Hill, 1990), 577, and Bibby and Posterski, *The Emerging Generation*, 103.

expectations similar to those of their parents. Furthermore, adolescents tend to find friends who are already like them, that is, those who have similar tastes in music, dress, interests, and activities. They then influence each other to become even more alike.[42]

Peer activity helps equip the adolescent with necessary interpersonal skills and prepares the individual for successful adult relationships. In sum, healthy peer relationships provide a foundation upon which social skills necessary for adulthood are developed, as well as mechanisms that help loosen dependencies on parental guidance and support.[43] The creation of an adolescent subculture is essentially an attempt to establish identity. One learns from peers to wear the right clothes and hairstyles, speak the teenage argot or lingo, and listen to the "in" music.[44] Finally, friends are also a source of enjoyment, self-esteem, intimacy, popularity, and emotional security.

Youth workers can have a major impact on how adolescents respond to parents and peers in their search for identity. Through religious education young people should first be reminded of the powerful impact that friends and peers can have on the shaping of their lives, and that this impact can be either positive or negative. They need to understand the value of peers but know when to go against them. Second, adolescents should be encouraged to choose friends whose values and behaviors are congruent with those of their family and church. Third, teenagers should be taught that as they grow in their independence, they are still called to honor and obey their parents. In addition, adolescents must be encouraged to value their parents' judgments and insights.

To illustrate how teenagers are often influenced by others, and how difficult it is to determine who is giving good advice and who is giving bad advice, play the following game. Have a person wait outside while the room is being set up. Place a variety of obstacles around the floor such as bottles or small pails. Blindfold the person waiting outside and have him or her come in. Choose three people to give good advice and three to give bad advice on how to cross the room without knocking over any of the obstacles.

---

42. Papalia and Olds, *A Child's World,* 579.
43. Guerney and Arthur, "Adolescent Social Relationships," 92.
44. Jack O. Balswick and Judith K. Balswick, *The Family* (Grand Rapids, Mich.: Baker, 1991), 137.

The blindfolded persons do not know who is giving the good suggestions and who is leading them astray. Whether the blindfolded persons can cross the room without knocking over any obstacles depends upon whom they decide to listen to. They may decide they can make it on their own and listen to no one at all. Have several individuals try to cross the room. Afterward, ask the group members questions like the following:
• *To the blindfolded persons:* How did you decide whom you would listen to? How did you feel when you followed someone's direction, only to find out it was bad advice?
• *To the friends and foes:* What tactics did you use to keep the person on or off the correct course?
• *To the whole group:* How is this situation like the world we live in? How do our friends and peers try to influence us? How do our parents try to influence us? How can we learn to stay on the best course?[45]

The youth group itself should be a place where adolescents can find acceptance with Christian peers. This is a setting where healthy and godly standards should be stressed, and where positive peer pressure is fostered.

Gaining Independence From Parental Control

In establishing their personal identity, adolescents need to exert their independence.[46] Adolescents must learn to act independently and make decisions for themselves; they must give up the identity of "the Browns' little boy" or the "Clarks' little girl" and establish their own identity. If this issue is not resolved, the adolescent cannot be expected to achieve healthy heterosexual or peer relationships, confidently pursue a vocation, or achieve a sense of identity.[47]

This creates tension for both parents and children. Teenage children vacillate between breaking away from parents and being dependent on them; parents are often torn between letting their children go and keeping them dependent. Autonomy, however, need not demand that parental ties be broken entirely. While responsibility for decisions concerning

---

45. Mike Yaconelli and Jim Burns, *High School Ministry* (Grand Rapids, Mich.: Zondervan, 1986), 244–45.

46. Ibid., 139.

47. John J. Conger and Anne C. Petersen, *Adolescence and Youth,* 3d ed. (New York: Harper & Row, 1984), 231.

day-to-day activities shifts gradually from parents to children, certain emotional attachments between parents and children can remain constant as behavioral autonomy is slowly achieved.[48] Still, adolescents must give up much childhood dependency, learn self-sufficiency and self-reliance, and come to identify with their parents more as friends and confidants.[49]

While a certain amount of conflict between parents and adolescents can be anticipated during this process, open defiance or rebellion should not be seen as the norm. For example, an empirical research study of early and preadolescents by the Search Institute found that while parent-child conflict increased slightly between each of the fifth through the ninth school years, only a minority of the respondents reported major conflicts with parents.[50] For the most part clashes between parents and teenagers are not over major issues such as economics, religion, or politics. Rather, most arguments are over mundane matters such as schoolwork, chores, friends, dating, curfews, and personal appearance—issues that can be resolved with less trouble than is often assumed.

How can the achievement of autonomy be made as smooth as possible for both parents and adolescents? First, adolescents and adults must remember that gaining independence from parents is a normal part of the developmental process. Activities such as independent thinking, spending more time with peers, and establishing new behaviors should not necessarily be seen as defiance, rejection, or rebellion. In fact, the teenager cannot become a fully mature adult without having achieved a certain degree of self-reliance nor without parents accordingly offering decision-making privileges to the youth.[51]

Jack and Judy Balswick liken the process of gaining autonomy to that of driving a car. Teenagers are often restless because their parents are in the driver's seat. Parents, on the other hand, are concerned that their children's restlessness and questioning of established norms are a sign of rejection of them and their values. For the most part, they go on to suggest that the adolescent children want nothing more than to get

---

48. Benson, Williams, and Johnson, *The Quicksilver Years,* 36.
49. Thornburg, *Development in Adolescence,* 171.
50. Benson, Williams, and Johnson, *The Quicksilver Years,* 38.
51. Stephen A. Small, Gay Eastman, and Steven Cornelius, "Adolescent Autonomy and Parental Stress," in *Journal of Youth and Adolescence* 17, (October 1988), 377–91.

behind the wheel—to gain more control over their life and participate in determining where it is going.[52]

Parents walk a fine line between giving their teenage children appropriate independence, yet protecting them from the possibility of making immature or bad decisions. The kind of parenting that seems to provide the best balance is an authoritative style that portrays warmth and acceptance; assertiveness regarding rules, norms and values; but also a willingness to listen, explain, and negotiate.[53] The change from dependence to independence proceeds smoothest if parents are moderate in their disciplinary practice, not overly restrictive and not extremely permissive.[54]

Youth religious educators and parents should see this change from dependence to independence as a transformation, rather than a radical change. As children move into early adolescence, parents should allow them more and more freedom to make their own decisions. As the adolescent matures, increasing responsibility and autonomy should be given, although involving adolescents in decisions relevant to them does not mean that the parents surrender final authority on important family matters. It is simply a recognition of the reality of the teenager's intellectual abilities to understand, contribute, and have opinions.[55]

Timothy Foster suggests a strategy of parenting he calls "freedom within boundaries," an approach that ideally begins with a child at about 18 months. The child has freedom of choice within boundaries, and if she steps out of the boundaries is disciplined. When a child is 5 years old, she may choose what kind of cereal to eat for breakfast, although the child is not likely to be given the option of not having breakfast. By the time the same child is 16, she should be given the freedom not to have breakfast if she so chooses.

The difficulty for many parents is realizing that these boundaries move so that by the time the child is seventeen, relatively few rules are left. At that point parents should use the little influence they have left on really significant issues of life. Length of hair, argues Foster, hardly qualifies as a significant issue, and it is a way for a child to express his uniqueness. It is unfortunate, he goes on to say, that so many family nights are ruined

---

52. Balswick and Balswick, *The Family*, 137.
53. Papalia and Olds, *A Child's World*, 573.
54. Balswick and Balswick, *The Family*, 141.
55. Guerney and Arthur, "Adolescent Social Relationships," 90–91.

by parents trying to exert too much control on their teenagers rather than focusing on preparing them for adulthood.[56]

Youth religious education activities can help parents ready adolescents for responsible positions in the church and society by involving them in responsible leadership positions. Many youth programs, argue Jack and Judy Balswick, do a good job of entertaining members and keeping them busy but do relatively little in empowering them to be effective leaders and ministers within the church community.[57] In positions of leadership, adolescents are forced to learn how to make decisions, keep commitments, use their gifts, abilities, and talents, and develop personal confidence and self-esteem. As mentioned elsewhere in this book, teenagers can provide leadership in a number of ways: leading small groups, teaching classes, heading up service projects, or coordinating meetings and activities, to name a few.

Identity Formation and Vocation

Part of identity formation is becoming a more productive person in society in terms of being a worker and economic provider. The problem of deciding on and preparing for a vocation represents one of the major developmental tasks for adolescents. Furthermore, vocational identity represents an integral part of their overall sense of who they are.[58]

It is important to make a clear distinction among three words often mistakenly used as synonyms for one another: *vocation, occupation,* and *career.* The term *vocation* is used in a broad sense and refers more to a particular course or state in life. In the context of one's religious faith, it may even allude to a life calling from God. Vocation speaks more of what an individual is than what he or she does specifically in terms of work. It suggests one's choice of life's central purpose and life-style.[59] For example, one may be a clergyperson, a doctor, or even a housewife. Or one might work with the sick and the outcasts on the streets of Calcutta, as does Mother Teresa. Generally, this does not specifically tell us what that person does in the work world. Is the clergy person a pastor of a

---

56. Timothy Foster, *Called To Counsel* (Nashville, Tenn.: Oliver-Nelson, 1986), 172.
57. Balswick and Balswick, *The Family,* 146.
58. Conger and Petersen, *Adolescence and Youth,* 446–48.
59. Richard Olson, *A Job or a Vocation* (Nashville, Tenn.: Thomas Nelson, 1973), 7; Thomas F. Green, *Work, Leisure, and the American Schools* (New York: Random House, 1968), 76–77.

church, a youth minister, a pastoral counselor? Is the businessman a
restaurant owner, a consultant, or president of a company?

Occupation refers more specifically to the work or employment in
which a person engages—bank teller, waiter, mechanic, or high school
teacher. The concept of *career,* on the other hand, denotes the idea that
there is a certain consistency over the lifetime in a person's relation
to work.[60] For example, a person may have a career in education that
includes multiple jobs or occupational changes. The person may have
held several teaching positions, spent some time as a principal or vice-
principal, and retired as a college professor.[61] There is the notion that
an individual progresses through a series of phases associated with
upward mobility, achieving greater responsibility, mastery, and financial
remuneration.[62]

Why is it that one's vocation and related occupation are so closely tied
to identity development? The importance of vocation to one's identity
formation cannot be overstated. Having a job that society values does
much to enhance self-esteem and assists in the development of a secure
and stable sense of identity. On the other hand, if one senses that his or
her employment is not meaningful to society, there may be resentment,
doubt, a loss of self-esteem, or even a dropping out of the work world.
Two important aspects of most people's working lives are that their job
or employment ties them into the larger system of society and gives
them a sense of purpose in life.[63] Furthermore, what one does for a
living is a primary source of information about values, social class, and
education.[64]

Choosing a vocation or occupation in our rapidly changing culture
proves to be much more complicated than it was prior to the Industrial
Revolution, when young men and women began their vocational roles
as early as 12 or 13 years old. At that time children had little, if any,
input into the process, as parents usually dictated what their vocation or

---

60. Charles Healy, *Career Development: Counseling Through the Life Stages* (Boston:
Allyn and Bacon, 1982), 13.

61. When I use the term "vocation" I will usually be referring to one's central purpose
and life-style as expressed by occupations and career one chooses.

62. Judith Stevens-Long, *Adult Life,* 2nd ed. (Los Angeles: Mayfield, 1984), 194.

63. Ibid.

64. Patricia M. Raskin, "Identity and Vocational Development," in Alan S. Waterman,
ed. *Identity in Adolescence: Processes and Contents* (San Francisco: Jossey-Bass, 1985),
26.

occupation would be, and in many cases it simply meant assuming the occupational role of the parent.[65]

Some researchers today suggest that vocational choice in contemporary Western societies is developmental in nature and begins in childhood. Eli Ginsberg and his associates describe the process of choosing a vocation as taking place in three specific stages. Up to about age 11, children are in the *fantasy period*. During this initial period children assume that they can do anything, but there is no serious or realistic testing of occupational choices. Children are in a play orientation and choices are made within a child's world, not the actual world they will eventually function in.

The second stage is the *tentative period*, and occurs between ages 11 and 18. During this time young people realize that they will have to make decisions about selecting a vocation or occupation. It is a time when individuals assess their skills, capabilities, and interests, as well as academic and training possibilities.

The *realistic period* takes place in late adolescence and early adulthood. It is a time when possibilities are narrowed and commitment to final choices of vocation and occupation take place. This stage is further broken into an *exploratory* phase, where adolescents acquire information about vocational and job opportunities; a *crystallization phase*, where there is the narrowing down of alternatives; and finally *specification,* at which point decisions are made to pursue particular vocations and job possibilities.[66]

Establishing a vocation in life or choosing an occupation is becoming increasingly difficult as our society grows more complex, more specialized, and more technologically oriented.[67] The *Occupational Outlook Handbook* describes over 300 occupations—covering well over 104 million jobs, or 91 percent of all jobs in United States.[68] Furthermore, the kinds of skills the workplace requires are changing as new technologies are developed.

---

65. Gary M. Ingersoll, *Adolescents in School and Society* (Lexington, Mass.: D.C. Heath, 1982), 127.

66. The theory is summarized by Ingersoll, *Adolescents in School and Society,* 133–35. Another important theory of vocational development is offered by Donald Super, "A Theory of Vocational Development," in *American Psychologist* 8, (1953), 185–90.

67. Conger and Petersen, *Adolescence and Youth,* 451.

68. *Occupational Outlook Handbook,* 4th ed. (Washington, D.C.: Department of Labor, 1994).

Part-time work is one way that adolescents explore possibilities in life vocation and occupation. However some psychologists disagree on the value that part-time work has on adolescent development and argue that extensive involvement in the workplace may in fact interfere with the development of healthy autonomy and social responsibility of adolescents.[69] These experts suggest that teenagers who work are no more independent in making financial decisions than those who do not, that jobs are largely irrelevant to future careers, and that work is likely to interfere with schooling. The benefits of working include the development of personal responsibility and self reliance, a better understanding of others and the world of work, and increased autonomy.[70]

How do parents affect vocational and occupational plans and ambitions of teenagers? The research suggests that financial support and encouragement of parents are highly influential in aspiration and achievement of career and higher education.[71] A review of related empirical research studies found that a father's occupation exerts significant influence on the career choice of sons, though not daughters. For example, sons of scientists, lawyers and physicians are more likely to enter these professions than young men of similar socioeconomic status. Several reasons are given for these tendencies: 1) a greater opportunity to learn about the father's occupation as compared to others, 2) a greater access to the occupation, 3) strong parental motivation (and in some cases pressure), and 4) the communication of values from father to son.[72]

The mother is influential in shaping vocational attitudes as well. For example, female adolescents whose mothers are employed outside the home are also more likely to view work as something they would like to do when they are married and become mothers. Furthermore, the vocational aspirations, attitudes, and accomplishments of girls will be influenced by the mother's attitude toward employment, her degree of

---

69. Ellen Greenberger and Laurence Steinberg, *When Teen-agers Work* (New York: Basic Books, 1986), 47.

70. Fred W. Vondracek and John E. Schulenberg, "Adolescence and Careers," in Richard M. Lerner and Nancy L. Galambos, eds., *Experiencing Adolescents* (New York: Garland, 1984), 341.

71. Papalia and Olds, *A Child's World,* 552.

72. Summarized from Conger and Petersen, *Adolescence and Youth,* 463–64. This book on the psychology of adolescence includes an excellent review of the literature related to adolescent vocation.

accomplishment and satisfaction in her work, and her ability to combine the roles of worker, mother, and wife.[73]

Gender also affects vocational and occupational plans of adolescents. Traditionally, women have been socialized to find their identity in the role of wife-mother-homemaker. Those who did enter the work force were limited to clerical fields, semiskilled jobs, and service jobs. Today, however, women are making significant inroads into job markets such as law, medicine and business, once considered exclusively male occupational areas.

It should be noted, however, that while in the 1970s most adults supported women's entry into the work force, the pendulum seems to be swinging in favor of the stay-at-home wife and mother. Empirical research by George Barna found Americans favor the model where the mother stays at home with the children by a four-to-one margin.[74]

How can a youth program help adolescents achieve identity through vocation and occupation? First, churches could sponsor vocational fairs, where representatives of different vocational and occupational fields come to talk and answer questions. Second, youth workers could organize exploration groups where adults from the church meet with small groups of young people who are interested in their particular vocations.[75]

Adolescents should also be aware of the options in higher education. Too often high school graduates have not explored the various possibilities for post-high-school training and are not aware of the offerings of different types of postsecondary schools. They should understand the benefits and drawbacks of attending private colleges, community colleges, or large universities, and should learn which would be most beneficial for their particular situation.

The youth worker should be prepared to counsel young people in choosing the appropriate educational route for achieving vocational and occupational goals. Other suggestions include visiting college and university campuses with students and inviting representatives of post-secondary schools or colleges to address youth groups.

Adolescent Sexuality and Identity

Among the many developmental changes that characterize puberty and adolescence, none is more dramatic or more closely related to

---

73. Ibid., 468–69.
74. George Barna, *The Future of the American Family* (Chicago: Moody, 1993), 184.
75. Steele, "Identity Formation Theory and Youth Ministry," 97.

identity formation than is sexuality.[76] Achieving personal sexual identity means coming to terms with one's maleness or femaleness, biological maturation, and the sexual differences that are accelerated during puberty.

The most profound and noticeable transformations in the teenager are probably the biological changes. The physical and sexual changes that take place during the early and middle adolescent years occur at a rapid pace; only during infancy does a person undergo a comparable period of extensive and accelerated change.[77]

The term given to this period of significant change is *puberty*. Puberty is the stage of development in which sexual characteristics and features begin to show and mature. During puberty a sudden increase in height occurs, and the bodily characteristics of boys and girls become increasingly differentiated. Boys develop broader shoulders and experience an overall gain in muscle development, while girls develop more rounded hips and undergo breast development. Boys begin to grow facial hair and experience a voice change. In both sexes genitals increase in size and pubic hair develops; girls experience their first menstruation and boys their first ejaculation. These physical changes require significant adjustment by teenagers, as a number of other areas are affected, including body image, self-image, relationships with peers and parents, sexual feelings, and moods.[78]

When adolescents are early or late in their maturation process, they can be significantly affected psychologically and emotionally. For boys, being an early physical maturer is associated with a more positive perception by self and others, while being late is associated with a poorer evaluation by self and others. The "on-time" developers fall somewhere in between these two extremes. It appears that maturing early has clear psychological and sociological advantages for boys.[79]

---

76. Conger and Petersen, *Adolescence and Youth,* 272.

77. See Ingersoll, *Adolescents,* 29; Thornburg, *Development in Adolescence,* 54; Maryse H. Tobin-Richards, Andrew M. Boxer, Suzanne A. McNeil Kavrell, and Anne C. Petersen, "Puberty and Its Psychological and Social Significance," in Richard M. Lerner and Nancy L. Galambos, eds., *Experiencing Adolescents* (New York: Garland, 1984), 17, for helpful descriptions of puberty and sexual development.

78. Ibid.

79. Tobin-Richards et al., "Puberty and Its Psychological and Social Significance," 30–31.

For girls, being early or late in physical maturity is associated with more negative attitudes and feelings than being on time. Early physical and sexual maturation for a girl may carry explicit sexual meanings and generate unwelcome or inappropriate social responses. Early biological maturers may be tempted to identify with older female adolescents who may not reciprocate their attention. Late physical and sexual maturers may experience the ridicule or teasing of friends, or suffer considerable anxiety as sexual development is delayed.[80]

It is common for preadolescents and adolescents to have concerns or questions regarding their body and sexuality. For example, adolescents whose physical and sexual development are not "on time" need comfort and reassurance that they are indeed "normal." The feelings, thoughts, and behaviors that accompany puberty are unfamiliar and sometimes confusing. Yet most adolescents lack information about pubertal changes and what puberty involves. However, the better prepared for puberty a child is, the more positive the experience will be. It is important that preadolescents know not only what puberty entails in terms of physical change but also what feelings and emotions are attached to these changes and anticipated changes.[81]

The task of preparing children for puberty belongs primarily to parents, though most are uncomfortable discussing issues related to sex, and in many cases ignore this responsibility entirely. Churches could make this task easier by providing seminars or classes whereby parents are equipped or prepared to talk to their preadolescents about such matters. It is imperative that youth workers share with parents the responsibility of helping adolescents work through issues related to sexual identity and development.

It is in the adolescent years that one's sexual orientation is usually manifested. Either an individual will be heterosexual, that is, sexually interested in members of the opposite sex, or homosexual, interested in members of the same sex. While most adolescents are heterosexual, many young people, more boys than girls, have one or more homosexual experiences.[82] Why do some young people become attracted to the same sex? A number of possible causes are cited by experts. Some

80. Ingersol, *Adolescents,* 38–39.
81. Tobin-Richards et al., "Puberty and Its Psychological and Social Significance," 40.
82. Ingersol, *Adolescents,* 191–92 summarizes some of the empirical findings related to adolescent homosexuality.

adolescents are not secure in their sex-role identification, while others have had homosexual experiences and convince themselves they are not attracted to the opposite sex. For still others, homosexuality has been learned or they have been conditioned toward homosexual behavior. Paul Meier and associates recognize the possibility of genetic influence on homosexuality but argue that even if such an influence could be proven, it would be erroneous to blame sinful behavior on "bad genes."[83] Psychologist Gary Collins argues that homosexuality is learned and offers several theories as to how this happens: certain parent and family relationships, fear of the opposite sex, and willful choice of homosexual actions.[84]

Gender-Role Identity

Closely related to the issue of sexual identity is gender-role identity. This refers to the accepting and assuming of sex roles, or behaviors and characteristics considered appropriate and desirable by society for males and females. In North American societies, autonomy, independence, dominance, aggression, and the inhibition of emotion are expected of males, while females are expected to be warm, nurturant, emotionally expressive, dependent, and interpersonally competent.[85] Furthermore, occupational roles have been classified as masculine or feminine. Traditionally, occupations requiring administrative responsibility and strength have been seen as masculine, while roles that are passive in nature and involve the caring for others have been viewed as feminine.[86]

Considerable debate exists as to whether gender roles and orientations are innate or environmentally conditioned. One cumulative empirical research study found significant differences between school-age boys and girls in three areas—girls have greater verbal ability, while boys excel in visual-spatial tasks and mathematics. The authors attributed differences partially to biological factors but emphasized the role of socialization as well.[87] Other experts agree that biological forces such

---

83. Paul D. Meier, Frank B. Minirth, Frank B. Wichern, and Donald E. Ratcliff, *Introduction to Psychology and Counseling,* 2nd ed. (Grand Rapids, Mich.: Baker, 1991), 272.

84. Gary R. Collins, *Christian Counseling* (Dallas: Word, 1988), 282–85.

85. Ingersoll, *Adolescents,* 119.

86. Ibid., 131–32.

87. Eleanor E. Maccoby and Carol N. Jacklin, *The Psychology of Sex Differences* (Stanford, Calif.: Stanford University, 1974).

as sex hormones and brain differences play a significant role in differentiation, although they also argue that these forces interact significantly with the environment. The resultant effects are that there are some tasks males do better than females, and vice versa. Some argue that better mathematics skills by boys should be attributed exclusively to environmental factors such as parental expectations.

Carol Gilligan suggests that women have a special innate nature that is different from men and that these differences be seen in a positive light. According to Gilligan, the male moves toward justice, rights, and detachment, while the female is predisposed toward attachment, intimacy, and relationships.[88]

Perhaps the most helpful approach is a holistic one that sees gender dimorphism or differences as best explained by the co-influence of biological, psychological, and sociological forces. In other words, differences between males and females are best understood to be the resultant effects of predetermined, innate characteristics combined with external influences such as parental and social expectations.

This holistic approach finds opposition from much of the feminist movement, which feels that there is neither biological nor social justification for identifying gender-specific roles or categories. However, sociologist Hans Sebald suggests that this feminist view is leading our society toward an abandonment or radical modification of traditional sexroles and an emergence of a nonsexist style of human interaction. He goes on to say that "whatever the future, at this time there is a significant eroding of the traditional stereotypes. Sex-role blueprints have become blurred, and prediction of a person's behavior on the basis of gender is no longer as reliable as it used to be."[89]

Females have felt the bulk of this blurring of gender roles. While the role of the male has remained relatively unchanged, the female role has experienced significant transformation in the 1970s and into the 1990s. This includes increased premarital sexual activity among women, a more competitive attitude of females, an influx of women into the once male-dominated professions, an increase in the number of women in higher education, and overall delays in childbearing. Some of the effects of gender-role changes are harmful, as females are now exposed to some of

88. Carol Gilligan, *In a Different Voice* (Cambridge, Mass.: Harvard University, 1982).
89. Sebald, *Adolescence,* 47.

the same tensions that males experience. These negative effects include a rise in the suicide rate of females, a general worsening self-image of young women, and an increase of violent crimes performed by women.[90]

Charles Sell suggests the breakdown of traditional roles of husband as leader and provider, and wife as homemaker has created a significant amount of confusion, conflict, and controversy in marriages. First, without the traditional understanding of husband and wife roles, which includes submission of the wife to the husband, a striving for power may dominate the relationship. For some women, getting a job may be a strategy to give them leverage in financial decisions. Second, getting a job outside the home may be a striving for significance. For them, caring for children full time is not as fulfilling or rewarding as it was for women in the past.

Third, for many women the movement from the traditional role of the male as sole provider has resulted in more work. While many women have increased their work outside the home, most men have not increased their share of the domestic tasks. Thus women often have two full-time careers, one outside the home and one inside.

Fourth, by questioning their roles in the home, women have forced men to reconsider their roles. With the traditional notions of manhood under attack, there has been considerable restlessness and questioning on behalf of men. Finally, couples are forced to search for new ways to solve conflicts and maintain marital harmony, as they are stripped of customary guidelines to order their relationships.[91]

The overall consequence of these significant changes is that many young women are no longer moving into traditional female roles but are working out a variety of role combinations and possibilities. For some, it is making a choice between carrying out the traditional roles of marriage, motherhood, and homemaking, or completing an education and establishing a career. For others, it is combining motherhood and homemaking with career. For an increasing number of females, it is planning their lives in phases: for example, education, work experience, career, marriage, motherhood, reeducation, and reentry into the work force.[92]

Teenage girls will need help as they face the difficult task of choosing from the multiple options and demands society has placed on them. The

90. Ibid., 47–52.
91. Charles Sell, *Family Ministry,* 2nd ed. (Grand Rapids, Mich.: Zondervan, 1995), 44–45.
92. Ibid., 53.

message society gives them is that they can have it all—family, education, career—but the result is often frustration and stress. Adolescent girls must be reminded that they must not overextend themselves and should pursue a path of moderation.

For male adolescents, it means they should be prepared for changing roles as well. Males must play, for example, a more significant role in parenting. Fathers need to be jointly involved in the efforts of childrearing. The parenting contribution made by the father must be significant enough that deep emotional bonds with his children are made.[93] It also means that young men must abandon the discriminatory attitude that women are generally inferior to men in important aspects of personality and capability.[94]

For both adolescent males and females, it means recognizing the important distinctions between men and women and at the same time encouraging individuals to meet their potentials and goals in life through equal opportunities and responsibilities.[95] Achieving the true ideal of Christian womanhood and manhood will be a difficult and sometimes confusing task for adolescents in today's world. It remains, however, a critical aspect of developing one's identity.

A Personalized Faith

One of the most important tasks related to identity achievement is the appropriation or internalization of one's faith system. In other words, teenagers must come to the point where they personalize their faith. James Fowler, in his theory of faith development, suggests that in the adolescent years aspects of faith such as values, commitments, and beliefs are central to the formation of identity.[96] V. Bailey Gillespie suggests that early youth provides an important setting for faith since faith formation is strongly related to the achievement of identity and self-autonomy.[97]

---

93. Balswick and Balswick, *The Family,* 166.
94. George Rekers, *Shaping Your Child's Sexual Identity* (Grand Rapids, Mich.: Baker, 1982), 15.
95. Balswick and Balswick, *The Family,* 169.
96. James W. Fowler, "Faith and the Structuring of Meaning," in Craig Dykstra and Sharon Parks, eds., *Faith Development and Fowler* (Birmingham, Ala.: Religious Education Press, 1986), 29–30.
97. V. Bailey Gillespie, *The Experience of Faith* (Birmingham, Ala.: Religious Education Press, 1988), 126.

Definitions of "faith" abound. Clearly, the most discussed definition of faith and faith development is that of James Fowler, who sees faith as the way to put meaning into life.[98] While Fowler contributes much to the understanding of faith development, his definition of faith has some shortcomings. Fowler is not concerned so much with the content or substance of faith as he is with the activity or process of faith making or putting meaning into life. Faith is not always religious in its content or context and to ask serious questions of oneself or life does not necessarily mean to elicit questions concerning religious beliefs or commitment.[99] While helpful in understanding faith formation, his definition is clearly more psychological than theological in nature. More will be said of Fowler and his helpful contributions to the understanding of faith development, shortly.

From a theological perspective, faith is seen as an activity of the person in response to the redemptive work of the Holy Spirit in one's heart.[100] In understanding faith as a human activity and response to a divine work, it is defined here as the religious aspect of life that includes such dimensions as beliefs and convictions, attitudes and values, and behaviors and life-style.[101] It is a complex activity that is made up of three interactive domains: the intellectual, the emotional, and the volitional.[102]

The Intellectual Domain: The *intellectual,* or cognitive, domain is concerned with the knowledge of faith. It includes the content, or the beliefs and convictions that form the foundation of one's religion and faith. Perry Downs describes Christianity as a "propositional religion with truth to be known."[103]

Often what is believed and adhered to in the preadolescent and early adolescent years, however, is that which is handed down from

---

98. James W. Fowler, *Stages of Faith* (San Francisco: Harper and Row, 1981).

99. Ibid., 4.

100. See Steele, *On the Way* (Grand Rapids, Mich.: Baker, 1990), 102, and Perry G. Downs, "Faith Shaping: Bringing Youth to Spiritual Maturity," in Warren S. Benson and Mark H. Senter, eds., *The Complete Book of Youth Ministry* (Chicago: Moody, 1987), 50.

101. Craig Dykstra, "Faith Development and Religious Education," in Craig Dykstra and Sharon Parks, eds., *Faith Development and Fowler* (Birmingham, Ala.: Religious Education Press, 1986), 252–53.

102. Steele, *On the Way,* 102–104; Downs, "Faith Shaping: Bringing Youth to Spiritual Maturity,"; John Westerhoff, *Will Our Children Have Faith* (San Francisco: Harper-Collins, 1976), 91, describe faith in accordance to these three categories.

103. Downs, "Faith Shaping: Bringing Youth to Spiritual Maturity," 50.

parents, teachers, pastors, and youth workers. Preadolescents are what developmental psychologist Jean Piaget calls *concrete* thinkers. At this stage of development thinking is limited to the here and now, to concrete objects and situations. There is relatively little capacity to do personal critical reflection or independent and abstract thinking.

At about age 12, when children move into early adolescence, they enter what is called the *formal operations* stage. At this point, thought, as Fowler puts it, takes wings.[104] The developing cognitive or thinking skills begin to be characterized by the ability to carry out abstract thought and to go beyond the here and now in thinking. Adolescents can hypothesize and suppose situations, which means they can now concern themselves with national and international affairs. They ask questions about meaning and values of human existence; they imagine the ideal—the ideal family, the ideal church, the ideal world. And they can understand, in the words of William Yount, the "un-concrete" world of spiritual matters.[105]

It is here that a number of faith development theorists better help us understand faith shaping, especially as it relates to identity formation. James Fowler argues that in developing a faith system teenagers first go through a stage he calls the *synthetic-conventional* (age 12 years on). It is synthetic in that it is the drawing together of distinct and different elements into a new whole or unity. It is conventional in that the beliefs of the individual conform to or are shaped and pulled together by, significant others: family, peers, clergy, and the like.[106] John Westerhoff calls this type of faith *affiliative,* characterized by a strong sense of belonging and a need for the interaction of significant people.[107] In other words, faith is not based on self-reflection alone.[108] The greatest danger for teenagers at this stage of development is that their faith is secondhand.

The next stage of development according to Fowler, is characterized by an *individuative-reflective* faith and normally emerges at about age 17 or 18. This faith is individuative in the sense that it is a faith that is one's

---

104. Fowler, *Stages of Faith,* 71.
105. William Yount, *Created to Learn* (Nashville, Tenn.: Broadman & Holman, 1996), 91.
106. Fowler, *Stages of Faith,* 151–73.
107. Westerhoff, *Will Our Children Have Faith,* 94.
108. Yount, *Created to Learn,* 125.

own, and is reflective in the sense that an individual who has moved into this stage has personally examined and critically thought out what he or she believes. The adolescent has begun to take seriously the burden of responsibility for his or her personal beliefs, attitudes, and life-style.[109] It is this firsthand faith, as youth ministry expert Duffy Robbins puts it, that we want to see our teenagers come to.[110]

With the development of cognitive skills and the resultant ability to internalize one's faith, a number of implications for the youth religious educator appear. To begin with, rather than being frustrated when students ask questions, express doubts, or challenge the teachings of the church, the youth worker should in fact be doing all he or she can to encourage such activity. The wise youth worker will welcome difficult questions, remind adolescents that it is not wrong to have doubts about his or her faith, and encourage youth to grapple with theological and life-related issues.

Adolescents should be taught to do independent and critical thinking, which means religious educators of youth should avoid spoon-feeding youth and simply filling them with content through the overused lecture method. Too many religious educators tell youth what to think, without teaching them how to think and far too many youth workers are concerned with telling young people what to believe, without enabling them to develop a firsthand faith of their own. The *Effective Christian Education Study* of mainline churches by the Search Institute found that only 45 percent of the youth say their church encourages them to ask questions, and just 42 percent say their church challenges their thinking.[111]

One way religious educators of youth can help move adolescents toward higher levels of thinking and better equip them to grapple with the tough issues of faith is by employing Benjamin Bloom's taxonomy of cognitive functioning.[112] Bloom and his associates have identified six levels of thinking. In order of complexity from the lower to higher

---

109. Fowler, *Stages of Faith,* 174–83.
110. Duffy Robbins, *The Ministry of Nurture* (Grand Rapids, Mich.: Zondervan, 1990), 63.
111. Eugene C. Roehlkepartain, *The Teaching Church* (Nashville, Tenn.: Abingdon, 1993), 206.
112. Benjamin Bloom et al., *Taxonomy of Educational Objectives. Handbook 1: Cognitive Domain* (New York: David McKay, 1956).

levels they are: 1) *knowledge* (remembering or recalling information); 2) *comprehension* (rephrasing the information, giving a description in one's own words); 3) *application* (applying previously learned information to solve a problem or determine a correct answer); 4) *analysis* (identifying motives, reasons, or causes; using available information to reach a conclusion); 5) *synthesis* (producing original communication, making predictions); 6) *evaluation* (judging the merit of an idea or an aesthetic work, based on specific criteria). By asking adolescents questions that go beyond the knowledge and comprehension levels, the youth religious educator enables teenagers to probe, reflect, and think about their walk with God, their faith, and their beliefs. Figure 2.2 includes examples of questions at the various levels of thinking.

Figure 2.2
Bloom's Taxonomy of Thinking and
Religious Education of Youth

Level	Type of Skill	Sample Question/Statement
Knowledge	Remembering Recalling Recognizing	Recite the definition of faith given last week.
Comprehension	Understanding Describing	Explain faith in your own words? What do you think Jesus means when he says . . . ?
Application	Implementing Solving	How could you apply Jesus' principle "love your enemy" to a situation at school?
Analysis	Identifying Concluding	What evidence can you find that supports the idea "money is the root of all evil"?
Synthesis	Producing Predicting	Construct a collage of pictures that represent your ideas, feelings and values concerning . . . What would it be like if . . . ?
Evaluation	Judging	Which is better . . . ? Why would you favor . . . ?

A natural part of adolescent faith development is doubt or a questioning of one's faith. The newfound cognitive skills that teenagers acquire
(Piaget's *formal operations*), along with their need to establish independence from their parents, will likely result in some form of questioning
of the faith system they have developed to this point. This should not
be seen as a spiritual problem, but rather as a normal phenomenon of
adolescent development.[113]

Perry Downs offers the following suggestions for the youth worker
who is helping adolescents struggling with doubts or who are troubled
over difficult questions of faith:

• *Remind adolescents that doubt is not a sin.* The Bible provides examples of followers of God who doubted. The Old Testament book
of Jeremiah provides a clear example of the prophet's struggle with
doubt (Jeremiah 20:7–8, 14–18). Likewise, John the Baptist expressed
his doubt when he questioned if Jesus was the Messiah (Matthew 11:1–
6). Neither is doubt the same as unbelief. Os Guinness argues: "Doubt
is not the opposite of faith, nor is it the same is unbelief. Doubt is a state
of mind in suspension between faith and unbelief so that it is neither
of them wholly and it is each only partly. This distinction is absolutely
vital because it uncovers and deals with the first major misconception
of doubt—the idea that in doubting a believer is betraying faith and
surrendering to unbelief. No misunderstanding causes more anxiety and
brings such bondage to sensitive people in doubt."[114]

• *Provide a safe context where doubts can be expressed.* If adolescents
get the message that it is wrong to doubt, they may go elsewhere with
their questions. By accepting their questions, and even encouraging them
to doubt, the youth religious educator can provide a safe context in which
doubts and questions can be raised.

• *Provide answers for some of their questions.* This does not mean that
the religious educator should quickly provide the answer so the doubt
may be quickly resolved. But the adult youth worker should be familiar
with the basic issues of apologetics, the rational defense of Christianity.
In some cases the religious educator might direct the youth toward
sources that might help the questioning person find helpful answers.

• *Provide the teenager with a real Christian experience.* While it is

---

113. Downs, "Faith Shaping: Bringing Youth to Spiritual Maturity," 50.
114. Os Guinness, *In Two Minds* (Downers Grove, Ill.: InterVarsity, 1976), 27.

true that doubt is an intellectual issue, adolescents are also very much experience oriented. If the doubting youth has a place where he or she is accepted and supported, if it is a place where the presence of God is felt, the teenager has a basis for belief that transcends the intellectual.[115]

One youth group has a unique manner of addressing the tough intellectual questions of faith that adolescents grapple with. Periodically they have a "Skeptics Night Out," where they submit questions anonymously. These questions are addressed one at a time, either by a panel of individuals or by an appointed person. This could be the youth worker, pastor, or anyone else who has a solid knowledge of the Christian faith and church doctrine, the way adolescents think, and the honest ability to admit he or she does not have all the answers.

Questions might range from How do we know we can trust the Bible? to What about the claims of evolution? to Can God forgive any sin? Youth group members are encouraged to bring their nonchurched friends from school so that there is an added measure of authenticity to these sessions.[116]

Gillespie accurately argues that freedom is an essential ingredient in people who want to personalize their faith, and we must at some point allow our adolescents freedom of choice. We cannot make our beliefs theirs.[117] Eugene Roehlkepartain suggests that the thinking climate within a youth religious education program can be evaluated and adjusted by struggling with a series of questions:[118]

• *To what degree are questions encouraged or discouraged?* If a teenager asks a question concerning faith, is he or she affirmed or discounted? Is it safe to ask any kind of question?

• *How does the church congregation handle diverse opinions?* It is said that when all think alike, no one thinks much. By stifling diverse thoughts, youth religious education programs discourage critical thinking.

• *Are youth group members challenged to examine their faith and lifestyles?* Is faith simply an intellectual exercise or does it challenge teenagers to develop and change? Are youth challenged to think about

115. Ibid., 56–57.
116. Robbins, *The Ministry of Nurture,* 154.
117. Gillespie, *The Experience of Faith,* 130.
118. Eugene C. Roehlkepartain, "The Thinking Climate: A Missing Ingredient In Youth Ministry," in *Christian Education Journal* 15, (Fall 1994), 53–63.

the implications of faith on school, family relationships, recreation, vocation, dating, and other domains of life?

• *Do youth religious educators and other adults model a thinking faith?* When adolescents observe their pastors, religious educators, parents, and other adults in the church, do they see people who are actively thinking about their faith and faith-related issues?

• *Are adolescents given answers, or are they led to discover answers for themselves?* Are youth given the skills to discern truth, think reflectively about their faith, and come to their own conclusions on critical issues?

The Emotional Domain: A second dimension of a personalized faith is the *emotional* or affective. This is that part of one's faith that is related to how he or she feels: the emotions, attitudes, and values. It refers to the conviction or passion one has about that of which he or she has knowledge. While the intellectual, or cognitive, domain is linked with the head, the emotional, or affective, domain is linked to the heart.[119] It is the part of faith that embraces and personalizes that which one believes with the head. Westerhoff suggests that perhaps we become too concerned too early with the activities of thinking in religious education and forget that the affections are just as important as the intellectual. In fact, in terms of faith the actions in the realm of affections are prior to the acts of thinking.[120]

What kind of experiences heighten the emotional element of the faith experience? Opportunities for experiencing the awe, wonder, and mystery of God abound in wilderness camping and outdoor activities such as hiking, cross-country skiing, rock climbing, canoeing, and backpacking. Participation in worship and prayer, as well as in the arts such as drama and music, gives adolescents opportunities for enhancing religious affections and facilitating the presence of faith. Journaling is a particularly good way to nurture reflection on how the adolescents feel about their religious experiences. Two suggestions for journaling are 1) reading a Psalm a day and jotting down thoughts on what was read; 2) writing one's own psalms.[121]

Finally, classroom procedures that promote active learning such as role-playing and simulation games, help adolescents identify their feel-

---

119. James Michael Lee, *The Content of Religious Education* (Birmingham, Ala.: Religious Education Press, 1985), 196.

120. Westerhoff, *Will Our Children Have Faith,* 94–95.

121. Robbins, *The Ministry of Nurture,* 65–66.

ings related to the faith experience. *Role-play* is the process of assigning participants roles of people in hypothetical or real situations.[122] In role-playing, youth explore life-related problems or issues by spontaneously acting them out and then discussing the enactments. Together, participants can explore feelings, values, attitudes, as well as strategies for solving problems.[123]

For example, assign the role of a skeptic or non-Christian to a capable individual—one who might clearly understand and be able to articulate questions in opposition to the Christian faith. Have others take turns trying to convince the skeptic to embrace the Christian faith. Following a role-play such as this, the teenagers can talk about the interaction, look for solutions to problems they encounter, and explore the feelings of the people whose roles they have assumed.[124]

Marlene LeFever suggests that role-play is a beneficial and powerful teaching tool for the following reasons, several of which are related to the affective domain of faith shaping:[125]

• By observing what teenagers say in the role-play, the youth religious educator is able to determine what the needs of the youth are.

• Through the role-play and subsequent discussion, students may find answers to their problems or questions.

• Role-play affords teenagers an opportunity to experience new, unusual, or problem situations in a protected, caring, environment.

• Role-play allows youth to experience and articulate their feelings.

• Role-play often deals with questions or issues youth have had but have not dared to mention.

• Teenagers learn to identify with the feelings and experiences of others.

Simulation games or activities try to reproduce some aspect of reality such as poverty, world hunger, or power struggles, often an event that is out of reach or beyond the adolescent's own life experience because of time, environment, or circumstances.[126] Because simulation activities

---

122. Marlene D. LeFever, *Creative Teaching Methods* (Elgin, Ill.: David C. Cook, 1985), 94.

123. Bruce Joyce and Marsha Weil, *Models of Teaching,* 3d ed. (Englewood Cliffs, N.J.: Prentice-Hall, 1986), 241.

124. LeFever, *Creative Teaching Methods,* 94.

125. Ibid., 94–98.

126. LeFever, *Creative Teaching Methods,* 149; Wayne Rice, John Roberto, and Mike Yaconelli, *Creative Learning Experiences* (Winona, Minn.: Saint Mary's Press, 1981), 110.

teach experientially, participants are likely to feel much more intently than if they were merely receiving information. For example, try the popular "World Hunger" simulation. Upon arriving at a banquet, group members are given a ticket signifying what they will eat. A large percentage will eat crackers and water and represent the millions of people who go to bed hungry each night. Another group might be fed plain rice, representing the multitudes who have enough food to live, but not in overabundance. Another group of teenagers might be given a full course meal, obviously representing those who have the luxury of having an abundance of food available to them. Expect some from the "poor" tables to come begging at the "rich" tables. Be prepared too for some anger to be expressed because of the unfairness of the situation. After the meal is eaten, the adolescents can not only discuss their thoughts on world hunger but express their feelings as well, which will surely be influenced and affected by their allotment of food at the banquet.[127]

Wayne Rice, John Roberto, and Mike Yaconelli offer the following suggestions for the effective use of simulation activities in youth religious education:[128]

• *Simulation activities should be placed within the proper context of the learning experience.* Simulations should never be used simply to fill time. Rather, they should be used as a portion of the whole learning experience.

• *Build in adequate time for debriefing and reflection.* Many simulations are powerful in their impact on the feelings of participants. Consequently, it is important to discuss the experience and to take time for the ventilation of the feelings generated.

• *Schedule in time for developing a plan of action.* If the youth group has just experienced the hunger simulation described above, sending everyone home without discussing a plan of action is achieving only part of the goal. Ideas of what can be done in response to what has been learned should be brainstormed.

• *Provide opportunity for a variety of viewpoints to be shared and digested by each individual.* Learning takes place even when the results are not precisely the same as those anticipated by the facilitator, and

---

127. A helpful book on simulation games is Richard Reichert, *Simulation Games for Religious Education* (Winona, Minn.: Saint Mary's Press, 1975).
128. Rice, Roberto, and Yaconelli, *Creative Learning Experiences,* 110–12.

results will be different every time the activity is played. Large groups might be broken down into smaller groups of four or five, to optimize the possibility of individual participation in discussion.

• *Make every effort to play the simulation in an environment conducive to the particular activity chosen.* Often the atmosphere or environment is critical to the effect of the simulation. If the activity is simulating, for example, an underground church in a Communist country, the impact will be enhanced by creating surroundings that help the participants sense the reality of worshipping in seclusion and in fear of authorities.

• *Choose an activity respectful of the people you are working with.* Some simulation activities are more difficult to learn than others; some take more time than others. Make sure the activity respects the ages and learning capacities of the group members.

The Volitional Domain: Real religious faith is more than just knowing or feeling. The "crowning aspect" of faith, as Perry Downs puts it is the *volitional.*[129] It is the choice of the will to live or act out in obedience through one's life-style that which is believed (intellectual) and valued (emotional). Jesus refers to this element of faith when he says "If you love me, you will obey what I command" (John 14:15, NIV).

A critical component of the religious education of youth is giving the skills and confidence to examine options and make life-style choices that are pleasing to God. Unfortunately, scripture does not always give us clear instruction on how to respond in every ethical or moral situation. Consequently, churches and parents tend to take away from adolescents the freedom of making their own life-style choices. Adults often want to make life painless as possible for teenagers by making choices for them, even to the point of establishing a censoring list of what movies to watch or songs to listen to. Once again, Gillespie points out that freedom is a very important reality in faith shaping. He says "it is an essential ingredient in people who want to personalize faith. We are well aware that freedom always implies some limitations. But for religious people, freedom implies the possibility to make personal choices, or at least perceive that the choices are personal and free."[130]

While age and situation must be taken into consideration, effective religious education ministry of youth must include teaching adolescents

---

129. Downs, "Faith Shaping: Bringing Youth to Spiritual Maturity," 50.
130. Gillespie, *The Experience of Faith,* 130.

to make wise and well thought out life-style choices. In regard to choice
of music, for example, rather than censoring certain songs for listening,
why not give adolescents some tools or criteria for examining lyrics
and music?

Case studies provide adolescents the opportunity to work through
some of the difficult life-style decisions and choices in the youth group
setting before they have to face them on the streets or in the locker room,
where there is considerably less support.[131] Chet Meyers and Thomas
Jones describe the case study as a narrative of an actual event that brings
learners and teachers together in an attempt to examine, discuss, and
suggest solutions to real-life problems and situations. The case study is
designed so that adolescents can identify with a particular situation and
the individuals described in it. The ideal studies will present a dilemma
or difficult situation that youth religious educators hope will stimulate a
variety of responses and suggestions for action from teenagers.[132]

The format for employing the case study follows a clearly defined
path: 1) participants receive information about the case and study it
for themselves 2) they then participate in group discussion, together
exploring possible solutions or answers to the dilemma, and finally, 3)
they reflect on the case, summarizing the possible solutions, as well as
thoughts on their actions, attitudes, and behaviors.[133] Here is a short
case study on dating:

*The Sanderson family thought Gary was a fine young boy. Their
15-year-old daughter Mindy, however, was forbidden to date him.
Gary was Chinese. He was adopted by the Whites when he was
only a few months old. He grew up in a typical suburban church
where most of the members were Caucasian. For the most part, the
church had accepted him in spite of his nationality; that is, until
he wanted to date Mindy Sanderson. Sandersons were prominent
church members; Mr. Sanderson served on the church board and
his wife was the church organist. The whole church was talking.
The Sandersons considered leaving the church. They were not
going to allow their daughter to date someone who was Chinese
or who was of any other minority group. It was fine for Gary to*

131. Robbins, *The Ministry of Nurture*, 154.
132. Chet Meyers and Thomas B. Jones, *Promoting Active Learning* (San Francisco:
Jossey-Bass, 1993), 103–4.
133. Ibid., 106.

participate in the church and they were glad he was a Christian.
However, when it concerned their daughter, it was a totally different
matter. [134]
- *What should Mindy do? What are her options?*
- *What are her responsibilities to her mother and father?*
- *What would you say to her parents?*

Youth Specialties' *Tension Getters* books are helpful resources for
case studies designed to help youth come to terms with difficult life-style
issues. These books include case studies that present real-life problems
and predicaments, such as cheating or abortion, and are ideal strategies
to be used as discussion starters, to introduce role-play, or to set the
scene for a skit or dramatic situation. [135]

Certainly, some youth will make life-style decisions that may not
be pleasing to youth workers or parents, but in the long run they can
learn to reason in a mature and biblical manner. It is unfortunate that in
the religious education of youth, well-meaning and loving teachers and
workers often short-circuit the faith development of youth by placing
prohibitions rather than nurturing mature decision making and providing
good models for living. [136]

Self-Esteem and Identity

One of the most important psychological aspects of identity is self-
esteem, defined as one's attitude toward self. In fact, William Glasser
argues that there are two basic psychological needs of people: love and
self-esteem, or self-worth. These, he adds, are the two pathways to the
successful achievement of identity. [137] Usually, self-esteem is thought
of in evaluative terms. A person may be described as having either a
positive or negative self-esteem; either an accepting or a critical view
toward self.

An adolescent's self-esteem is shaped by a number of factors including treatment by parents, a perception of his or her own body

---

134. Adapted from Wayne Rice and Mike Yaconelli, *Tension Getters* (Grand Rapids,
Mich.: Zondervan, 1981), 49.

135. Rice and Yaconelli, *Tension Getters*; Wayne Rice and Mike Yaconelli, *Tension*
Getters Two (Grand Rapids, Mich.: Zondervan, 1985).

136. Gillespie, *The Experience of Faith,* 131.

137. William Glasser, *Schools Without Failure* (New York: Harper and Row, 1969),
12–15.

development and physical attractiveness, evaluation by peers, and a response to the standards portrayed by society. Parents can foster a negative self-esteem by abusing or unduly punishing a child, berating, rejecting, or criticizing, comparing a child with others, and by placing unrealistic expectations on a son or daughter.[138]

Some relevant empirical research indicates that during early adolescence, self-esteem tends to become more negative than during childhood or late adolescence. Girls, especially, may look at their bodies and feel unsatisfied with what they see. Weight, in our society, is a particularly important component as to how a girl feels about her body. Society places a strong emphasis on slimness, thus the heavier a girl is, or thinks she is, the more dissatisfied with herself she becomes.[139] The self-starving disorder of anorexia nervosa is often related to self-esteem. Most common among girls and young women of middle and upper classes, anorexics place tremendous pressure on themselves to be slim. This is often a response to society's concept of being slender equated with being beautiful and adored, and fatness equated with being ugly and unloved.[140]

An adolescent also perceives himself or herself as attractive, successful, or acceptable because of the responses of others, especially peers.[141] Most people take seriously the opinions of others about them, and these opinions become part of the definition of themselves.[142]

Finally, personal competence contributes to one's self-esteem. When an adolescent is successful in sports, academics, music, or whatever, there is a greater likelihood that the individual will feel confident about himself or herself. Likewise, experiences of failures or incompetencies will lead to low self-esteem.[143]

In his extensive study of church-going adolescents, Merton Strommen found one cry of teenagers to be the cry of self-hatred, characterized by distress over personal faults, lack of self-confidence, and low self-regard. He concluded that one in five church youth harbors thoughts of

---

138. Bruce Narramore, *You're Someone Special* (Grand Rapids, Mich.: Zondervan, 1978), 79.
139. Tobin-Richards et al., "Puberty and Its Psychological and Social Significance," 29–30.
140. Barbara Newman and Philip Newman, *Adolescent Development* (Columbus, Ohio: Merrill, 1986), 142.
141. Ibid., 277.
142. Ibid., 279.
143. Ibid., 281.

severe self-criticism.[144] Other studies indicate that as many as 95 percent of the population (including adults) feel inferior and inadequate.[145] Adolescents with low or poor self-esteem are more susceptible to peer pressure, are more likely to engage in at-risk behaviors such as alcohol and drug abuse, are more suicidal, and are more likely to seek acceptance through sexual activity.[146]

Most youth experience periods of feeling quite worthless, especially when they experience difficulties in their relationships with friends or fail to measure up in school or in activities such as sports and music. Such feelings usually pass, but if they persist and dominate the adolescent, they can become destructive and interfere with many aspects of life such as peer relationships, studies, and spiritual development. These adolescents need special attention.[147] Jerry Aldridge identifies four basic requirements for the development of positive self-esteem in adolescents: a sense of belonging, a feeling of individuality, the opportunity to choose, and the presence of good models.[148]

Building a Sense of Belonging: Adolescents often feel lonely and isolated from other people, but this is especially so for youth suffering from low self-esteem.[149] A youth ministry to adolescents who feel isolated and poorly about themselves begins with adult workers who demonstrate and model the warmth and empathy of a concerned person. Many times the teaching procedures and programs that are offered matter little to the teenager with low self-esteem, if the worker/adolescent interaction does not establish a warm relationship. The effective relationship means communicating to youth that they are loved, that they are important, and that they do have potential.[150]

Low-esteem youth also need a community or small group where they can sense they are accepted.[151] For larger youth groups, it may be necessary to systematically break the group into smaller units. These

---

144. Merton P. Strommen, *Five Cries of Youth,* 2nd rev. ed. (San Francisco: Harper and Row, 1988), 18–23.

145. Collins, *Christian Counseling,* 313.

146. Ray Johnston, *Developing Student Leaders* (Grand Rapids, Mich.: Zondervan, 1992), 21.

147. Strommen, *Five Cries of Youth,* 21.

148. Jerry Aldridge, "Preadolescence," in Donald Ratcliff and James A. Davies, eds., *Handbook of Youth Ministry* (Birmingham, Ala.: Religious Education Press, 1991), 107.

149. Strommen, *Five Cries of Youth,* 24.

150. Ibid., 37–38.

151. Ibid.

small groups of six to eight might meet once a week in homes or meet on a regular basis in conjunction with large group functions. It is important, however, that the small group membership remain constant for a period of time (perhaps six months or a year), so a sense of belonging or community can be nurtured.[152]

Finally, avoiding unnecessary competitive activities and comparisons is important in working with youth who have difficulties with low self-esteem and have trouble experiencing a sense of belonging. Merton Strommen suggests that competitive activities such as "head-trip" discussions and competitive sports tend to encourage unfavorable comparisons and threaten some youth.[153] While competition cannot be avoided entirely, youth ministries should stress cooperative activities and games that neutralize the superior skills of some of the participants. For example, rather than playing a regular softball game that emphasizes the skills of the athletes while isolating those who cannot catch and hit the ball so well, try modifying the game by using a whiffle ball and plastic bat. Add a further dimension to the game by requiring batters and fielders to get inside a large garbage bag, forcing them to hop rather than run to the ball and bases. Or try three-legged soccer. Participants on each team are paired off and instructed to tie their adjacent legs together. Team members are only allowed to kick the ball with the "middle" leg. These modifications bring the athletic and nonathletic participants much closer together in skill levels and add a new dimension of humor and fun to the games.[154]

Developing Individuality or Uniqueness: While adolescents have a strong need to belong, they also have the need to be distinct or unique. However, one of the primary distinctives of adolescents with low self-esteem is that they tend to perceive themselves as having little worth or importance.[155] Furthermore, they often lack self-confidence and live

---

152. See David R. Veerman, *Small Group Ministry with Youth* (Wheaton, Ill.: Victor, 1992), for helpful ideas on using small groups in youth ministry.

153. For additional comments on the negative aspects of competition see Strommen, *Five Cries of Youth*, 38; Anthony Campolo, *The Church and The American Teenager* (Grand Rapids, Mich.: Zondervan, 1989), 21–22; Aldridge, "Preadolescence," 108.

154. See Wayne Rice and Mike Yaconelli, *Play It* (Grand Rapids, Mich.: Zondervan, 1986) for some ideas for noncompetitive games. Another helpful book on cooperative sports and games is Terry Orlick, *The Cooperative Sports and Games Book* (New York: Pantheon, 1978).

155. Strommen, *Five Cries of Youth*, 23.

in fear of failing or being humiliated by making a mistake or blunder. Adolescents with low self-esteem may also be convinced that they lack talent or abilities, yet realize their dependence on the praise of others.[156]

A sense of individuality and uniqueness can be enhanced in youth ministry settings by encouraging adolescents to express their own ideas. Parents and youth workers alike should be encouraged to listen to the viewpoints of teenagers even when they differ from one's own.[157]

Likewise, teenagers should be encouraged to share their talents and abilities. It may be difficult, however, to get low-esteem youth to involve themselves in activities where they might fail. They tend not to try out for the school play, or work on important committees, or join in a volleyball or softball game.[158] They should know that they are loved and accepted even if they make mistakes or their performance lacks a certain amount of quality.

Getting adolescents involved in the leadership level of youth ministry will provide valuable benefits in the areas of self-esteem and individuality. Involvement in leadership will help young people feel significant and responsible, enable them to gain competence in certain skills, and help them develop character.[159] Allow the adolescent leaders a certain amount of freedom so that they can perform their duties with a measure of individuality. Teenagers need opportunities to explore and implement their newly discovered thinking and problem-solving skills in order to enhance their sense of competency.[160]

Most important, young people should achieve a sense of uniqueness by recognizing who they are in relationship to God. Adolescents should understand that they are created in God's image (Genesis 1:26), they are the pinnacle and culmination of His creation (Psalms 8:4–5), purchased by the blood of Christ (I Cor. 6:20; I Peter 1:18–19), and proclaimed to be of great value by Christ (Matthew 6:26). Because we are created in God's image, we possess great significance, worth, and value.[161]

Encouraging the Ability To Make Choices: Aldridge suggests a third essential to healthy self-esteem is the ability to make personal decisions

---

156. Ibid., 21–22.

157. Jerry Aldridge, *Self-Esteem: Loving Yourself at Every Age* (Birmingham, Ala.: Doxa Books, 1993), 87.

158. Aldridge, "Preadolescence," 108.

159. Johnston, *Developing Student Leaders,* 20–21.

160. Aldridge, *Self-Esteem: Loving Yourself at Every Age,* 88.

161. See Narramore, *You're Someone Special,* for a biblical perspective on self-esteem.

and maintain a certain amount of control over the environment. The ability, and consequently the privilege, to make choices increase as a child grows in age and maturity. Adolescents can be given increasing responsibility in participating in the decision-making processes of the youth group.[162] According to Stanley Coopersmith, an essential component to a healthy self-esteem is power.[163] Holding positions of leadership allows youth to feel that they are making important decisions, thus giving them a sense of power.

It is important, however, that when youth group members are asked to participate in decision-making activities that they be listened to when they contribute worthwhile insights and information. Youth, especially those with low self-esteem may become annoyed or hurt when adult leaders ask for their input and then fail to respond to what the youth have shared.[164]

Providing Good Role Models: The final requirement for the development of healthy adolescent self-esteem is the presence of good models.[165] For adolescents, models include parents, teachers, church workers, employers, and certain peers. One of the primary roles of the volunteer or full-time youth worker is that of modeling. Donald Posterski, who has done extensive studies on the Canadian youth culture suggests adults ponder the question Does my behavior deserve to be duplicated?[166] He goes on to say that adults who hope to serve the best interests of youth will lead the way with their living; they will model what matters. Adults who have high aspirations for the younger generation will give them something worth watching.[167]

CONCLUSION

This chapter has explored the critical and arduous adolescent task of identity formation. From the material presented in this chapter it is

---

162. Aldridge, "Preadolescence," 109.
163. Stanley Coopersmith, *The Antecedents of Self-Esteem* (Palo Alto, Calif.: Consulting Psychology Press, 1967).
164. Maria Edwards, *Total Youth Ministry* (Winona, Minn.: Christian Brothers Publications, 1980), 31.
165. Aldridge, "Preadolescence," 109.
166. Reginald W. Bibby and Donald C. Posterski, *Teen Trends* (Toronto, Ont.: Stoddart, 1992), 320.
167. Ibid.

clearly evident that identity achievement is not a single-faceted under-taking; rather, it is a highly complex and interactive process by which the individual establishes his or her personal goals, values, beliefs, and even life-style.

In an increasingly complex, fast-paced, and stressful world adoles-cents seek answers to questions such as Who am I? and How do I fit in? The task of the youth religious educator is to assist adolescents in achieving a sense of identity by focusing on issues related to autonomy, vocation, sexuality, gender roles, religious faith, and self-esteem.

3

Adolescence and the Contemporary Family

Of the numerous groups to which adolescents belong, the family clearly is the most significant in affecting and shaping their lives. Family dynamics penetrate the very personality of an individual, significantly influence the manner in which a teenager weathers the storms of adolescence, and have a profound bearing on how a young person positively emerges into young adulthood. No other social institution or group offers an adolescent what a family does: security, affection, emotional support, and protection against a harsh and sometimes cruel world.

Furthermore, empirical research indicates that critical family issues are related to a number of youth crises and destructive patterns, such as suicide, premarital sexual activity, running away from home, substance abuse, and low self-esteem. Thus, it is not only fitting, but imperative, that any discussion of contemporary youth issues includes the effects the family has on the adolescent.

THE RAPIDLY CHANGING AMERICAN FAMILY

The traditional concept of family in the United States and Canada as well as much of Western culture finds its roots in Judeo-Christian heritage and has been based on the ideal of families as conjugal units. Historically, the wife was primarily a homemaker, the husband was the chief source of economic income and main source of authority, and children were a source of pride and satisfaction, expected to carry on

66

the cycle of marriage and procreation. Often families included close relatives such as grandparents, uncles, and aunts, which meant there were generally many adults who served as role models and guardians, and shared in the child rearing process.

In the first half of the twentieth century in America, the extended family was all but replaced by the nuclear family—normally one adult of each sex and two or three children. However, since the 1960s, the family has seen even more radical changes, to the point that some insist we can no longer speak of a typical family or that the family is no longer a viable unit.[1]

The most dramatic change comes in regard to society's view and practice of divorce. In 1885, the rate of divorce per 1,000 people was 0.6. That rate has risen steadily and peaked in 1980 when there were 5.2 divorces per 1,000. In 1991 the rate was 4.7 per 1,000, or 1,187,000 divorces.[2] Another trend that has considerably altered the shape of the family is the choice to remain single. The single or unmarried adult population includes those who have never been married, as well those who are divorced, separated, and widowed, and is the fastest growing family type in America.

Because of these trends, children are now being reared in a variety of situations. Many, of course, are still a part of a family that includes a biological mother and a biological father, but even in many of these cases both parents work full time. Other families include at least one parent who has been married before; sometimes both have been married several times. A growing number of families are headed by a single-parent— either a divorced parent or a "never been married" mother. Babies born to single women now represent over 25 percent of all newborns—the highest proportion ever.[3] There are also a growing number of homosexual "marriages," some of which involve the rearing of children. It is estimated that only 41 percent of the youth we work with will reach age 18 having lived in a traditional two-parent family.[4]

---

1. Hershel D. Thornburg, *Development in Adolescence,* 2nd ed. (Monterey, Calif: Brooks/Cole, 1982), 148.

2. U.S. Bureau of the Census, *Statistical Abstract of the United States:* 1993 (113th edition.) Washington, D.C.: U.S. Government Printing Office, 1993, 103.

3. Ibid., 69.

4. Merton P. Strommen, *Five Cries of Youth,* 2nd rev. ed. (San Francisco: Harper and Row, 1993), 64.

While research indicates that instability of the family and breakup of marriages have negative and destructive repercussions, there are those who acclaim and promote the transitions in family structure as described above. As early as 1972, reactionaries, especially feminists, expressed opposition to the traditional heterosexual marriage as the basis for rearing children and establishing family life. One source proposed, "The end of the institution of marriage is a necessary condition for the liberation of women. Therefore, it is important for us to encourage women to leave their husbands and not live individually with men. We must build alternatives to marriage."[5] A decade later, another writer argued that the significant changes the family has been going through should stimulate interest in new family processes and in trying new family structures such as cohabitation, part-time marriages, communes, cooperatives, and postmarital singlehood.[6]

In a 1992 edition focusing on the century to come, *Time* magazine featured an article on the family titled "The Nuclear Family Goes Boom!" The article not only predicted significant changes to come but portrayed the nuclear family in a cynical and sardonic manner. The very term nuclear family, suggests the writer, gives off a musty smell and eventually will not be seen as normal, but rather as a fascinating anomaly. In the future, she says, the family will look like this: "The family of the 21st century may have a robot maid, but the chances are good that it will also be interracial or bisexual, divided by divorce, multiplied by remarriage, expanded by new birth technologies—or perhaps all of the above. Single-parents and working moms will become increasingly the norm, as will out-of-wedlock babies, though there will surely be a more modern term for them. The concept of the illegitimate child will vanish because the concept of the patriarchal nuclear family will vanish."[7]

This grim analysis of where the family is today and where it may be in the years to come is a bleak reminder to the church of the formidable yet indispensable task it has of making sure the family is not rendered obsolete. While the nuclear family will not cease to exist, as many social scientists would like to suggest, we must be cognizant of the

---

5. N. Lehmann and H. Sullinger, *The Document: Declaration of Feminism* (Minneapolis, Minn.: Powderhorn Station, 1972), 11–12.

6. Thornburg, *Development in Adolescence,* 148.

7. Claudia Wallis, "The Nuclear Family Goes Boom!" in *Time* (Fall Special 1992), 42–44.

fact that many of the children and adolescents we work with will be products of nontraditional families. In addition, these youth will be shaped largely by those cultural influences that are antithetical to Judeo-Christian teachings and values.

Much of the effectiveness of youth ministry now and in the future will be contingent on the church's and youth religious educator's capacity to work with parents and to strengthen the family. Researcher George Barna says the battle and opportunity for the future will be to redefine the family in a sensible manner and to insist that the standards of God's Word become the basis for family policies, systems, and teachings.[8]

THE TRAUMA OF DIVORCE

Divorce is more common today than it ever has been in the past, not only in North America but in other parts of the world as well. It can be predicted with a good degree of certainty that at least two out of every five marriages will end in separation or divorce.[9] Divorce has literally ravaged the American family, and the instability of the institution of marriage is a matter of great concern for the church and those who do religious education with adolescents.

Empirical research studies indicate that divorce has negative effects on both the emotions and behavior of children and adolescents. One of the most significant empirical research endeavors on the impact of divorce on children and teenagers was a 10-year study carried out by Judy Wallerstein and Sandra Blakeslee. As a result of their research on 131 children from 60 families, they concluded that while most men, women, and children appear outwardly to get their life on track within two and one-half to three and one-half years, the profound internal changes that people experience in the wake of divorce are never lost.[10] "Children's fundamental attitudes about society and about themselves can be forever changed by divorce and by events experienced in the years afterward. These changes can be incorporated permanently into their developing characters and personalities. The post divorce family and the

---

8. George Barna, *The Future of the American Family* (Chicago: Moody, 1993), 38.
9. Charles M. Sell, *Family Ministry,* 2nd ed. (Grand Rapids, Mich.: Zondervan, 1995), 42.
10. Judy S. Wallerstein and Sandra Blakeslee, *Second Chances* (New York: Ticknor and Fields, 1989), xii.

remarried family are radically different from the original intact family. Relationships are different. Problems, satisfactions, vulnerabilities, and strengths are different. People may get their lives back on track, but for most the track runs a wholly different course than the one they were on before divorce."[11]

Among the conclusions of this study are the following:
• Children of all ages tend to feel intensely rejected when their parents divorce.
• Children tend to feel intense loneliness as most of the supports fall away.
• Many children tend to feel guilty, and think that it is their duty to bring the marriage back together.
• The severity of a child's reaction at the time of the divorce is not indicative of how a child will fare years later. Some of the most troubled children turned out emotionally healthy a decade later, while some of the least troubled were in much poorer shape ten or fifteen years later.
• Ten years after the divorce, nearly half of the boys (now between 19 and 29) were unhappy, lonely, and had few, if any, lasting relationships with women.
• Thirty-seven percent of the children of divorce had severe problems adjusting; 29 percent were coping but not recovered, while another 34 percent adjusted adequately.

Other empirical research studies have made similar discoveries. In their study of divorce, Cline and Westman found 52 percent of the families continued to have hostile encounters requiring court intervention after the divorce. Nearly all of these interactions involved the children in some manner.[12]

In his carefully conducted study of church youth, Merton Strommen was able to make several generalizations based on comparisons between young people who experienced divorce and those who did not. Youth whose parents are divorced or separated
• are more bothered by lack of family unity and more likely to report family pressures;

---

11. Ibid.
12. David W. Cline and Jack C. Westman, "The Impact of Divorce on the Family," in *Child Psychology and Human Development* 2, (Winter 1971), 78–83.

- have a lower estimate of self worth;
- have more difficulty in school studies;
- demonstrate a lower interest in religious matters.[13]

Researcher George Barna found that divorced parents were less likely to spend time with their children than married parents, in seven of eight areas. These areas are[14]

- watching television,
- doing homework or educational activities,
- going out for a fun meal together,
- driving to a special place that would be of interest to the kids,
- playing a sport together,
- experiencing a cultural activity together, and
- going to a movie.

The only item where there was no significant difference was "spending more than 30 minutes at a time talking about life."

Children of divorce will usually encounter a number of negative emotions and feelings as they attempt to cope with the trauma of divorce. Some of the most common reactions are:[15]

- guilt (I am the cause of the divorce),
- denial (this is not really happening),
- fear (what will happen to me),
- shame (I am not like other teenagers who have two parents),
- confusion (I do not know who to believe),
- sadness (I cannot allow myself to be happy now),
- depression (it is hopeless),
- hurt (someone I love has disappointed me),
- blame (one of my parents is responsible for this), and
- anger (I cannot change anything and it is not fair).

Occasionally teenagers will report a positive feeling of relief; relief that the fighting and hostilities have ceased and that their parents are taking some steps to end the tension that has existed.

How can the youth religious educator effectively work with adolescents from divorced homes? It is essential that adolescents verbalize

---

13. Strommen, *Five Cries of Youth*, 44.
14. Barna, *The Future of the American Family*, 87.
15. Velma T. Carter and J. Lynn Leavenworth, *Caught in the Middle: Children of Divorce* (Valley Forge, Pa.: Judson, 1985), 81 ff.

their feelings related to their parents' divorce. While a youth worker can encourage teenagers to talk about their feelings by spending individual time with them, it might be better to have them join support groups where they can talk to other teenagers who have divorced parents. A youth ministry support group is a small group of five to ten individuals who share a common problem or need (in this case the commonality is divorced parents), meet on a regular basis, and covenant to give emotional, spiritual, and even physical support to each other in their struggles and hurts. Support comes by sharing their experiences, learning from one another, offering suggestions to group members, giving encouragement to each other, talking about their problems, and praying for each other. Support groups might also engage in recreational activities such as attending a baseball game together or going bowling.[16]

A critical but often overlooked dimension of youth ministry is working with parents. In the context of divorce, the youth religious educator might encourage adolescents and their parents to speak openly about the divorce and related issues. For example, they should talk about the future, including the parents' intentions for remarriage, living arrangements, financial arrangements, and the possibility of moving. These are all major concerns for the teenage children, but, unless urged, parents may avoid talking about them.[17]

As mentioned above, what teenagers experiencing divorce need most is a listening ear and someone to say "I understand how you are feeling." However, there are some words of advice the sensitive youth worker can share with these hurting adolescents.[18]

First, find someone to talk to. Besides the youth worker, they might seek out some other teenagers who have endured their parents' divorce.

Second, do not blame yourself. Many adolescents identify themselves as a reason for the divorce of their parents. While children may have agitated the situation or caused some family disruption, parents are adults and accountable for their own actions.

---

16. It is important not to confuse a support group with psychotherapy and counseling groups. Counseling and psychotherapy groups usually focus on the alleviation of some type of problem and are professionally led. Support groups are usually led by people struggling with the same issues as group members.

17. G. Wade Rowatt, *Pastoral Care With Adolescents in Crisis* (Louisville, Ky.: Westminster/John Knox, 1989), 87.

18. Adapted from H. S. Vigeveno and Anne Claire, *Divorce and the Children* (Glendale, Calif.: Regal, 1979), 113–24.

Third, do not take sides or try to retaliate against one or both of your parents. Retaliation often comes in the form of refusal to communicate with or see a parent.

Fourth, resist the temptation to isolate yourself. While some private time of reflection is important, shutting themselves in a room and pouting or allowing themselves to get depressed is unhealthy for teenagers.

Fifth, try not to agitate the situation. Perhaps the thinking is "If I stir up enough trouble, they will get back together." However in such family situations, there is enough trouble and disharmony already.

Finally, look for help and friendship in the right places. Church youth groups, Christian friends, Christian camps, and good sports programs can all be effective in providing the teenager with healthy surroundings.

The "divorce panel" is a teaching procedure that Mike Yaconelli and Jim Burns suggest can help all youth group members better understand the effects of divorce. It can be a supportive experience for youth whose parents are already divorced, it can help teenagers currently going through a divorce experience to better understand what is happening, and it can teach other youth group members how to help a friend whose parents are divorced or divorcing.

The first step is to ask several teenagers whose parents are divorced to serve on a panel. Give them a list of possible questions, so that they can make a decision as to whether they can handle the experience. If they decide the activity would be too difficult for them, give them the privilege of declining.

Select an adult to moderate the panel. This person should be sensitive to the pain that most adolescent children of divorce would be experiencing. Make sure the moderator does research and is well prepared in understanding the effects of divorce.

Here are some sample questions youth members might ask of the panel:

• How did you find out your parents were going to get a divorce?
• Did the way in which you were told of your parents' divorce help or hinder your acceptance of it?
• Did your role in the family change in any way after the divorce? How?
• What kinds of things did friends and peers do or say in response to the divorce? Is there anything you wish they had done or said?[19]

---

19. Adapted from Mike Yaconelli and Jim Burns, *High School Ministry* (Grand Rapids, Mich.: Zondervan, 1986), 193–94.

FAMILY CONFLICT AND PROBLEM SITUATIONS

As unfortunate and difficult as divorce is for many adolescents, acute family problems are not confined to children of divorce. For many youth, home life is characterized by parent-youth conflicts, father absenteeism, abuse, distrustful parents, or overly authoritative parents. Merton Strommen insists that the most poignant cry of adolescents is that of despair or sheer frustration that comes from living in atmospheres of parental hatred and distrust.[20] Such distress sometimes results in running away from home, suicide or attempted suicide, delinquent behavior, and/or low self-esteem.

Strommen's study of church youth found that one in five teenagers can be placed in the category of a troubled-home situation. These "psychological orphans," as he describes them, demonstrate four major characteristics:[21]

• family pressures such as divorce or separation of parents, illness, financial pressures, father absenteeism, unemployment, death, and parent-youth strife;

• distress over parental relationships such as lack of communication and understanding with parents, feelings of being treated as a child, overly strict parents, and parental distrust and rejection;

• family disunity, including a lack of closeness and oneness of family members; and

• lack of concern among members—some troubled youth do not see their parents as caring people. Some of these family situations will be explored in this section.

Stressed and Dysfunctional Families

In addition to divorced families, there are a number of other family types that might be considered stressed or dysfunctional in nature. Most stressed and dysfunctional family situations lead to some at-risk behavior on behalf of the teenager. Some of the family situations that may place all family members—but certainly adolescent children—under moderate to extreme stress are single-parent families, blended families, latchkey families, substance-abusing families, families experiencing violence and conflict, and father-absent families.

---

20. Strommen, *Five Cries of Youth,* 41.
21. Ibid., 44.

Single-Parent Families: One of the most troublesome and widespread family dysfunctions is the single-parent family. In the United States approximately 25 percent of the children under 18 live in a single-parent home, the majority of these living with the mother.[22] The effects of living in a single-parent household can be quite devastating. One study found that children of single mothers were more likely

- to have repeated a grade in school,
- to have been expelled from school, and
- to have been treated for emotional and behavioral problems, than those living with both biological parents.[23]

Merton and Irene Strommen compared responses of single-parents to those parents of intact families (where there has not been separation, divorce, or death), in regard to the well-being of their children. More single-parents than parents of intact families

- rated their child in the direction of being disobedient, rebellious, likely to get in trouble, disrespectful of authority, and not a good student;
- used extreme measures of discipline—either by being too lenient or reacting in anger by yelling or hitting the child; and
- were less active in church and community organizations—something which held true for their children as well.[24]

The Search Institute compared at-risk behaviors of children from single-parent families to those living in two-parent families. The researchers concluded that youth in single-parent families are, on the average, clearly more at risk than adolescents from two-parent families. For example, the percentage of adolescents who have experienced intercourse at least twice rises from 35 percent (two-parent families) to 53 percent (one-parent families). The percent of adolescents who have attempted suicide once or more jumps from 12 percent (two parents) to 19 percent (one parent). On twenty at-risk behaviors (other behaviors include illicit drug use, alcohol use, binge drinking, depression, fighting, theft, school absenteeism), this pattern remains consistent. The authors conclude that whether we are looking at males or females, younger or

---

22. U.S. Bureau of the Census, *Statistical Abstract of the United States: 1993,* 64.

23. Deborah Dawson, "Family Structure and Children's Health and Well-Being: Data From the 1988 National Health Interview Survey on Child Health," in *Journal of Marriage and The Family* 54, (August 1991), 573–84.

24. Merton P. Strommen and A. Irene Strommen, *Five Cries of Parents* (San Francisco: Harper & Row, 1985), 25.

older adolescents, whites or ethnic minorities, teenagers in one-parent families tend to engage in risk-taking behaviors with greater frequency than do adolescents in intact two-parent families.[25]

An effective way to work with single-parent teenagers is to involve them in the larger church community. One strategy is to divide the church into "family pods" where people of different ages and family structures are clustered in "family" groups for lessons, socials, and other activities.[26] In these group structures single-parent adolescents have the opportunity to be in close proximity to intact families.

A "buddy program" is a good way to provide opposite-sex role models for adolescents. In this program, adults in the church or parish volunteer to periodically spend time with single-parent teenagers.[27] If, for example, a male adolescent is in a home without a father, a man in the church would volunteer to do something with this young person from time to time. They might attend a baseball game, go fishing, work on a car, or play tennis. The activities they engage in would depend on the interests and abilities of the parties involved.

Blended Families: Blended families, also known as reconstituted or stepparent families, are those in which one or both of the remarried partners bring children into the new family relationship. As divorce and remarriage become more common, the number of children living in blended families progressively increases. Approximately one third of the children born in the early 1980's can expect to live with a stepparent before they reach the age of 18.[28]

Citing a Search Institute study, Merton Strommen reported more adolescents in stepfamilies evidenced deviant behavior, erotic activities, parent-youth conflict, and identity and achievement problems. In addition, more of these youth felt they received less parental affection and nurturance, and either more authoritarian or permissive treatment.[29]

---

25. Peter L. Benson and Eugene C. Roehlkepartain, *Youth in Single-Parent Families* (Minneapolis, Minn.: Search Institute, 1993), 7–8, 17.

26. Diane L. Pancoast and Kathy Bobula, "Building Multigenerational Support Networks," in Diana S. Richmond Garland and Diane L. Pancoast, eds., *The Church's Ministry With Families* (Dallas, Tex.: Word, 1990), 180.

27. Sell, *Family Ministry,* 330.

28. Mark Fine and Lawrence Kurdek, "The Adjustment of Adolescents in Stepfather and Stepmother Families," in *Journal of Marriage and the Family* 54, (November 1992), 725.

29. Strommen, *Five Cries of Youth,* 65.

Several additional problems may emerge in reconstituted families. First, children may become confused living with a stepmother or step-father, while their biological parent lives elsewhere. In other words, a difficulty may exist in determining the proper relationship between the child and stepparent, and divided loyalties will certainly exist. A second source of difficulty may be an unrealistic expectation on the part of the stepparent, such as the equal sharing in each other's lives. Finally, stepchildren are often more tolerant of the mistakes of their natural parents than those of stepparents. Thus, they may enter a blended family situation with suspicion, overcautiousness, and resentfulness. Stepparents may initially try very hard to be loving and caring but when rebuffed tend to retreat to a less active parenting role.[30]

Once again, ministry and religious education to youth must include ministry to parents. How parents handle the dynamics of a blended family powerfully impacts the spiritual and emotional development of their adolescent children. Needed for both adolescents and parents of single-parent and blended families are classes on relating to one another, creating a close family life, communicating with one another, and, most important, how to pray and share their faith with one another.[31]

Parent education has become extremely popular in churches. Many such programs focus on teaching parents attitudes, knowledge, and skills critical to successful adolescent rearing. Parents learn how to listen to their teenage children, how to communicate so that they will be heard, how to effectively discipline, how to instill responsibility in adolescents, and how to nurture spiritual growth.[32]

One such program is the Parent Effectiveness Training (PET) program developed by Thomas Gordon. Convinced that most parents desire to rear emotionally balanced children but often lack the knowledge and skills to do so, Gordon developed a systematic program of training for the task of parenthood. In these classes parents are taught effective forms of communication such as active listening, empathetic open-ended questioning, and reflecting of feelings. They also learn methods

---

30. Jack O. Balswick and Judith K. Balswick, *The Family* (Grand Rapids, Mich.: Baker, 1991), 267–69.

31. Strommen, *Five Cries of Youth,* 66.

32. Diana S. Richmond Garland, "Developing and Empowering Parent Networks," in Diana S. Richmond Garland and Diane L. Pancoast, eds., *The Church's Ministry With Families* (Dallas, Tex.: Word, 1990), 92.

of preventing conflicts between parents and children as well as conflict resolution.[33]

Parents in all types of family structures must see the need for developing and nurturing a supportive network of relationships for themselves and their children. Parent networks are initiated by linking parents with one another so that they can share common problems, questions, concerns, experiences, and activities. The following activities might be included in a supportive parent network:[34]

• Contact and become acquainted with the parents of their teenage children's friends.
• Talk with other parents about some of your concerns (What movies are you allowing your children to watch? What guidelines or rules do you have for dating?).
• Meet together to talk over shared concerns: (e.g., drugs and alcohol in the school).
• Swap services such as chaperoning activities or transporting children to school or church activities.
• Cooperate to offer alternative activities to those in which parents feel their teenagers should not be involved (such as a party instead of a rock concert).
• Offer each other help in times of crisis (perhaps a meal during sickness).
• Provide nurture and support to the adolescent children of others.[35]

Latchkey Families: On any given weekday in the United States and Canada, between the hours of 3:00 P.M. and 6:00 P.M., millions of children and young adolescents are left without adult supervision. In the United States, estimates of the number of latchkey children vary from 2 to 15 million, or 7 percent to 45 percent of all elementary children. However, there are also appreciable numbers of preschool children and adolescents who are in such self-care, and authorities maintain that the number of latchkey children will continue to increase.[36] Latchkey families are those in which the parents are not available to their children before or after school and on school holidays. Latchkey children are so

---

33. Thomas Gordon, *Parent Effectiveness Training: The Tested New Way to Raise Children* (New York: Peter H. Wyden, 1970).
34. Garland, "Developing and Empowering Parent Networks," 91–101.
35. Ibid.
36. Frances Smardo Dowd, *Latchkey Children in the Library and Community* (Phoenix, Ariz.: Oryx Press, 1991), 6–7.

named because they often wear a house key on a chain or string around their neck to let themselves in their homes independently after school.[37] At least three factors contribute to the latchkey phenomenon. First, the number of mothers in the work force continues to grow. Second, single-parent families have become the norm. Third, there is a lack of affordable child care available.

With the increasing number of children and adolescents supervising themselves, professionals interested in the welfare of children have raised concern as to the consequences of being in self-care. Frances Dowd summarizes the detrimental impact of the latchkey experience on children and adolescents:[38]

• a high incidence of loneliness, fear, stress, and conflict;
• increased use of drugs and alcohol;
• unsupervised television viewing;
• increased sexual activity;
• risk of safety (research indicates that children are more likely to be seriously injured when they do not have an adult caregiver available);
• difficulties in school.

Many parents, but especially single-parents, agonize over the fact that they have many demands on them and do not have adequate time for supporting and exercising proper supervision over their children and teenagers. Given the fact that many parents have no choice in the matter of work and that the number of latchkey children will rise, it is time for churches and youth religious education programs to consider the possibility of after-school programs. While many organizations and institutions are offering supervision and activities for elementary-age children, there are few programs offered to teenagers.

Youth ministries that desire to take advantage of the opportunity to reach out to adolescents of latchkey families might consider the following activities in an after-school program:

• sports and games,
• tutoring and homework assistance,
• counseling,
• music and art, and
• Bible studies.

---

37. Ibid., 3.
38. Ibid., 13–18.

Substance-Abusing Families: Children and adolescents from homes of drug- or alcohol-abusing parents are at extreme risk for abuse, neglect, and emotional damage. Parental drinking and drug use patterns are a very important influence on adolescent substance abuse.[39] Empirical studies further relate substance abuse of parents to family problems such as physical abuse[40] and denial of clothing, food, and education to children.[41] Children of alcoholic parents may also exhibit antisocial behavior, experience problems with the law, and have difficulties at school.[42]

Two self-help or recovery groups that operate throughout the United States and Canada for family members of alcoholics are Alateen (for teenage children of alcoholics) and Al-Anon (for family and friends of alcoholics). In these recovery groups family members of alcoholics meet together much like the twelve-step program of Alcoholics Anonymous.[43] Participants learn about alcoholism, exchange feelings and experiences, are helped to increase their self-esteem, and are taught to rely on a higher power. Through the sharing of common problems, members of alcoholics' families find that they are not alone and that they do have the power and ability to cope with and overcome their difficulties.[44]

Parental Violence and Conflict: Strommen insists that by far the most decisive variable in identifying hurting youth and families is exhibited

---

39. Judith R. Vicary, "Adolescent Drug and Alcohol Use and Abuse," in Richard M. Lerner and Nancy L. Galambos, eds., *Experiencing Adolescents* (New York: Garland, 1984), 158.

40. Ruth Kempe and C. Henry Kempe, *Child Abuse* (Cambridge, Mass.: Harvard University Press, 1978), 69.

41. Wayne Worick and Warren Schaller, *Alcohol, Tobacco and Drugs* (Englewood Cliffs, N.J.: Prentice-Hall, 1977), 10.

42. Rosalie Jesse, Adrienne McFadd, Gloria Gray, and Steven Bucky, "Interpersonal Effects of Alcohol Abuse," in Steven Bucky, ed., *The Impact of Alcoholism* (Center City, Minn.: Hazelden, 1978), 58–61.

43. Alcoholics Anonymous is a popular recovery program for alcoholics that is based on twelve steps developed by Bill Wilson. The 12-step format has been adapted for a myriad of other dysfunctions and addictions. These support and recovery groups are easily put into a Christian context by making it clear that the "Higher Power" they refer to is Jesus Christ.

44. For information concerning Al-Anon and Alateen write Al-Anon Family Group Headquarters, One Park Avenue, New York, N.Y. 10016. To find out what recovery groups are available in your area, check the local mental health office. These organizations are usually listed in the telephone directory.

when parents are at odds with each other. Conversely, one of the predictors of greater family unity is the degree of parental accord. Strommen found that only about half of the population of church youth reported harmonious accord between their parents.[45] According to another study of church youth by the Search Institute, serious conflict and violence are regular occurrences in 5 to 10 percent of the homes, and less frequent in many more.[46]

The degree of violence between spouses correlates directly with the severity of the child's problems, including destruction of the child's self-esteem and confidence, vulnerability to stress disorders, and other psychological disturbances.[47] In the aforementioned Search Institute study, a measure of spousal violence was constructed and compared to other elements of family life. The investigators found that family harmony, high quality of life, and family closeness were unlikely to accompany a family life characterized by violence. On the other hand, abuse of the child, coercive methods of discipline, and child-authority conflict were often present.[48]

Father Absenteeism: With the diminishing presence of the traditional family, father-absenteeism is on the increase. In most cases father-absenteeism occurs because of divorce and separation, but even with intact families, father-absence has become more frequent (the father who spends little or relatively little time with his family). In fact, Christopher Anderson asserts that almost every adult American alive today has been reared in his or her father's absence.[49] Thus, in many, if not most, homes, parenting is primarily the task of the mother.

When the father's presence is not felt at home, development of traits such as independence and achievement orientation are impeded,[50] and there is increased likelihood for delinquency.[51] The effects of father

---

45. Strommen, *Five Cries of Youth,* 53–54.

46. Peter Benson, Dorothy Williams, and Arthur Johnson, *The Quicksilver Years* (San Francisco: Harper and Row, 1987), 194.

47. J. Jeffries McWhirter et al., *At-Risk Youth: A Comprehensive Response* (Pacific Grove, Calif.: Brooks/Cole, 1993), 52.

48. Benson et al., *The Quicksilver Years,* 194–95.

49. Christopher Anderson, *Father, the Figure and the Force* (New York: Warner, 1983), 37.

50. Hans Sebald, *Adolescence,* 3d ed. (Englewood Cliffs, N.J.: Prentice-Hall, 1984), 42.

51. Michael Lamb, "Fathers and Child Development: An Integrative Overview," in Michael Lamb, ed., *The Role of The Father in Child Development* (New York: John Wiley and Sons, 1981), 28.

absence on boys includes a deterioration of school performance,[52] dependent and submissive personality features,[53] and a retardation in sexrole and masculinity development. It also appears to be a major factor in the development of homosexuality among males.[54] Teenagers who experience father-absenteeism in one form or another especially need male youth workers who serve as role models and provide the presence of a father figure.

Parent-Teen Conflict

It is not uncommon for teenagers to be at odds, at least to some degree, with one or both of their parents. Strommen, for example, found that one in four teenagers reported trouble getting along with the father, and of these nearly half were at odds with the mother.[55] Another study found that only half of the teenage population surveyed claimed they were very close to their parents. Furthermore, the strength of the relationship deteriorated as the teenager grew older.[56]

Not everyone agrees that a struggle between parents and their teenage children is inevitable or an accurate characterization of adolescence. In fact, there is more evidence than concerned parents realize, indicating that teenagers are often satisfied with their parents as well as with their family situations. For example, the Search Institute found that for young adolescents at least, there is relatively little parent-youth conflict. Although the amount of conflict increases slightly between each of the school years from the fifth through the ninth, only a minority of young adolescents reported any major conflict. When parents were questioned, similar findings were evident.[57]

Psychologist Albert Bandura argues that the "storm and stress" of adolescence—which includes conflict with parents—is largely exaggerated, and that in most middle-class families both parents and teenagers are relatively satisfied with their relationships with one another. In his study of young boys, Bandura found that 1) the parents tended to be

52. Ibid.

53. Sebald, *Adolescence*, 42.

54. Henry Biller, "The Father and Sex Role Development," in Michael Lamb, ed., *The Role of the Child in Child Development* (New York: Wiley, 1981), 320–35.

55. Strommen, *Five Cries of Youth*, 47.

56. Barna Group, *Today's Teens*, 8.

57. Benson et al., *The Quicksilver Years*, 38.

trustful of their children, 2) independence was largely completed before adolescence, and 3) the boys tended to choose friends who shared similar value systems and behavioral norms. His conclusion was that intergenerational conflict was minimal.

Bandura explains some of the difference between his theory and traditional thinking: 1) nonconformity and fad behavior is wrongly characterized as rebellion, 2) the media mistakenly sensationalize the storm and stress view of adolescence, 3) generalizations have been made from studies of delinquent adolescents, and 4) accepting the self-fulfilling prophecy that if youth are expected to be rebellious, they will be.[58] Bandura would not leave us with the notion that adolescence is free from stress or without conflict; rather, he suggests that much of the conduct of teenagers that is characterized as rebellious is consistent with natural adolescent development and normal social behavior. For example, it is entirely appropriate for adolescents to need space away from the family, to experience mood changes, to spend more time with peers, and to adhere to beliefs different from those of their parents.

Although there may be much truth to the notion that parent-youth conflict is overly exaggerated, and while serious antagonism may not be the mark of many relationships, most families will experience at least some conflict. In other words, a certain amount of strife between teenagers and their parents is inevitable. The intensity of this conflict will likely be progressive—that is, it will increase with the age of the adolescent.[59] There are several reasons one can anticipate a certain amount of conflict or struggle between parents and teenagers during the adolescent years, including overprotection, parental distrust, rigid authoritarianism, poor parent-teen communication, and the adolescent struggle for autonomy.

Parental Overprotection: As adolescents grow older, they become increasingly independent, meaning parental influence wanes. Many parents, however, have a difficult time adjusting to the fact that their teenagers are no longer little children. Thus, from the perspective of most adolescents, much parent-teen conflict exists because parents treat them like little children.

---

58. Albert Bandura, "The Stormy Decade: Fact or Fiction," in Rolf E. Muuss, ed., *Adolescent Behavior and Society,* (New York: Random, 1971), 22–31.
59. Benson et al., *The Quicksilver Years,* 39, and Sebald, *Adolescence,* 134.

Overprotective parents offer consistent support, but they do so with many rules and regulations, inappropriate emotional involvement, and high levels of anxiety. These parents might be comparable to a mother or father bear, protecting their child against a hostile environment.[60] While the inclination to protect is a parental instinct, and a certain amount of protection is desirable and admirable, overprotection can be life-denying to the adolescent child. It robs the teenager of natural social, spiritual, and intellectual development, and of course is the source of much conflict in the life of the youth.

Distrustful Parents: Feelings of mistrust by parents of their teenagers are a potent factor in family conflict, says Merton Strommen. In fact, his study found that parental distrust is nineteen times more likely to predict family disunity than divorce. His empirical data also demonstrates a positive correlation between suicide and a youth's feeling of being distrusted. In other words, the percentage of teenagers who consider killing themselves grows in direct relation to a teenager's feeling of being distrusted. Conversely, parental trust—along with open communication and parental accord—is singled out as a strong predictor of family unity.[61] In a survey of professional workers (i.e., counselors), respondents identified "a sense of trust" as fourth in a list of fifty-six characteristics of a healthy family.[62]

Parents should be encouraged to allow their adolescent children to move toward a healthy independence. They should give teenagers age-appropriate choices and hold them responsible for the consequences of their choices.[63] In addition, parents should allow teenagers greater involvement in decision making in family matters, although parents do not surrender final authority on such issues.

Rigid Authoritarianism: The overstrict home is characterized by a lack of discussion of problems (only being told by the parents), nagging and prying by parents, the assumption that teenagers must always be told what to do, disapproval of friends, and a power struggle between parents and teenage children.[64] Overly rigid parents may appear cruel

---

60. McWhirter et al., *At-Risk Youth,* 58.

61. Strommen, *Five Cries of Youth,* 51–54.

62. Dolores Curran, *Traits of a Healthy Family* (San Francisco: Harper & Row, 1983), 99.

63. Reginald W. Bibby and Donald C. Posterski, *Teen Trends* (Toronto, Ont.: Stoddart, 1992), 216.

64. Strommen, *Five Cries of Youth,* 48.

in their interactions with their children, have a large number of rules and regulations, and enforce them in a cold, rigid, and precise manner. Sometimes these parents appear to enjoy punishing their adolescent children for misbehavior.[65]

Youth reared in an overly strict, authoritarian home are more likely to reject traditional moral standards, involve themselves in acts of rebellion, and reject a personal faith.[66] These young people may also display fear and rejection of authority figures or adopt highly delinquent behavior.[67] Finally, an overly authoritarian home life may contribute to running away. Homes of many runaways are characterized by excessively rigid family rules and regulations, and little or no planning or sharing of family activities and responsibilities.[68]

Some adolescents may perceive that they are in a situation in which their parents are overly strict when, in fact, that is not the case. Sometimes negative peer influence is the cause of a teenager's notion that his or her parents are overly strict. The youth religious educator can play a significant role in helping misguided teenagers to understand the importance of parental authority and guidelines, as well as the need to obey and respect all authority. For example, if a young teenager comes to a youth worker complaining about her curfew time being unfair, the worker can explain to the adolescent why this parental regulation is not only fair, but important. The youth worker might encourage the adolescent in understanding that such parameters exist out of the love her parents have for her and are designed to protect and nurture her.

It should not be inferred, however, that there should be a lack of parental control in the home. While adolescents in an overly strict home may develop undesirable behaviors, the same is likely when overpermissiveness is the norm. Ideally, parents should strike a balance between exercising consistent and firm rules and discipline, and trust and freedom appropriate to the age, maturity, and demonstrated responsibility of the teenager. Strommen determined from his study of adolescents that teenagers given authoritative and firm guidelines along with increasing freedom to make personal decisions were more likely to reflect a strong

---

65. McWhirter et al., *At-Risk Youth,* 57.
66. Strommen, *Five Cries of Youth,* 49.
67. McWhirter et al., *At-Risk Youth,* 59.
68. Ann Burgess, *Youth At Risk: Understanding Runaway and Exploited Youth* (Washington, D.C.: National Center for Missing and Exploited Children, 1986), 10.

self-esteem, embrace the Christian faith, and become more involved in serving other people.[69]

Poor Communication: In a revealing study of 3,000 teenagers and their families conducted by Gordon Sebine, 79 percent of the parents involved reported that they were communicating well with their teenagers. On the other hand, in a complete reversal, 81 percent of the teenagers said that their parents were not communicating with them.[70] This study indicates first, that there is little common understanding between parents and teenagers as to what good communication is, and second, that a large percentage of adolescents recognize the need for better communication in the home.[71]

Other empirical studies divulge information that suggests parent-teen communication to be a major source of family trouble. The Barna Research Group found that among teenagers whose fathers are living in the home, the average amount of time spent with the father discussing things that matter to the teen is less than 40 minutes per week (that amounts to a little over five minutes a day). With the mother, the teen averages 55 minutes per week.[72] Fathers have long been know as shirkers of the responsibility of communicating with their children—excusing themselves because of their jobs and because males are supposed to be less intimate and relational than females.

This communication problem is no doubt compounded by the fact that today many mothers are likewise absorbed in the pursuit of careers and higher education. One-third of the church youth in Strommen's study were bothered by their inability to communicate with their mother.[73] Peter Benson, Dorothy Williams, and Arthur Johnson conclude from their empirical research study of early adolescents that both parents and young people want to talk about issues, interests, and problems, but in only a few families does this take place, and then it is not often or long enough.[74]

---

69. Strommen, *Five Cries of Youth,* 49.

70. Cited in Gary Dausey, "Communication Killers," in Jay Kesler, ed., *Parents and Teenagers* (Wheaton, Ill.: Victor, 1988), 226.

71. See Blake J. Neff, "Communication and Relationships," in Donald Ratcliff and James A. Davies, eds., *Handbook of Youth Ministry* (Birmingham, Ala.: Religious Education Press, 1991), 162.

72. *Today's Teens: A Generation in Transition* (Glendale, Calif.: The Barna Research Group, 1991), 10.

73. Strommen, *Five Cries of Youth,* 47.

74. Benson et al., *The Quicksilver Years,* 212–13.

The results of poor communication between teenagers and their parents may be more severe than either parents or youth workers realize. A study of runaways in Los Angeles County revealed that almost three-quarters of the young people said they ran away because of communication problems with their parents—more than those who identified divorce or separation, physical abuse, or sexual abuse.[75] A similar investigation by Ann Burgess for the National Center for Missing and Exploited Children found that almost all of the runaways in her study had engaged in a serious argument with one or both parents.[76]

One of the goals of religious education should be to assist in the improvement of communication between teenagers and their parents. Blake Neff suggests using the following strategies to enable the youth religious educator to accomplish this goal:[77]

1. *Model effective communication.* The youth worker will want to begin by modeling effective communication skills to both the adolescents in the youth group and their parents. Reading nonverbal messages, speaking through appropriate touch, making good eye contact, and asking open ended questions (questions that cannot be answered with a simple yes or no) are some techniques that will aid greatly in teaching communication skills.

2. *Develop a ministry of presence.* Communication and relationships go hand in hand; thus, the youth religious educator must concentrate on simply being available to the teenager or parent. By this ministry of presence, the youth religious educator says, "I care about you and I am interested in being a part of your world." Often the most effective time a youth worker can spend with either parents or teenagers will be outside of the formal educational setting. Meeting with a youth group member over the lunch hour or in a restaurant after a youth meeting are effective ways to develop relationships. The youth worker will do well to realize that parents too, have interests outside the church. Finding out what these interests are and finding ways to participate in them help the youth worker earn the right to gain an audience with parents. Special attention should be given to search out and identify the interests of parents who are not a part of the regular church community.

---

75. Jack Rothman, *Runaway and Homeless Youth* (New York: Longman, 1991), 75.
76. Burgess, *Youth At Risk,* 10.
77. Neff, "Communication and Relationships," 174–75.

3. Educate in communication. Many young people and parents are either unsure of what effective communication is or have never taken the time to learn effective communication skills. An effective church ministry to youth and their parents might include programs that teach communication skills such as nonverbal communication, listening and attending, and asking questions.[78]

4. Facilitate communication. Often church ministries and programs minimize communication between young people and their parents. The effective youth religious educator will plan for some intergenerational activities that bring parents and teens together. Fathers and sons might do some outdoor or adventure camping together, while mothers and daughters meet for a luncheon. A sport such as a softball or volleyball is a possibility. Another idea might be an open or panel discussion on an issue that is pertinent to both parents and adolescents such as choice of music or substance use and abuse.[79]

Struggle for Autonomy: In 1952 developmental psychologist Robert Havighurst drew up a list of developmental tasks appropriate to the various stages of life. He described a developmental task as a task that arises at a certain period in the life of an individual, of which successful achievement leads to happiness and to success with subsequent tasks, while failure leads to unhappiness, disapproval by society, and difficulty with later tasks. Several of the tasks identifiable with adolescence are related to the gaining of autonomy from parental control. These include achieving emotional independence from parents, achieving assurance of economic independence, selecting and preparing for an occupation, and preparing for marriage and family life.[80]

Unfortunately, while gaining autonomy is a natural part of adolescent development, it is often an origin of conflict between adolescents and their parents, and a source of stress for both. In fact, Anna Freud

---

78. The youth religious educator who would like to teach parent-youth communication skills will find some helpful insights in Jay Kesler, ed., *Parents and Teenagers* (Wheaton, Ill.: Victor, 1988), chapter 9. See also Andrew Wolvin and Carolyn Gwynn Coakley, *Listening,* 4th ed. (Dubuque, Iowa: Wm. C. Brown, 1992).

79. For additional insights on intergenerational ministries and religious education, see Sell, *Family Ministry;* M. Scott Miles, *Families Growing Together* (Wheaton, Ill.: Victor, 1990); James W. White, *Intergenerational Religious Education* (Birmingham, Ala.: Religious Education Press, 1988).

80. Robert J. Havighurst, *Developmental Tasks and Education* (New York: Longmans, Green, 1952), 6–96.

concluded that it may not be the teenager who experiences the greater stress but rather the "parents who need help and guidance so as to be able to bear with him [because] there are so few situations in life which are more difficult to cope with than an adolescent son or daughter during the attempt to liberate themselves."[81]

Stephen Small and associates discovered that while mothers and fathers experienced an equal amount of stress resulting from adolescent autonomy, they experienced stress for two very different reasons. Fathers reported greater stress as a result of nonadherence to parental advice and the adolescent's involvement in deviant behaviors. Mothers, on the other hand, were stressed more because of their child's desire and demands for more autonomy.[82]

The task of growing up includes acquiring the skills to act independently, making one's own decisions, and being accountable for one's own actions. Gaining autonomy includes the letting go of absolute control by parents and the assuming of more responsibility by the adolescent. It is a gradual process that begins in preadolescence and gradually gains momentum through the teenage years.

The adolescent or young adult is developmentally successful when autonomy is achieved in three areas—the emotional, the behavioral, and the ideational. In regards to *affective* autonomy, the teenager lessens emotional ties to parents and family, and increases bonds of love, affection, care, and support with nonfamilial individuals. This is not to suggest that all bonds with parents will be severed. Attachments such as care and affection can and should continue to exist between parents and teenagers, but adolescents will become less dependent on parents as a primary or sole source of emotional support.

A second area of autonomy is *behavioral* in nature. The teenager has acquired both the skills and boldness to take part in activities or tasks he or she wants to. For example, the adolescent should now be able to drive the car, hold down a job, go shopping alone, or prepare a meal. Along with the ability to carry out tasks or activities without direct parental supervision comes increased decision-making freedom.

---

81. Quoted in Stephen A. Small, Gay Eastman, and Steven Cornelius, "Adolescent Autonomy and Parental Stress," in *Journal of Youth and Adolescence,* 17, (October 1988), 377–91.
    82. Ibid.

Finally, *ideational* autonomy is achieved, whereby the adolescent works through and establishes personal convictions and beliefs.[83]

Stress between parents and adolescents may emerge because, although self-governance and independent decision making are expected and normative, there may be disagreement between parent and adolescent as to the speed and circumstance with which these new forms of behavior are assumed.[84] For example, a teenage daughter may feel that upon receiving her driving license she should be able to drive the family car without supervision. Her parents, on the other hand, may insist that she does not drive the car unsupervised until she turns 17.

The difficult task for parents is in finding the right balance between freedom and control. If too much control on behalf of the parent is a source of parent-adolescent conflict, too much or unbridled freedom may result in irresponsibility or abusive behavior on behalf of the teenager.

The goal of moving a son or daughter toward healthy autonomy actually starts in the preteen years when parents gradually give children age-appropriate choices. For example, while a mother may dictate what a 6-year-old wears to school, a preadolescent 12-year-old should be given a certain amount of freedom in choice of clothes. As preadolescents move into the teenage years, they should be given more freedom to make their own decisions on matters. Adolescents should be given freedom to make decisions related to eating and sleeping. As long as they are eating nourishing foods, they might be allowed to choose their own diet. Perhaps they could also be included in planning the family menus and cooking the food.[85]

However, teenagers must realize that consequences come with these choices, so rather than nagging about completing homework, perhaps occasional reminders coupled with comments regarding the consequences of not being diligent with studies is a more appropriate approach for the parent. Ultimately, the only way to really learn how to make independent decisions is to actually make them, and then live with the consequences.[86]

---

83. Sebald, *Adolescence,* 133.

84. Small, Eastman, and Cornelius, "Adolescent Autonomy and Stress," 379.

85. An excellent source of help for moving a teenager toward autonomy is Ronald Koteskey, *Understanding Adolescence* (Wheaton: Victor, 1987).

86. Ibid., 36.

Teenagers can also be given greater involvement in family decision making. They might be included in planning vacations, choosing a particular place of worship, or making decisions about moving. It should be understood that involving adolescents in making decisions relevant to them does not mean that parents relinquish final authority on family matters. Nor does it mean, as mentioned earlier, that emotional support is altogether withdrawn. It does mean, however, that there is less telling and more empowering and equipping. It is the parents' responsibility to make sure the adolescents have sufficient information related to the issue at hand, and allow the teenager to make the decision.[87]

Child Abuse

One of the unfortunate tragedies facing children and adolescents today is abuse. Statistics indicate that the rate of child abuse is on the upswing. It is almost impossible, however, to know whether there is actually an increase in abuse or if there are other factors that simply make it appear to be so. First, it is difficult to determine if rates of reported abuse are due to an actual increase of abuse, or due to an increased sensitivity of professionals working with children and adolescents and their families. Second, a continual change in the definition of child abuse, along with constant revisions of laws related to abuse, tend to broaden the definition of child abuse.

There are four major types of abuse: *sexual, physical, parental neglect,* and *emotional.* Sexual abuse is defined as the exploitation of an adolescent for the sexual gratification of an adult, and includes fondling of the genitals, exhibitionism, incest, and rape.[88] Physical abuse includes harmful actions such as slapping, choking, punching, cutting, or burning. Parental neglect involves the harming of an adolescent through lack of care or supervision. Emotional abuse refers to parental behavior and actions that jeopardize a teenager's patience, ability to set reasonable goals, interpersonal skills, or self-esteem.[89] It includes punishing normal social behaviors and consistently putting the adolescent in negative light.

---

87. Ibid.
88. Robert L. Burgess and Rhonda A. Richardson, "Child Abuse During Adolescence," in Richard M. Lerner and Nancy L. Galambos, eds., *Experiencing Adolescents* (New York: Garland, 1984), 127.
89. Ibid., 128.

There are problems with both defining abuse and subsequently accurately estimating or reporting the incidence of abuse. At what point does parental discipline become abusive? Must a parent's behavior result in injury in order to be considered abusive? At what point should a distinction be made between abusive and nonabusive behavior of parents?

Perhaps more difficult than defining the issue of child abuse is measuring the occurrence or incidence of abuse. Part of the problem lies in the fact that there appear to be no clear distinctions of what constitutes child abuse and what constitutes neglect. More significant is the problem of underreporting. While all states have passed legislation requiring the reporting of child abuse and neglect, fewer than one-fourth of all cases are actually reported.[90] Nonetheless, in spite of the ambiguity of defining and identifying cases of abuse, there is substantial evidence available suggesting adolescent abuse is a serious problem. In 1992 public social service and child protection agencies in the United States reported 2,694,000 cases of child abuse or neglect, a rate of 42 out of every 1,000 children.[91] A large proportion of these abused children were adolescents.

Sexual Abuse: While it is very difficult to talk about, and more difficult for a society to acknowledge that it exists, sexual abuse of children and youth is a common occurrence in the United States. While there are no national statistics on incidence of sexual abuse, some researchers believe that it is more widespread than physical abuse. Numbers fluctuate wildly with estimates ranging from 1.9 to 1,000 incidences per million, however, the most recent estimates on the incidence of child sexual abuse are between 132,000 and 138,000 per year.[92] The greater proportion of offenses are committed by family members. Of these, father-daughter incest accounts for 75 percent of the family-related sexual abuse cases, with mother-son, father-son, mother-daughter, and brother-sister accounting for the remaining fourth.[93] Experts estimate that 90 women out of every 1,000 have been sexually victimized by a

90. Ibid., 129.

91. This is according to the April 1992 survey conducted by the National Committee for the Prevention of Child Abuse, and reported in the American Humane Association Fact Sheet #1 (February 1993).

92. The figures are reported in a *Fact Sheet on Child Sexual Abuse*, published by The National Resource Center on Child Sexual Abuse, Huntsville, Ala.

93. C. Henry Kempe, "Sexual Abuse, Another Hidden Pediatric Problem," in Joanne Valiant Cook and Roy Tyler Bowles, eds., *Child Abuse: Commission and Omission* (Toronto: Butterworths, 1980), 100.

family member, and 5 to 10 women out of every 1,000 have had an incestuous relationship with their father at some point in their childhood or adolescent years.[94]

The number of reported cases of sexual abuse is only the tip of the iceberg, as many incidences go unreported. Fear of social disapproval, embarrassment and shame, and the fact that no physical harm may have been done, discourage many children and adolescents from reporting sexual abuse. They may feel that their parents will blame them, may be apprehensive over losing their family, feel guilty themselves for any pleasure they might have experienced, fear repercussions from the perpetrator, or experience shame as a result of the experience.

Incest in the United States seems to be on the increase in recent years, and significant changes in family life and structure might be a contributing factor. Henry Kempe, an expert on various kinds of child and adolescent abuse, argues that rising divorce rates, birth control, abortion, and an increasingly more tolerant view of sexual acts between household members who are blood related are likely contributors to the increased rate of sexual abuse.[95]

As one might naturally expect, the effects of sexual abuse in the teenager are devastating. Some of the consequences are as follows:
• serious rebellion, especially against the mother;
• unforgiveness (girls may eventually forgive their fathers, but rarely forgive their mothers who failed to protect them);
• serious delinquency;
• extremely low-self esteem ("I am a whore");
• prostitution and running away;
• chronic depression, social isolation;
• pregnancy, venereal disease, and drug abuse.[96]

Sexual abuse is linked to running away from home. According to an empirical study of runaway youth by Ann Burgess, 70 percent of the female runaways and nearly 40 percent of the male runaways had been sexually abused.[97] Yet another study found that one-fourth reported that they ran away from home because of sexual abuse.[98]

––––––––

94. David Finkelhor, "Psychological, Cultural and Family Factors in Incest and Family Sexual Abuse," in Cook and Bowles, eds., *Child Abuse: Commission and Omission*, 263.
95. Kempe, "Sexual Abuse, Another Hidden Pediatric Problem," 100.
96. Ibid., 104.
97. Burgess, *Youth At Risk*, 11.
98. Rothman, *Runaways and Homeless Youth*, 75.

The consensus in the past among researchers has been that the majority of incestuous families come from the lower end of the socioeconomic scale. More recent studies indicate, however, that sexual abuse crosses all social strata, and there is a growing awareness of middle-class incest.

The first task of the youth worker is identifying adolescents who have suffered from some form of sexual abuse. Teenagers may make it rather difficult to detect that sexual abuse has taken place. While victims often want to be identified and assisted, the embarrassment of letting others know may cause them to cover it up. Youth workers might use questionnaires to discover high-risk adolescents. Whether the issue is sexual abuse, suicide, or drug abuse, a personal response sheet that gives adolescents an opportunity to identify their involvement with the issue is a helpful technique. Information should remain anonymous unless students choose to fill in their name and indicate that they would like an opportunity to meet with a counselor.[99]

A critical responsibility of the youth worker is to understand the legal responsibility in reporting sexual abuse. In all states and most countries, sexual abuse is a criminal act, yet youth workers are not required in all states to report abuse. However, there are states, such as California, where law requires the reporting. Youth workers should contact their local police department or social service agencies to obtain information and requirements regarding reporting in their area. Every state has at least one agency mandated to receive and investigate reports. The agency is usually called the Department of Social Services, Department of Protective Services, or Department of Children and Family Services.[100] Persons who report in good faith—that is, have an honest belief that a child is being sexually abused—are immune from civil and criminal court action, even if the report proves to be in error.

Prevention of sexual abuse may be enhanced by teaching children and adolescents about their bodies and appropriate sexual behavior. Being taught how to say no to sexual advances and how to ask for help when they need it may help many teenagers to defend themselves against

---

99. The suggestion is given by Rich Van Pelt, *Intensive Care* (Grand Rapids, Mich.: Zondervan, 1988), 157.

100. The American Humane Association operates the National Resource Center on Child Abuse and Neglect and can offer more information on what you can do. The number is 1-800-227-4645.

incestuous sexual abuse.[101] All children, even the very young, can learn the following rules:

• You have rights to the privacy of the parts of your body that are covered by a bathing suit.

• No person has a right to touch your body in any place that you do not want touched.

• You are an individual and have the right to say you do not want that kind of touch.[102]

Physical Abuse: Research investigations of rates of physical abuse of children and adolescents describe varying degrees of incidence, with some estimations as high as 1.5 million cases of physical abuse per annum.[103] In a 1967–68 study, it was estimated that there were only 6,000 to 7,000 cases reported annually in the United States. Even allowing for underreporting, the researcher concluded that physical abuse could not be considered a major cause of mortality or morbidity of children in the United States.[104]

In a subsequent study, however, it was found that nearly three-fourths of all parents had used violence on their children at some time. Nearly half reported that they had pushed or shoved their child, and another fifth admitted hitting their children with an object. Most disturbing was the fact that 4 in 100 parents had engaged in kicking, biting, punching, beating, or using a knife or gun. Over half of the 10–14-year-olds and a third of the 15–17-year-olds had been abused in some manner.[105] The Search Institute study of students in grades five through nine (approximating the ages 10 to 14), asked parents if they got angry enough to hurt their children. Approximately one-third of the respondents indicated this was so: "once in a while," "sometimes," "often," or "very often."[106]

---

101. For information and publications on sexual abuse call or write The National Center on Child Sexual Abuse, 107 Lincoln Street, Huntsville, Ala. 35801. The telephone numbers are: (205) 534-6868; for information service 1-800-534-7006.This center provides information and publications on child sexual abuse.

102. Margaret O. Hyde, *Sexual Abuse: Let's Talk About It* (Philadelphia: Westminster, 1984), 22.

103. Richard Gelles, "Violence Toward Children in the United States," in Cook and Bowles, eds., *Child Abuse: Commission and Omission*, 36.

104. David Gil, *Violence Against Children* (Cambridge, Mass.: Harvard University Press, 1970), 138.

105. Murray Straus, Richard Gelles, and Suzanne Steinmetz, *Behind Closed Doors: Violence in the American Family* (Garden City, N.Y.: Anchor, 1980).

106. Benson, Williams, and Johnson, *The Quicksilver Years,* 191.

Many children and adolescents most unfortunately learn to accept abuse as the norm and learn to live with it. Often adolescents grow up accepting beating as a part of their parent's rights in child rearing. Furthermore, abused teenagers adopt a wait-and-see attitude and hope the conflicts will not develop into further violence.[107]

The consequences of child abuse greatly exceed the immediate pain and suffering a young person might experience. One review of pertinent research identified the following characteristics of abused children:[108]
• they are aggressive and full of hatred;
• they are uncontrollable, negativistic, and subject to severe temper tantrums;
• they are lacking in impulse control;
• they are emotionally disturbed, with behavior problems;
• they are withdrawn and inhibited;
• they have cognitive and neurological deficits.

Another tragedy of physical abuse is the runaway. Ann Burgess discovered that a third of the runaways in her study had been physically beaten at home,[109] while Jack Rothman found that over a third ran away because of physical abuse.[110] Finally, the effects of physical abuse go far beyond adolescence, as many abused teenagers grow up to become abusive parents themselves and the cycle of abuse continues.

Many empirical research studies have attempted to identify or discover the relationship between various demographic characteristics and abuse. One of the most extensive attempts in the United States was a national study which identified family structure as a significant factor. Over 29 percent of the sample lived in homes without a father or father substitute, while 12 percent were without a mother. Nearly 20 percent of the mothers and 2 percent of the fathers were separated, divorced, deserted, or widowed. This study also found that both the educational level and occupational status of these parents were fairly low. Only 6 percent of the parents fell into a professional, technical, or managerial occupational status. Only 52.5 percent of the fathers and 30 percent of

---

107. Kathleen Galvin and Bernard Brommel, *Family Communications* (Glenview, Ill.: Scott, Foresman, and Co., 1986). 184.
108. Thomas Reidy, "The Aggressive Characteristics of Abused and Neglected Children", in Cook and Bowles, eds., *Child Abuse: Commission and Omission*, 471–77.
109. Burgess, *Youth At Risk*, 11.
110. Rothman, *Runaways and Homeless Youth*, 75.

the mothers were employed throughout the year. The overall conclusion of this revealing study was that child abuse was concentrated among the socioeconomically deprived segments of the population.[111]

While certain studies do indicate a higher rate of incidence at the lower end of the socioeconomic ladder, some researchers suggest this is not so. Theo Solomon, for example, argues that the problem is common to parents of all economic and educational levels, and that institutions are more likely to intervene in the more visible and vulnerable lower classes than in the affluent.[112] It is probably best concluded that the majority of deprived families do not abuse their children, and some well-to-do parents do.

The youth worker's responsibility in responding to physical abuse is similar to those already identified under the topic of sexual abuse. The youth religious educator must initially identify the indicators of physical abuse and neglect:[113]

• welts and bruises on the body from being hit;
• lagging in social development;
• poor hygiene (dirty teeth, offensive body odor);
• hunger and thirst, indicating deprivation of nourishment;
• failure to attend school regularly;
• change in school performance;
• lagging in physical development, weight loss;
• fatigue or listlessness;
• fear of family members or caregivers;
• stomachaches or abdominal pains that may come from physical injuries, but may also be psychological symptoms;
• low self-esteem.

Logically, consideration should be given to preventive measures.[114] One of the key factors in abusive parenting is that the parents often lack the appropriate knowledge of child rearing, and that their expectations, attitudes, and parenting techniques set them apart from nonabusing

---

111. Gil, *Violence Against Children,* 108–11.

112. Theo Solomon, "History and Demography of Child Abuse," in Cook and Bowles, eds., *Child Abuse: Commission and Omission,* 67.

113. Lucy Dekle Braun, *Someone Heard . . .* (Winter Park, Fla.: Currier/Davis, 1988), 9.

114. There are a number of organizations that are dedicated to the prevention and treatment of child abuse. One such center is The Kempe National Center, 1205 Oneada St., Denver, Colo., (303)321–3963.

parents.[115] In addition, and as mentioned earlier, many abusers represent dysfunctional families. Churches should encourage family education, as well as requiring premarital counseling for adolescents and young adults preparing for marriage. A suggestion is that while such programs should be geared to the strengthening of "normal" families, they could also serve as a screening device for the identification of dysfunction in any area of individual and family.[116]

Most abusive parents are themselves emotionally crippled because of circumstances they experienced in their childhood and adolescence— many, abused themselves. Abusive parents are further described as isolated, lonely, and lacking in support. Support groups can provide these individuals with an immediate support system and an opportunity to reduce their overwhelming sense of aloneness.[117] Parents Anonymous is a national association of support groups patterned after Alcoholics Anonymous, available to help parents who abuse their children.

There is no single format that characterizes support groups. Some gather simply to discuss issues of common interest, while others spend large amounts of time in Bible study and prayer. But whatever the process or design of the small group, a common purpose is to offer emotional and spiritual support to the group members. Often the supportive element of these groups is enhanced by interaction and socializing that occurs before and after the formal meeting time and between meetings.[118]

Runaway Youth

Another of the frightening and tragic consequences of family conflict and breakdown is the runaway youth. Although it is difficult to determine exactly how many children and teenagers are runaways, it is evident that this is reaching alarming proportions. One source estimates that there are 700,000 to 1 million runaway youth between 10 and 17, per year.[119] Another cites a figure in excess of 1,155,000 runaway and homeless youth annually in the United States, but adds that researchers consider this a conservative estimate.[120]

---

115. John Spinetta and David Rigler, "The Child Abusing Parent," in Cook and Bowles, eds., *Child Abuse: Commission and Omission,* 139.

116. Gil, *Violence Against Children,* 146.

117. Strommen and Strommen, *Five Cries of Parents,* 183–84.

118. Robert Wuthnow, *Sharing the Journey* (New York: The Free Press, 1994), 69.

119. Burgess, *Youth At Risk,* 3.

120. Rothman, *Runaways and Homeless Youth,* 19.

While adolescents offer a number of reasons for running away from home, most run away because of family conflict. In a study of runaways at a shelter in Toronto, the following profile emerged:[121]
- Almost all the runaways had a serious argument with one or both parents.
- Fifty percent reported verbal abuse.
- Only 6 in 10 recalled being happy for more than three days at a time.
- Seven in 10 believed they disappointed their families.
- Seventy-three percent had been physically beaten.
- Seven in 10 females, and 4 in 10 males reported having been sexually abused.

In addition it was found that the runaways in this study did poorly in school, had trouble with authorities, fought with peers, and many came from broken homes. Surprising was the fact that most of the runaways in this study came from financially stable homes. Not surprising was the fact that for 60 percent of these youth, religion was of limited or no importance to their families.

A study of Los Angeles County runaways identified the following reasons for leaving home:[122]
- communication difficulties with parents (73 percent),
- divorce or separation (55 percent),
- physical abuse (39 percent),
- sexual abuse (26 percent),
- wants to be on his or her own (18 percent).

As difficult as the home life may be for many runaways, life on the street is significantly worse. Most turn to crime, drugs and sex as a means of coping with their situation. Most have some sexually transmitted disease, and many of today's runaways test positive for the AIDS virus.

Adolescents who engage in severe conflict with their parents are strong runaway candidates and youth workers should endeavor to identify these teenagers. In addition to arguing and fighting with parents, signs to look for are unhappiness, depression, insecurity, impulsiveness, and wrestling with problems that seem unmanageable.

Some churches and youth ministry organizations may be in a position to work with runaway teenagers. One such operation is Helping Hands,

---

121. Burgess, *Youth At Risk,* 9–13.
122. Rothman, *Runaways and Homeless Youth,* 75.

an arm of Catholic Charities. Helping Hands has field offices near bus terminals and train stations, and sends out two-people teams (a male and a female) to try to identify new runaways. Their goal is to take young people off the streets and steer them back home or put them into a program or shelter. They are not a treatment center or shelter, just an intermediate step in helping young runaways get their lives back together. This kind of outreach to teenagers is not for every parish or youth ministry program. However, for certain churches that are in the proximity of metropolitan streets, have the financial sources to support such a youth-related ministry, and have a passion and vision to reach the inner city, this type of ministry could prove extremely effective.[123]

INFLUENCE OF PARENTS ON ADOLESCENT BEHAVIOR

While some parents seriously question the impact they really do have on their teenage children, adolescents are, in fact, highly dependent on parents as role models in many areas: in acquiring norms and values, in their personality development, in making major life decisions, and in less significant matters such as dating and dress. While parents receive, as one might expect, stiff competition from peers, studies consistently demonstrate that youth credit parents as a primary source of influence. For example, the 1985 study by Reginald Bibby and Donald Posterski asked Canadian high school students to what extent they thought their life was influenced by other people or forces. Parents were ranked as the most influential, as 85 percent of the respondents credited the way they were brought up, while only 73 percent acknowledged the impact of their friends.[124]

According to the Search Institute study of early adolescents, respondents viewed parents as the most likely source of help; about half would turn to parents on every problem mentioned. Peers were the second choice as a source of help. A noteworthy observation, however, is that there was a steady decline in parental influence as age increased, coinciding with a corresponding increase of peers as a source of help.[125]

---

123. For more details on this outreach ministry, Rothman, *Runaways and Homeless Youth,* 21–23.

124. Reginald W. Bibby and Donald C. Posterski, *The Emerging Generation* (Toronto, Ont.: Irwin, 1985), 101–102. This was a national study of Canadian high school students. It was not limited to church attenders.

125. Benson, Williams, and Johnson, *The Quicksilver Years,* 200–202. Respondents in this study were members of thirteen youth agencies, most of which were church related.

When teenagers were asked by the Barna Research Group as to who has "a lot of influence" on their thoughts and actions, 70 percent credited their mothers. Sixty percent said their fathers significantly influenced the way they thought and acted, while only 52 percent credited friends with a similar type of influence. However, when asked whom they often sought for help or encouragement, mothers ranked a distant second (54 percent) to friends (72 percent). Only 38 percent said they often went to their father for help. Thus, according to this empirical study, while teenagers may tend to seek out friends over parents for help and encouragement, they admit that parents ultimately have a greater impact over their lives in terms of influencing their thought and behavior patterns.[126]

In the national study of Canadian youth by Bibby and Posterski, teenagers rated parents high as a source of counsel when it came to items such as spending money, what's right and wrong, school concerns, and career decisions. Parents scored much lower on relationships, sex, having fun, and major problems.[127] Another empirical study by Hans Sebald found peers to have more influence over decisions related to social activities, but in regard to major issues such as career or finances, parents had more of an impact in the decisions teenagers made.[128]

When comparing mothers and fathers, it appears that mothers tend to have more influence than fathers in most areas of the lives of their teenage children. Bibby and Posterski discovered that teenagers not only perceived the mother as a greater source of influence in making choices and decisions than the father, but also tended to turn to mother more often than to father when facing problems and looking for moral guidance.[129]

This was found to be true by the Barna Research Group as well.[130] Fathers may be seen as the primary breadwinner and the one in charge, but they are still perceived as distant to their teenage children and considerably less influential in the parenting role. In yet another study of adolescents and their choice of parental advice, researchers found that

---

126. Barna Group, *Today's Teens: A Generation in Transition* (Glendale, Calif.: The Barna Research Group), 23–24. This study is based upon a nationwide telephone survey of a random sample of teenagers.

127. Bibby and Posterski, *Teen Trends,* 205. The study is based on the responses of 3,600 public high school students.

128. Hans Sebald, "Adolescent's Shifting Orientation Towards Parents and Peers," *Journal of Marriage and The Family* 48, (February 1986), 5–13.

129. Bibby and Posterski, *Teen Trends,* 208.

130. Barna Group, *Today's Teens,* 24.

teenagers had an overwhelming preference to seek and follow mother's rather than father's advice.[131]

One area in which fathers may have a greater impact than mothers in shaping the lives of their teenagers is in religion and religiosity. While different conclusions have been reached, extensive reviews of studies by Dean Hoge and Gregory Petrillo[132] and Kenneth Hyde[133] noted that fathers were more influential than mothers in areas related to adolescent religiousness, such as participation in church-related activities or faith development.

Several parenting principles and procedures emerge from these studies. First, when it comes to being involved in the life of their teenagers, parents should enter at the points of least resistance or those junctures where adolescent children will be most likely to invite or receive parental participation. Once they have entered, they may move into areas normally reserved for their friends and peers. For many parents, fathers especially, sports are a natural entry into their teenagers' lives. Bowling, tennis, fishing, hunting, biking, backpacking, and softball offer some ways to spend time together. For some girls, perhaps shopping is a natural point of entry into their lives. For families whose children are involved in activities such as organized sports, music, or drama, efforts should be made by both mothers and fathers to attend performances and games as much as possible.

Second, parents should not expect to be the only source of influence in the lives of their teenagers. Wise parents will recognize that adolescents are moving from dependence to independence, and whether they like it or not, will be influenced by friends and other adults. Parents might be more comfortable with the new influences in their sons' or daughters' lives if they know a little bit about them. Parents should make an honest effort to get to know their teenagers' close friends, perhaps to the point of having an open-home policy.

---

131. A. L. Greene, "Age and Gender Differences in Adolescents' Preference for Parental Advice," *Journal of Adolescent Research* 5, (October 1990).

132. Dean R. Hoge and Gregory H. Petrillo, "Youth and the Church," in *Religious Education* 74, (May-June 1979), 305–13; Dean R. Hoge and Gregory H. Petrillo, "Determinants of Church Participation and Attitudes Among High-school Youth," in *Journal for the Scientific Study of Religion* 17, (1978), 359–79.

133. Kenneth E. Hyde, *Religion in Childhood and Adolescence* (Birmingham, Ala.: Religious Education Press, 1990), 233–35.

Third, parents, especially fathers, must make greater efforts to be involved in the lives of their teenage children. This means more and deeper meaningful interaction in all dimensions of life—including the physical, emotional, and spiritual. Many families today are accomplishing aspects of this by returning to meaningful supper or dinner hours where all members are encouraged to be present. With the television turned off, they talk about their day's events, read a chapter of a book, or discuss the world news.[134] It is important that teenagers get focused, one-to-one attention. This might come in the form of a father-daughter outing, a father-son backpacking trip, or a mother-daughter luncheon.

Fourth, parents should be reminded that the positive influence they have on their teenagers comes as much or more through consistent modeling as it does through verbal efforts to advise or instruct. For example, Hoge and Petrillo found that the very strong influence parents have on their teenagers' participation in church-related activities comes mostly through their own behavior rather than through a conscious effort to socialize their children into the church.[135]

Finally, youth workers should attack the myth of "quality time"— the ill-conceived notion that suggests that a little bit of *meaningful* time is sufficient for a healthy parent-child relationship. While it is important that the time parents spend with their adolescents is quality in nature, it takes time, effort, and sacrifice of other desires and pleasures to develop strong parent-adolescent relationships. Strong families do things together, whether it be work, play, or the sharing of meals.

CONCLUSION

The purpose of this chapter was to identify critical family issues and the effect they have on adolescents and adolescent development. It must be remembered, however, that not every family in America is in turmoil and conflict, and not every teenager is at odds with one or both of the parents. If, according to Strommen, one youth in five is from a troubled home, then four in five are from at least reasonably healthy family situations (this is not to say that there may not be some

---

134. Dave Arp and Claudia Arp, *60 One-Minute Family Builders* (Nashville, Tenn.: Thomas Nelson, 1993), 18.

135. Dean R. Hoge and Gregory Petrillo, "Determinants of Church Participation and Attitudes Among High School Youth," 359–79.

arguments, conflicts or disagreements—47 percent admit there are some differences).[136] Over two decades ago, Roy Zuck and Gene Getz found that seven out of ten young people who attended church stated that the relationships between themselves and their parents were adequate. They also cited a 1966 *Newsweek* article which reported that a heavy majority of teenagers got along just fine with their parents.[137]

In 1991 the Barna Research Group found that this attitude had changed only slightly, as six out of ten teenagers said they were very satisfied with their current family situation.[138] In the Search Institute study of pre- and early adolescents, nearly three-quarters of the respondents said "There is a lot of love in my family."[139]

Unfortunately, many parents feel ill equipped to do an effective job of parenting. When 10,467 parents in an adolescent-parent study were asked to rank the importance of sixteen values, one that received top attention was "to be a good parent." Yet four out of five parents said that "to be a good parent is one of the hardest things in life I do."[140] While parenting is one of the most important and difficult tasks parents will face, it is one of the few responsibilities of this magnitude that does not require formal training or equipping.

136. Strommen, *Five Cries of Youth,* 62, 54.
137. Roy Zuck and Gene Getz, *Christian Youth—An In-depth Study* (Chicago: Moody, 1968), 81.
138. Barna Group, *Today's Teens,* 9.
139. Benson, Williams, and Johnson, *The Quicksilver Years,* 103.
140. Strommen and Strommen, *Five Cries of Parents,* 12.

4

The Adolescent World
of Social Relationships

Adolescents live in an ever expanding world of relationships, membership groups, and social environments. As young people move from childhood, through puberty, and into adolescence, their web of social and interpersonal relationships broadens. In addition to the family, teenagers find themselves increasingly involved with friends and peers, schoolmates, and dating relationships.

The adolescent interests in new social relationships and involvement in expanding membership groups are natural, though they are often a source of consternation to parents and teenagers alike, but for different reasons. Parents sense a gradual loss in the influence and control they have on their adolescent children. For teenagers, friendships, dating relationships, and acceptance by peers become overriding concerns and are often cause for much anxiety as well as the sources of rejection, hurt, and frustration.

This chapter investigates the various types of social relationships and membership groups that help make up the burgeoning world of adolescence. In addition the chapter will address many of the issues that emerge in the lives of teenagers as they explore new dimensions of life.

THE INFLUENCE OF FRIENDS AND PEERS

While teenagers do not always like to admit it openly, they are greatly influenced by their family. But in the adolescent years there emerges a natural desire to distance themselves from parents and siblings while affiliating more with nonfamilial peers and friends. While parents continue to have a significant impact on their teenage children, peers are by far the greatest presence in the lives of adolescents.[1] This shift of significant others can be a source of conflict between youth and parents. Parents generally place a higher value on family relationships and activities, while teenagers more often than not choose friends over parents. Furthermore, there is the concern of adults that teenagers left to themselves will be "up to no good," and that peer relations are disruptive to healthy personal development and to the best interest of society.[2]

While there is some evidence that peer relationships may contribute to deviant behaviors, such as drug use or delinquency, friendship and peer associations serve a number of important functions in the socialization of adolescents.[3] First, they operate as a mechanism whereby dependence on parental support and guidance is gradually loosened. Second, the adolescent period is seen as one in which interpersonal skills necessary in adulthood are learned through peer relationships. Third, peer groups offer emotional support at a time when young people are often unsure of themselves, questioning how they fit into the scheme of things. Friends provide an opportunity to discuss pertinent issues and events such as dating, parents, and school. In short, peer groups and friends serve as a training ground for the development of social and personality skills that will be necessary to function in the world of adulthood, toward which they are moving.[4]

THE FRIENDSHIP FACTOR

One of the major findings of Reginald Bibby and Donald Posterski through Project Teen Canada was the high value Canadian teenagers placed on friendships. The researchers were so struck with their discovery that they were able to conclude that friendship is the glue that holds

---

1. Mihaly Csiszentmihalyi and Reed Larson, *Being Adolescent* (New York: Basic Books, 1984), 71; Barna Group, *Today's Teens* (Glendale, Calif.: The Barna Research Group, 1991), 11.

2. Csiszentmihalyi and Larson, *Being Adolescent,* 157.

3. Ibid., 156–57.

4. Louise Guerney and Joyce Arthur, "Adolescent Social Relationships," in Richard M. Lerner and Nancy L. Galambos, eds., *Experiencing Adolescents* (New York: Garland, 1984) 92–93.

Canada's youth culture together.[5] They reaffirmed this in their follow-up study seven years later.[6]

Why were Bibby and Posterski compelled to make such an assertion? When asked "How much enjoyment do you receive from the friendship?" more than 7 in 10 responding adolescents said they experienced "a great deal" of enjoyment from friendships. When ranked with other factors, friendship was found to be the greatest source of enjoyment, with music the only other factor that was close. In comparison, fewer than half of the respondents claimed a high level of enjoyment from parents, with mothers faring slightly better than fathers.[7] When Canadian teenagers were questioned about what was of value to them, friendship emerged as the trait most valued; 91 percent said this was "very important" to them. This was followed by being loved, a trait seen as very important by 87 percent. Compare these to family life (65 percent) and being popular (21 percent).[8] Between 1984 and 1992 the proportion of teenagers who viewed friendship as "very important" dropped from 91 percent to 84 percent.[9]

The high value Canadian youth place on friends and friendships is supported by other empirical studies on North American teenagers. For early adolescents in the Search Institute study, "Friends I can count on" were highly valued by 80 percent of the respondents. Only the factors "To get a good job," "To have a happy family life," and "To do well in school," ranked slightly higher. According to this study, to have friends appears slightly more important to girls than boys, and the value placed on friendships increases each year for girls, while for boys this remains constant.[10] When asked whom they enjoy being with more, fifth-year students tended to enjoy parents more than friends, but by the time they reached the ninth year in school, friends were clearly a greater source of enjoyment than parents.[11]

---

5. Donald C. Posterski, *Friendship: A Window on Ministry to Youth* (Scarborough, Ont.: Project Teen Canada, 1985), 7; Reginald W. Bibby and Donald C. Posterski, *The Emerging Generation* (Tononto, Ont.: Irwin, 1985), 98.

6. Reginald W. Bibby and Donald C. Posterski, *Teen Trends* (Toronto, Ont.: Stoddart, 1992), 199.

7. Bibby and Posterski, *The Emerging Generation,* 32.

8. Ibid., 17.

9. Bibby and Posterski, *Teen Trends,* 10.

10. Peter L. Benson, Dorothy L. Williams, and Arthur L. Johnson, *The Quicksilver Years* (San Francisco: Harper & Row, 1987), 25.

11. Ibid., 26.

The Barna Research Group addressed the value of friendship by asking teenagers how they spend their time in an average week. The average amounts of time designated for six activities are shown below:[12]

Adolescents not only spend a greater amount of time with their friends, but time with friends is considered the best part of their daily lives. Most of this time involves socializing—talking, joking, or simply "hanging out." Much of what they do is spontaneous, unrelated to the external requirements of adults and adult institutions. In most cases experiences with friends are more positive than negative, and time with friends is the best part of adolescents' daily lives.[13]

If friendship is, as Donald Posterski suggests, the centerpiece of the teenager's life, how should adult volunteer youth workers and youth pastors proceed to do youth ministry? First, adult youth religious educators must work hard at building friendships and nurturing relationships with youth. Second, youth workers must place a high priority on building group community. Third, a relationally warm climate must be created at all youth ministry events. Finally, the physical environment in which youth ministry takes place must appear attractive and friendly.

Building Relationships With Youth

The promotion of friends in the personal lives of teenagers often means the demotion of adults—including grandparents, teachers, ministers, and youth workers—as sources of influence and relationships.

Table 4.1
How Teenagers Spend Their Time
In an Average Week

Time with friends	15.3 hrs.
Time with family	13.7 hrs.
Leisure activities	12.0 hrs.
Working at a paying job	9.3 hrs.
Studying or doing homework	6.9 hrs.
Church activities or events	2.7 hrs.

12. Barna Group, *Today's Teens,* p. 11.
13. Csikszentmihalyi and Larson, *Being Adolescent,* 158–61.

While intergenerational relationships have always been strained, the degree of distance may be increasing. Researchers Mihaly Csikszentmihalyi and Reed Larson observe that while adolescents spend a significant amount of time in locations structured or supervised by adults, they spend relatively less time actually involved in adult-oriented activities. They add that adults as a whole invest relatively little time in being with young people.[14]

Effective ministry with youth, however, begins when an adult leader finds a comfortable way of entering into the life and world of an adolescent.[15] If we observe closely the ministry of Jesus, we see that personal relationships were at the core of his strategy. Whether He was confronting the Samaritan woman at the well on a hot afternoon (John 4), talking with the Pharisee Nicodemus at night (John 3), or praying with his closest followers (John 17), Jesus modeled a loving, relational style of ministry.

If youth religious educators are going to impact teenagers with the gospel of Christ, they must work hard at entering their world and building personal relationships or friendships with them. This aspect of youth ministry is what many youth workers call "contacting."[16] This dimension of youth religious education does not come without effort for many adult volunteers. Some adults may feel uncomfortable or awkward attempting to develop a relationship with a teenager, while others may simply be frightened or intimidated by adolescents and their world. And it is always possible that an adult worker will take the time and make the effort to reach out to a teenager, only to be rejected.

Religious educators of youth will find, however, that if they genuinely and honestly attempt to enter into the lives of adolescents through love and acceptance, there will be those youth who will respond. There are some basic principles that will help the adult youth worker to more effectively establish relationships with teenagers.

First, building friendships with youth does not involve stripping oneself of adulthood, and taking on the appearance of an adolescent. Young people do not expect adults to try to dress, talk, or act like

---

14. Ibid., 70–75.

15. Mark H. Senter III, "Axioms of Youth Ministry," in Warren S. Benson and Mark H. Senter III, eds., *The Complete Book of Youth Ministry* (Chicago: Moody, 1987), 202.

16. See Duffy Robbins, *The Ministry of Nurture* (Grand Rapids, Mich.: Zondervan, 1990), 180–81.

teenagers. What they do desire is for adults to feel comfortable around teenagers acting like teenagers. They also need adults who understand adolescents—their ways of thinking, their struggles, and their needs.

Second, there is no one correct way to enter into a teenager's world. The most comfortable way for an adult to earn the right to be heard by an adolescent will differ from individual to individual and situation to situation.[17] The best way to facilitate relationships with teenagers and get to know them better is by doing something with them. Find out what an individual likes to do and do it with him or her. Here is a list of suggestions that might trigger some additional ideas as to how a youth leader can spend time with a teenager:[18]

• Have a soft drink and fries together.
• Go bowling or skating.
• Go hiking or rock climbing.
• Play tennis.
• Attend a school event.
• Attend a professional or college sporting event.
• Go to a concert.
• Go to the mall.
• Shoot baskets.
• Go fishing.
• Tutor a teenager in a subject he or she is struggling with.
• Go to a movie.

Third, relational ministry will not occur unless an adult youth worker earns the right to be heard by a teenager. Many young people are simply looking for someone to love and accept them and to be available to them. Earning the right to be heard usually comes simply with the exercising of basic interpersonal skills. Relational people are sensitive to others' feelings and demonstrate a willingness to listen and talk to others. Relational people also reflect a caring attitude by implementing a few basic communication skills. Maintaining good eye contact is one way to show real interest in what another person is saying. Responding with nods and verbal interjections lets people know you are listening, and using appropriate touch such as a pat on the back or a shoulder hug demonstrates warmth and care.

17. Senter, "Axioms of Youth Ministry", 203.
18. See Robbins, *The Ministry of Nurture,* 186–87 for some additional ideas concerning contacting.

Community Building

Donald Posterski concludes that in the North American culture at large, people are increasingly more interested in relationships than with ideas and beliefs.[19] This is probably as true or more true of the youth subculture than of any other group of people. Teenagers today look for a place to belong, find friends, and build relationships first, and then to learn and grow. With this being the case, it is imperative that the youth religious educator place a priority on building community in the group. To build community is to foster a sense of belonging and to nurture meaningful and genuine interpersonal relationships.

Goals for Community Building: Wayne Rice, John Roberto, and Mike Yaconelli suggest that a youth group seeking to build community and nurture a relational type of ministry strive for the following goals:[20]

• *Affirmation:* Community members have the responsibility and priv- ilege to confirm one another's self-worth, as well as to acknowledge the gifts and abilities of each group member. When teenagers hear their peers and friends saying positive things about them they enjoy their participation in the group to a much greater degree and are more likely to share their deep feelings.[21]

• *Interdependence:* While it is easy for adolescents to be consumed with individual needs, the nature of community members is both to have needs and to be needed. The keys to healthy interdependence are mutual support, interaction, and reliance on one another.

• *Trust:* Before young people can rely on one another, they must be assured that the relationships are mutually valued. To trust means to be confident in the loyalty of another person in the youth community.

• *Potential:* The gifts and abilities adolescents possess as individuals often have to be recognized and drawn out by adult leaders and peers who care for them. As adolescents discover their potential, they can in turn recognize and affirm the potential in others. In this way, the community enables its members to actualize their potential.

Community Building Through Small Groups: One of the most ef- fective community-building models for youth religious education is

19. Posterski, *Friendship: A Window on Ministry to Youth,* 16.

20. Summarized from Wayne Rice, John Roberto, and Mike Yaconelli, *Creative Communication and Community Building* (Winona, Minn.: Saint Mary's Press, 1981), 42–43.

21. Denny Rydberg, *Building Community in Youth Groups* (Loveland, Colo.: Group, 1985), 19.

the small group. A small group can be the setting where a lonely or hurting teenager connects with someone else—another adolescent or perhaps a caring adult worker. One of the most helpful small-group strategies that works toward the goal of community building is that developed by Lyman Coleman. Coleman describes a process of small-group sharing that begins at a simple, nonthreatening level and moves toward a *koinonia* or depth Christianity. He likens this strategy to a baseball diamond. First base is history giving, where group members are asked to tell their spiritual story to one another. It is a time of getting acquainted through the sharing of where they have come from (the past), where they are in their spiritual journey (the present), and where they want to be (the future).

At second base small-group members need a sense of affirmation. The goal at this point is to give each group member some positive feedback and encouragement through statements such as "Thanks for sharing," "I appreciate what you shared," or "Your story is a gift to me because . . . ."

Once affirmed, says Coleman, small-group members are ready to move on to third base, where interaction at a deeper level takes place. Youth begin to trust each other with sharing about needs, hurts, aspirations, joys, frustrations, and doubts. Group members are asked to respond to questions like "What is God saying to you concerning . . . ?" or "What is keeping you from . . . ?"

Finally, small-group members reach home plate, or that depth of Christian community called *koinonia*. When this level of interaction is reached, group members serve and respect each other and experience a sense of belonging and bonding. Community has been achieved.[22]

Leading a small group, however, is not a task that comes easily to everyone, and effective leadership comes only with practice and experience. The principles identified below will help the small-group leader in the critical task of nurturing interpersonal relationships and deeper community in the youth group.

• *Choose a setting that is comfortable and conducive to sharing.* Physical environment is very important for a small group. Ideally a small group should meet in a warm, comfortable setting. Try to avoid large,

---

22. Lyman Coleman, *Serendipity Small Group Training Manual* (Littleton, Colo.: Serendipity, 1991), 15–16.

cold rooms like church basements and settings that provide too many distractions, such as restaurants. Homes provide the environment that is best suited to small groups.

• *Set up in an appropriate fashion.* Make sure your group sets up in a circular or U-shaped manner. It is important that the leader and each member can make eye contact with every other member. Try to avoid the use of sofas or easy chairs, as they sometimes allow members to get too relaxed or become too distant from the group.

• *Develop a relationship with each of the group members.* As a leader, it is important to get to know each of the group members. Always arrive early, so you can get to know any new attendees. Make sure they are properly introduced to the group.

• *Ask open-ended questions.* One of the keys, if not the key to effective group interaction and sharing, is being able to ask the right kinds of questions. Closed-ended questions should generally be avoided: those that can be answered with a yes or no, have one-word answers, or have a single correct answer. Open-ended questions generally have more than one correct answer, demand personal reflection, and will result in dialogue. Usually the best open-ended questions begin with *how* or *why,* and sometimes *what.*

• *Show interest in the speaker by using good listening skills.* A good small-group leader is a sensitive listener. Adolescents want more than physical presence in communication; they want the other person's psychological and emotional presence as well. Effective listening includes hearing what the speaker is saying, making good eye contact, and demonstrating interest in the speaker through the use of nonverbal responses such as nods or smiles.

• *Learn to read nonverbals.* Often people will say more with nonverbal expressions than they will with verbal. For example, a raise of the eyebrows or a particular head movement may indicate a group member wants to say something. It is important for a leader to be sensitive to these subtle signals.

• *Try to get balanced participation.* It is important that every member has an opportunity to contribute to the dialogue. For those youth who are quiet and tend not to participate, the leader has several options. First, look for nonverbal sparks of interest. Then when it looks like a quiet individual would like to contribute, offer a nonthreatening response like "John, were you going to say something?" A second approach would be to occasionally make a comment to the group like "You know, we would like to hear from everybody!" or "Every person's input is valued in this group!" Try to avoid putting individuals on the spot by asking them to answer a particular question. This can cause great anxiety for some young people, and such an experience may cause them to quit coming to the small group.

• *Discourage domination by individual group members.* For the dominating group member, your first tactic might be to avoid eye contact with this person, while at the same time offering other members an opportunity to contribute. Second, politely suggest to the whole group that you are looking for *everyone* to participate, hoping the dominating member will get the hint. If one individual continues to try to control the discussion, talk to this person outside of the group, thanking him or her for contributing to the discussion, but reminding the individual that such dominance is discouraging others from participating.

• *Resist the temptation to answer questions yourself.* When a question is raised or asked by group members, many leaders feel constrained to pontificate or answer the question themselves. Often a response by the facilitator will squelch group interaction. This is an ideal opportunity to nurture further group dialogue by throwing the question back to the group and encouraging members to interact with each other.

• *Do not be afraid of silence.* Often a question will be greeted with silence by group members. This often unnerves small-group leaders and they feel constrained to say something. Do not be afraid of a little silence. It is possible the small-group participants are thinking and they need a little time before responding. Give them time to ponder the question and then if nothing is said, rephrase the query.

Building Community in Large-Group Activities: Large-group activities and programs must also be opportunities for making friends and nurturing relationships.[23] Looking for opportunities to break the whole group into smaller clusters during youth group meetings and events is one way to accomplish relationship building. For example, a small-group experience designed to assist the youth-group members to learn more about each other and affirm one another's position in the Body of Christ is "The Football Game." Break the larger body into small clusters of four or five. Individuals then share where they feel they fit into the youth group or church body and why. One teenager, for example, might

---

23. Posterski, *Friendship: A Window on Ministry to Youth,* 21.

consider himself to be sitting on the bench, not very active. Another might consider herself a cheerleader, offering encouragement to the team but not participating directly. Other group members might identify with the coach, the quarterback, the trainer, or the spectators. Then give each member an opportunity to share where they would like to be in the picture, and why. This is an ideal way to help the young people visualize where they are today and where they would like to be in the future. You might also prepare a photograph or drawing of a football stadium with coaches, players, and spectators for each group, or provide a list of possible participants in a football game to choose from. Bring the experience to a close by having individuals affirm each other in prayer.[24]

Instead of playing team sports that stress competition and winning, such as volleyball or softball, try engaging the youth group in cooperative recreational activities that focus more on working together and the attainment of a group goal. One such noncompetitive activity is "The Platform Game," the object of which is to see how many people can fit on a platform at one time. Materials needed are:
• a sturdy piece of plywood approximately 3 feet by 3 feet depending on the number of people in the group;
• 4 bricks, one under each corner of the plywood; and
• a rope that is long enough to surround the platform with a 2½-foot gap between the rope and the platform.
The space between the rope and the platform symbolizes a deep shaft. If someone steps in the shaft or falls back into this area, he or she must try again to get on the platform. See how many people can pile onto the platform without falling into the shaft.[25]

Another activity that can illustrate the importance of community and relationships is the often used "Yarn Circle." Youth group members are asked to form a circle with their elbows touching. The person beginning the activity holds the end of the yarn and without mentioning the name of the person she is thinking of, states a quality or attribute the person has that contributes to the unity of the group. She then tosses the ball of yarn to another person who does the same. This process continues with each

---

24. Revised from Wayne Rice, John Roberto, and Mike Yaconelli, *Creative Communication and Community Building*, 42–43.

25. Two excellent sources for community-building activities are Wayne Rice, John Roberto, and Mike Yaconelli, *Creative Communication and Community Building*, and Wayne Rice, *Up Close and Personal* (Grand Rapids, Mich.: Zondervan, 1995).

person holding onto the yarn and throwing the ball to another person until each member is included in the yarn pattern. Note the beauty of the pattern that has been created. Then ask two or three of the youth to let go of the circle and step out. Notice how ugly the pattern becomes when some of the group members are missing. Tighten the yarn by moving back slowly and then ask two or more youth to drop out. Continue this process and ask the youth to observe what is happening to the pattern as more and more people remove themselves from the circle.

Read Philippians 2:1–8 and ask youth group members to pick out qualities and actions that contribute to group community. Talk about the scriptural teachings that could help your group attain unity and closeness. Close the session by thanking God for the contributions each member brings to the community of the youth group.[26]

Creating a Relationally Warm Climate

To reemphasize, programmed events must be seen as more than opportunities for teaching. They must be occasions for making friends and nurturing relationships.[27] In an insightful empirical study on the participation of youth in church-related activities, Dean Hoge and Gregory Petrillo found that a positive attitude toward church youth programs is almost synonymous with the friendliness and affirmation received from other youth group attendees.[28]

Regular youth group attendees should be encouraged to develop relationships with adolescents beyond their immediate circle of friends, and to reach out to newcomers and visitors. Sometimes, however, teenagers need to be taught how to communicate effectively with others and build interpersonal relationships. The following skills will help adolescents take the initiative in befriending and reaching out relationally to other adolescents.[29]

Remembering Names: One of the most effective ways of demonstrating interest in other people is by remembering and using their names. To

---

26. Taken from John Shaw, "Exercises for Building Unity in Your Group," in Lee Sparks, ed., *The Youth Group How-to Book* (Loveland, Colo.: Group, 1981), 36–37.

27. See also Posterski, *Friendship: A Window on Ministry to Youth,* 21.

28. Dean R. Hoge and Gregory H. Petrillo, "Youth and the Church," in *Religious Education* 70, (May-June 1979), 305–13.

29. Barbara B. Varenhorst, *Training Teenagers for Peer Ministry* (Loveland, Colo.: Group, 1988).

help youth group members become more conscious of the importance of names, spend some time talking about their own names by doing the following exercise. Have each member state his or her first, middle, and last name. Then talk about these names by answering questions such as: "How do you feel about the name you were given?" "Why were you given the names?" "Do you have any nicknames?" "What embarrassing or funny experiences have you had with your names?" "Of what nationality are they?" "Do you know why your parents gave you the name they did?" "What is the significance of any one of your names?" Choose the first person to begin, then have that individual choose the next person. Conclude the session by explaining the significance of names in Scripture. For example, Saul changed his name to Paul after his conversion. Jesus changed Simon's name to Peter, which means "rock" (John 1:35–42).

Listening: In order to practice care, concern, and understanding for others, we must learn how to be effective listeners. Listening is the communication tool that allows us to enter into another person's private world and helps us better understand what someone else is feeling or experiencing. Communication experts suggest, however, that while listening is the most fundamental and basic language or communication skill that we develop, it is the most neglected skill at all educational levels.[30] Therefore, young people, as well as the rest of us, need to be taught how to listen more effectively to others.

To help group members become better listeners and learn the important communication techniques of attending, clarification, and paraphrasing, try the following listening exercise. Divide the youth group members into pairs and ask one partner to begin by describing in detail, an important person (a parent, relative, coach, teacher, minister, friend, etc.) in his or her life. Encourage the listeners to *attend* or listen carefully to the speakers by facing them squarely, maintaining good eye contact, and leaning toward them slightly.

The listeners should be encouraged to ask questions for *clarification,* especially for vague phrases or words the speaker may have used. Good clarification statements are "I am not sure what you meant by that," or "Could you restate that and tell me a little bit more?"

---

30. Andrew Wolvin and Carolyn Gwynn Coakley, *Listening,* 4th ed. (Dubuque, Iowa: Wm. C. Brown, 1992), 18, 31.

When the speakers finish the account, the listeners should *paraphrase,* or tell back to the speakers in their own words the message they heard. The objective is not to repeat a detailed account but rather to feed back the heart of the message, particularly the feeling level of what was initially shared.

Conclude the learning experience with a debriefing time, giving the youth an opportunity to respond to and discuss their encounter. Ask questions like the following:

• In what ways did your listener show he or she was listening to you?
• Did the listener demonstrate a lack of interest or in any way make it difficult for you as the speaker?
• What suggestions could you give your listener that would make her a better listener?
• How would you rate yourself as a listener?[31]

Asking Questions: Sometimes adolescents find it difficult to initiate or carry on a conversation because they do not know how to find a bridge that connects to another individual. Use the following activity to teach them how to use questions that will help them carry out warm conversations.

Ask group members to think of an interest they have such as a hobby, recreational activity, or subject that gives them enjoyment and pleasure. Inform them that they may be asked to share their interest with the whole group. After they have had time to think, go in a circle, asking each person to identify his or her interest. After everyone has shared, choose the person with the most unusual or unique interest. Have the group members brainstorm questions they might ask this person about his interest, without the person answering at this time. Write the questions on the board precisely as they have been asked. When the group has run out of questions, ask the selected person to indicate only the questions he or she would prefer to answer. Now ask the members if they see any difference between the preferred questions and the others. The group will probably discover that the individual chose questions about personal feelings or achievements. Have the person answer the top-ranked questions and then see if the group wants to ask any more questions based on that answer.

---

31. This exercise was taken from Varenhorst, *Training Teenagers for Peer Ministry,* 43–45.

Follow up by describing four types of questions often used in conversation:

• *Closed-ended questions*—questions that require a one word answer such as "Do you like baseball?"

• *Open-ended questions*—"What is it you like about baseball?"

• *Informational questions*—questions that ask for factual information such as "Where did you live as a child?"

• *Feeling-level questions*—"How do you feel about living in California rather than Texas?" "How do you like attending your new school?"

Inform participants that most people prefer to respond to open-ended and feeling-level questions over closed-ended and informational questions. By asking open-ended and feeling-level questions, the questioner gives others the opportunity to provide more information and develop meaningful conversation, rather than short, specific answers.[32]

Welcoming Strangers to the Group: A difficult task for many adolescents (as well as some adults) is reaching out to strangers or people they do not know. Yet it is imperative that a youth group open its arms to new people. To help regular attendees realize the importance of accepting outsiders or strangers, let them experience firsthand what it is like to try to get into a group that will not accept them or how it feels to keep someone out. Choose one youth to stand outside of the group while other members stand in a circle and lock arms. Give the outsider about 30 seconds to try to get in while those in the circle do everything they can (without doing bodily harm) to keep the intruder from getting into the circle. The outsider may overpower the group and get in, but usually he cannot penetrate the circle and gives up. Have two or three people attempt to break into the circle.

Try to get the participants to apply the simulation activity to real life, where a stranger or visitor is trying to get involved in their youth group. Follow the activity by asking the participants some questions. To those trying to get into the group ask the following questions:

• If you failed to get into the group, how did you feel? Why did you give up?

• If you did get into the circle, what strategy did you use? Was it worth the effort? Did you feel accepted?

Ask the insiders questions such as these:

----

32. Ibid., 33–34.

• How did you feel as you kept the people from getting in?
• Were you concerned about the outsider's feelings in any way?
Ask the whole group questions like the following:
• How do you think a newcomer feels when she visits a group and members do not make her feel welcome?
• Why is it sometimes difficult to reach out to strangers?
• What can you do to help a visitor feel more comfortable or welcome?[33]

Breaking the Ice

Youth religious educators who want to encourage youth group attendees to interact with one another should give careful attention to the use of "icebreakers" or "crowd-breakers." These are games designed to open meetings and help group attendees get to know each other. Icebreakers help defuse any uneasiness or tension at the beginning of a session and are also an ideal way to get visitors and first-time attendees to mix with regular attendees in a nonthreatening manner.

For example, an often used icebreaker is the "Name Tag" game. Create name tags using biblical, historical, or contemporary celebrity names. As youth group members arrive for the group activity attach a tag to the back of each individual's shirt. Each individual is to try to find out his identity by asking questions which can be answered with a simple yes or no. Each participant is limited to three questions per person. As identities are discovered, have each member sit down until all have finished.[34]

Another good icebreaker is the "Match Mixer." Give each individual three 3 by 5 cards or slips of paper. Have the participants write something about themselves on each card. Suggest topics such as these:
• My most embarrassing experience is . . .
• My ambition is to . . .
• The person I admire the most is . . .
• My favorite recreational activity is . . .
• If I had a million dollars I would . . .

Collect the cards and redistribute three to each person (make sure no one has his or her own card). At a given signal each participant tries to match the three cards with the correct people by asking questions of

---

33. Ibid., 62–63.
34. Taken from John Bushman, "Breaking the Ice at the Beginning," in Lee Sparks, ed., *The Youth Group How-to Book* (Loveland, Colo.: Group, 1981), 13–14.

participants. Whoever first matches the three cards is the winner. Allow all the youth to finish matching their cards and, if time allows, let each member share his or her findings with the whole group.[35]

Creating an Environmentally Warm Climate

The environmental conditions of the settings where youth ministry takes place are critical in creating a relationally warm setting. James Michael Lee insists that the extent of an individual's learning depends on the power and nature of the environment, including the design and arrangement of the room in which the group activity is carried on.[36] Elements such as the size of the rooms, the decor, the floor coverings, and even the appearance of the building can influence the emotional climate and the process of relationship building. Church basements with cold concrete floors, drab walls with little or no wall ornamentation, exposed electrical wiring and ductwork, and hard metal folding chairs arranged in straight rows should be avoided.

Rooms used for youth ministry should be as warm, attractive, inviting, and comfortable as possible. What is communicated when one enters a meeting room? Does it feel warm and friendly or cold and rejecting? Is it a place for lectures and impersonal meetings, or is it a place where friends gather for warm fellowship and meaningful interaction? Often large homes with recreation rooms are ideal for youth-group activities and meetings. Homes usually communicate automatically a sense of warmth and friendliness.

PEER INFLUENCE

Since adolescents spend a significant amount of time with each other, it follows that peers exert a significant amount of influence in the shaping of conduct and value systems of teenagers. Empirical studies related to adolescent development identify several patterns in regard to peer influence.

---

35. Taken from Wayne Rice and Mike Yaconelli, *Play It* (Grand Rapids, Mich.: Zondervan, 1986), 152.

36. James Michael Lee, *The Flow of Religious Education* (Birmingham, Ala.: Religious Education Press, 1973), 65, 71.

First, as mentioned earlier, the strength of peer versus parental influence depends on the nature of the issue involved. A number of empirical research studies have found that when choices or issues pertain to long term and future aspirations such as school, moral and ethical issues, the choice of a part time job, and religious convictions, youth tend to seek out parental influence and advice. For status and short-term social values regarding length of hair, style of dress, or dating, adolescents tend to follow peers.[37] Thus, it appears that personal identity (Who am I?) is largely influenced by peers, while future identity (Who am I to be?) is influenced more by parents.[38]

Second, parents and peers will generally have more similarity than dissimilarity in moral orientation.[39] Contrary to what adults may think, most adolescents choose friends who have values and expectations similar to those of their parents. Thus disagreements, as already noted, will tend to be over minor issues such as music or dress.[40]

Third, the relationship of the adolescent to his or her parents affects the impact of peer influence. Peer-oriented adolescents are more likely to exhibit antisocial behavior than those who have strong relationships with their parents.[41] Furthermore, it appears that the tendency to conform to peer-group norms occurs only in the absence of monitoring by parents and teachers. In other words, the threat of exposure to adults has the effect of diminishing pressure to conform to the standards of peers.[42]

The presence of parents and other adults in the lives of teenagers is critical if young people are going to be equipped to withstand the negative pressures of their friends and peers. Again, it is normal for

---

37. Bibby and Posterski, *Teen Trends,* 205; Clay Brittain, "Adolescent Choices and Parent-Peer Cross-Pressures," in Rolf E. Muuss, ed., *Adolescent Behavior and Society* (New York: Random House, 1971), 230; Hans Sebald, "Adolescents Shifting Orientation Towards Parents and Peers," in *Journal of Marriage and the Family* 48, (February 1986), 5–13; Hans Sebald, *Adolescence,* 3d ed. (Englewood Cliffs, N.J.: Prentice-Hall, 1984), 230.

38. Cheryl R. Laus, Edward Lonky, and Paul Roodin, "Moral Reasoning and Behavior," in Richard M. Lerner and Nancy L. Galambos, eds., *Experiencing Adolescents* (New York: Garland, 1984), 244.

39. Ibid., 243.

40. Guerney and Arthur, "Adolescent Social Relationships," 96.

41. Ibid.

42. Urie Bronfenbrenner, "Response to Pressure From Peers Versus Adults Among Soviet and American Students," in Rolf E. Muuss, ed., *Adolescent Behavior and Society* (New York: Random House, 1971), 438.

youth to spend more time with their peers than with their parents. But, as Walt Mueller reflects, parents who choose to become overinvolved in work, recreation, and other activities are making the choice to spend less time with their family; they are, as a result, opening the door for their teenagers to spend more time with members of their peer group.[43]

Fourth, the influence of peers plays a greater role during the adolescent years than in either childhood or young adulthood. It is in the adolescent years that peer pressure reaches its greatest intensity. In their empirical study of preadolescents and early adolescents, Benson, Williams, and Johnson found the influence of peers to increase with each succeeding age.[44]

Philip Costanzo and Marvin Shaw extended their study into late adolescence and young adulthood and found a curvilinear pattern whereby peer influence peaked in early adolescence and declined in the later teenage years. This decline continued into the early adulthood years at which point individuals no doubt learned that there are some situations that call for conformity while others call for individual action.[45]

Louise Guerney and Joyce Arthur suggest that this shifting in loyalty from family to peers appears to be a necessary phase in the process of *individuation,* or the manner in which an adolescent becomes a separate, unique individual, with his or her own interests, identity, values, and personality. They go on to say that to develop a positive concept of self, the need for acceptance by peers increases with age, so that by the adolescent years it is the all-critical area for approval and acceptance.[46]

Finally, peer influence can be either positive or negative in nature. Peter Benson and his colleagues found that by and large pre- and early adolescents did not experience a great deal of peer pressure toward negative behavior. They did find, however, that at each age boys reported higher levels of negative peer pressure than girls.[47] Empirical research studies indicate that the influence of friends and peers indisputably

43. Walt Mueller, *Understanding Today's Youth Culture* (Wheaton, Ill.: Tyndale, 1994), 184.

44. Benson, Williams, and Johnson, *The Quicksilver Years,* 27.

45. Philip R. Costanzo and Marvin E. Shaw, "Parent and Peer Group Influences on Adolescents," in Rolf E. Muuss, ed., *Adolescent Behavior and Society* (New York: Random House, 1971), 246–49.

46. Guerney and Arthur, "Adolescent Social Relationships," 91.

47. Benson, Williams, and Johnson, *The Quicksilver Years,* 30.

contributes to deviant behaviors such as drug and alcohol use,[48] difficulties with teachers and school,[49] and delinquency.[50]

Negative peer pressure is of great concern to parents and youth workers alike. Adults often point to the negative effects of peer influence such as substance abuse, delinquent behavior, or rudeness. But adolescents can also influence each other in positive ways: to be compassionate, to share their faith, to pray and study the Word, to help those in need, to be friends to others, and to reach out to the lonely and hurting.

Klaus Issler and Ronald Habermas suggest that the church has the responsibility to provide positive modeling to young people through two sources: godly adults and godly peers. Many adult youth workers are recognizing the powerful impact adolescents can have on one another and are training their young people for what is called "peer ministry." Youth religious education experts consistently argue that ministry to teenagers is best done by other teenagers, not adults, and that youth ministries grow only as young people are equipped, encouraged, and released to do the work of ministry to their peers.[51] Merton Strommen concludes that adolescents, when properly trained, can become an important and effective resource for reaching lonely and alienated youth. He bases his assumptions on the results of a Search Institute study which tested the effectiveness of programs that trained high-school youth to reach out to the friendless.[52]

It then becomes the task of adult leaders to equip and disciple young people to carry out ministry to their friends and peers. This is the challenge Paul gave to Timothy when he said, "And the things you

---

48. Chris Lutes, *What Teenagers are Saying About Drugs and Alcohol* (Wheaton, Ill.: Tyndale, 1986), 24, 50; John A. Webb, Paul E. Baer, Charlene D. Caid, Robert J. McLaughlin, and Robert S. McKelvey, "Concurrent and Longitudinal Assessment of Risk for Alcohol Use Among Seventh Graders," in *The Journal of Early Adolescence* 11, (November 1991), 450–65.

49. Ronald L. Simons, Les B. Whitbeck, Rand D. Conger, and Janet N. Melby, "The Effect of Social Skills, Values, Peers, and Depression on Adolescent Substance Use," in *The Journal of Early Adolescence* 11, (November 1991), 466–81.

50. Sebald, *Adolescence,* 170.

51. See Ray Johnston, *Developing Student Leaders* (Grand Rapids, Mich.: Zondervan, 1992), 25; Barbara B. Varenhorst, *Training Teenagers for Peer Ministry* (Loveland, Colo.: Group, 1988), 10–11; Mike Yaconelli and Jim Burns, *High School Ministry* (Grand Rapids, Mich.: Zondervan, 1986), 106; Joan Sturkie and Siang-Yang Tan, *Advanced Peer Counseling* (Grand Rapids, Mich.: Zondervan, 1993), 9–11.

52. Merton P. Strommen, *Five Cries of Youth,* 2nd rev. ed. (San Francisco: HarperSan Francisco, 1993), 90–91.

have heard me say in the presence of many witnesses entrust to reliable men who will also be qualified to teach others" (II Tim. 2:2, NIV). It is also the strategy modeled by Christ as He spent the majority of his time and efforts in the choosing of his disciples, instructing them in the techniques of ministry, and sending them out to do ministry.

The following suggestions for a healthy peer ministry are offered by Mike Yaconelli and Jim Burns:

• Teenagers should not just *go* to the youth group, they should *do* the youth group. They should be given opportunities to use their gifts and abilities in youth ministry programs, rather than passively occupy seats and watch.

• Youth religious education ministry should provide plenty of small-group activities, the primary source of peer ministry opportunities.

• Youth should be encouraged to write letters, cards, and notes of encouragement to their peers.

• Youth ministry should involve adolescents in service projects such as feeding the hungry, tutoring immigrants, or visiting shut-ins.[53]

Yaconelli and Burns conclude that adolescents are the best programming resource an adult leader has and can participate in almost any aspect of a youth religious education ministry. This chapter, as well as other parts of the book, includes many suggestions for preparing and involving adolescents in peer ministry.

POPULARITY

Many researchers have noted that popularity is one of the most emphasized values among teenagers. For example, James Coleman, in a well-known survey of high school students, found a strong desire to be popular, a desire that was more intense for females than for males.[54] In a longitudinal study of suburban high school students taken between 1976 and 1982, Hans Sebald and Karen Krauss discovered the importance attached to being popular in high school. The 1976 responses to the question "How important is it to be liked and accepted by other teenagers?" showed that 47 percent felt it to be of "very great importance," 37 percent of "great importance," 14 percent of "some

---

53. Yaconelli and Burns, *High School Ministry,* 107.
54. James S. Coleman, *The Adolescent Society* (New York: Free Press, 1963), 30.

importance," and only 2 percent of "no importance." The 1982 study revealed a distribution of 17 ("very great importance"), 37 ("great importance"), 41 ("some importance"), and 4 ("no importance") percent on the same question. The 1982 study reported a sharp decrease in the "very-great importance" category and a marked increase in the "some-importance" category. However, when all categories reporting "importance" were combined, there was only an insignificant decrease from 98 to 95 percent from 1976 to 1982.[55]

Interestingly, not all research studies support the notion that popularity is highly valued by teenagers. According to a 1992 study by Bibby and Posterski, only 22 percent of Canadian youth viewed "being popular" as very important. Compare this response to freedom (86 percent) and friendship (84 percent), the items that ranked first and second as valued goals in life by Canadian youth.[56] The responses did not differ significantly from a 1984 study that asked the same question.[57]

In the study of early adolescents by Search Institute, "To be popular at school" was seen as important by a little less than half of the respondents; however, this response ranked near the bottom of 24 items. The desire for popularity did increase slightly, though, as the respondents got older.[58]

Teenagers seem to make a clear distinction between personal relationships or friendship, and being popular. Popularity may be seen more as pleasing or leading the crowd, whereas friendship is identified with intimacy and meaningful acceptance. This may very well represent a recent and positive trend, as earlier researchers noted popularity as one of the most emphasized values among teenagers. It may be that contemporary adolescents are not concerned with being popular as much as they are with fitting in and being accepted.[59]

Nonetheless, adolescents want to feel accepted by their peers, and often this is displayed through a seeking to be popular. However, one of the main prices of popularity, for either sex, is conformity, especially true of younger adolescents up to age 13. When respondents were asked by Sebald and Krauss, "What is expected of a teenager by his or her friends in order to be popular with them?" they ranked the conformity principle

---

55. Reported in Sebald, *Adolescence*, 228.
56. Bibby and Posterski, *Teen Trends*, 15.
57. Bibby and Posterski, *The Emerging Generation*, 17.
58. Benson, Williams, and Johnson, *The Quicksilver Years*, 92–93.
59. Sebald, *Adolescence*, 227.

first (that is, doing, speaking, thinking, dressing, etc., "our way"). The second criterion was "good personality"; third was "being yourself"; fourth was taking an interest in others and helping them; fifth was being honest and trustworthy.[60]

Rather than overindulging in conforming to harmful or questionable activities in attempts to gain popularity, adolescents should be encouraged to build meaningful friendships within and outside the youth group. The adult youth worker can assist youth group members establish deepening friendships by encouraging them to apply five steps suggested by Alan Loy McGinnis[61] and reaffirmed by Wayne Rice:[62]

• *Place a high priority on relationships.* Deep friendships require much time and effort and should not be taken for granted.

• *Cultivate transparency.* Learn to be open and honest with others; talk about what is on your heart.

• *Share your affections.* Tell your friends how you feel about them; that you like them and care for them.

• *Learn and offer the gestures of love.* Do things regularly for others that affirm the friendships. Giving a gift or taking a friend out for supper are examples of gestures of love.

• *Create space in your friendship.* Do not try to control, manipulate, or smother the other person. Strong relationships allow for both closeness and freedom.

Many teenagers go to great lengths to be accepted and affirmed by large groups of peers. They get a strong sense of security through an active social life and large groups of people. But as Alan McGinnis poignantly suggests, getting close to a few friends is far more important than receiving 400 Christmas cards every year.[63]

LONELINESS

Fifteen-year-old Trevor woke up with a dull, empty feeling in his stomach. It was time to get ready for another day at school, but it

---

60. Sebald, *Adolescence,* 228 and Jane E. Brownstone and Richard H. Willis, "Conformity in Early and Late Adolescence," in *Developmental Psychology* 4, (May 1971), 334–47.

61. Alan Loy McGinnis, *The Friendship Factor* (Minneapolis: Augsburg, 1979), 20–58.

62. Rice, *Up Close and Personal,* 128.

63. McGinnis, *The Friendship Factor,* 24.

*was the last thing in the world that he wanted to do. Trevor always
had a difficult time making friends and developing relationships.
But two months ago his dad was transferred to a new city and the
whole family, of course, was forced to move. This meant leaving the
few friends he had, his school where he had begun to feel somewhat
comfortable, and his youth group—the only place besides his home,
where he felt any measure of belongingness and acceptance. Now
Trevor was convinced that he did not have a friend in the world
and felt an intense loneliness he was sure could never go away.*

Loneliness has been called "the world's most common mental health
problem," "one of the most universal sources of human suffering," an
"almost permanent condition for millions of people,"[64] and an "emotional epidemic."[65] Robert Weiss, based on his empirical study of loneliness, estimates that 25 percent of the American population feels acutely
lonely at some time during any given month.[66] Gallup polls indicate that
as many as 30 percent of American adults have been lonely "for a long
period of time" with half of these people saying this experience has
affected their thoughts "a great deal."[67]

One might think that teenagers, with all the activities they are involved in and the people they are constantly with, are immune to the
trauma of loneliness. However, several research studies indicate that
between 25 and 45 percent of American teenagers experience serious
loneliness at some point during their adolescent years.[68] Samuel Natale,
in his insightful book on loneliness and spiritual growth, suggests that
adolescents are at a stage of life when they are extremely vulnerable to
feelings of loneliness.[69] Adolescence is normally seen as a time during
which friendships and relationships become more valued, peers become
increasingly significant, and the need for social acceptance is at its peak.

---

64. Cited in Gary R. Collins, *Christian Counseling* (Waco, Tex.: Word, 1988), 92.

65. Craig W. Ellison, *Loneliness: The Search for Intimacy* (Chappaqua, N.Y.: Christian
Herald, 1980), 17.

66. Robert Weiss, *Loneliness: Emotional and Social Isolation* (Cambridge, Mass.:
MIT Press, 1973).

67. *The Religious Life of Young Americans* (Princeton, N.J.: The George H. Gallup
International Institute, 1992), 12.

68. These figures are given by Craig W. Ellison, *Loneliness,* 18, who cites a paper
given by Tim Brennan titled "Some Social and Psychological Correlates of Adolescent
Loneliness" presented at the UCLA Conference on Loneliness in May 1979.

69. Samuel M. Natale, *Loneliness and Spiritual Growth* (Birmingham, Ala.: Religious
Education Press, 1986), 94.

For some teenagers, unfortunately, the adolescent years are spent in rejection, alienation, and loneliness. Religious educators of youth must enable youth to effectively deal with feelings of loneliness and help them understand their source. Furthermore, it is of utmost importance that youth ministry programs be designed and implemented so as to minimize the possibility of loneliness being perpetuated in the youth group setting.

Causes of Loneliness

Loneliness is an emotional state which involves a conscious lack of warmth, contact, and friendship.[70] It involves feelings of inner emptiness, isolation, and intense longings to be accepted by other human beings. Loneliness is not necessarily a matter of aloneness, for even people who are surrounded with others often feel alienated, left out, rejected, or unwanted. On the other hand, individuals can be by themselves and have no sense of loneliness whatsoever. Adolescent loneliness can have a variety of causes, most of which can be grouped into the following categories: 1) developmental, 2) psychological, 3) cultural, 4) social, and 5) spiritual.

Developmental Causes: Because adolescence is a period of profound physical, affective, and cognitive change and maturation, new capacities for intimacy and identity emerge. If the developmental needs for the intimacy and identity are not fulfilled, loneliness is often the result.

Intimacy includes the ability to be committed to close and lasting relationships, as well as the willingness to sacrifice and compromise as those relationships require.[71] One alternative to intimacy is isolation and loneliness. Francine Klagsbrun, in her book on youth and suicide, says that youth who have received little love from their earliest days have, in a sense, lost love before they have even found it. As adolescents, they may retreat into a fantasy world and isolate themselves from others. They are incapable of giving or receiving love and in the most severe cases they often become seriously depressed and suicidal, refusing to allow anybody to intrude on their lonely world.[72]

---

70. Ibid., 2.
71. Charles Sell, *Transitions Through Adult Life* (Grand Rapids, Mich.: Zondervan, 1991), 52.
72. Francine Klagsbrun, *Too Young To Die* (New York: Pocket Books, 1981), 46.

Merton Strommen says the issue of loneliness is not so much not having friends as the ability to commit oneself to others. To know the trust of deep attachments young people must entrust themselves to others and the inability to do so robs them of the affections they need so desperately. When they are unable to open their lives to others in caring and loving ways, they do not experience the love and affection of others and consequently suffer through the experiences of loneliness.[73] An ideal way for adolescents to learn to entrust and open themselves up to others is by engaging themselves in the ongoing life of a small group. A small group provides an opportunity to develop close relationships and offers a safe context for promoting and nurturing care and self-disclosure among members.

Identity achievement is another of the major tasks of adolescent development. This is the process, as described in chapter 2, whereby the individual is faced with the crises of answering the questions Who am I? Where have I been? and Where am I going? In the adolescent years the young person experiences the need and desire to be weaned from his or her parents while simultaneously feeling a linkage with them. No longer a child and not yet an adult, the adolescent agonizes over his or her identity in terms of a variety of roles and responsibilities. With struggle and a certain amount of emotional pain, the adolescent seeks identity in terms of sexuality, the opposite sex, peers, career, and self worth. Because the teenager often feels separated or somewhat disconnected to the security of what has been and at the same time is seeking new relationships and identity, it can be a time of severe loneliness and frustration.[74]

The youth group and adult youth workers can provide that sense of security that lonely, identity-diffused teenagers are searching for. Adult workers are advised to make special efforts to identify and spend time with lonely adolescents. While not allowing their time to be consumed with these individuals, youth workers must make sure these teenagers receive a certain amount of special attention and acceptance. This might include making sure lonely adolescents have opportunities to serve and to be involved, doing one-on-one activities with them, giving them a

---

73. Strommen, *Five Cries of Youth,* 25.
74. Harvey H. Potthoff, *Loneliness: Understanding and Dealing With It* (Nashville, Tenn.: Abingdon, 1976), 37–38.

phone call from time to time, sending them a note, or by simply talking to them during a youth activity. Youth workers must resist the temptation to focus only on the "attractive," successful, or identity-achieved teenagers.

Furthermore, the identity-seeking questions that teenagers are asking in the formative years of adolescence are best answered in the community or context of their friends and peers. Samuel Natale suggests that the peer group offers many positive contributions to the growth toward identity. During this period of alienation from parents and family, the peer group, in this case made up of youth group members, offers teenagers a forum in which they can communicate with people of their own age. There is a sense of security in sharing problems and tough questions with friends and peers they know well and feel they can trust. In a healthy community, adolescents can also experience the feeling that they are needed, a feeling that is critical for a healthy self-concept.

Finally, and most important, the youth group can reinforce the norms and values that have been taught by parents in the family context. In this sense, youth group members provide a social environment in which adolescents' identities are shaped, and they decide what kind of persons they will become.[75]

Psychological Causes: In some cases certain psychological predispositions lead adolescents toward loneliness. Loneliness tends to appear more in adolescents who have low self-esteem, lack self-confidence, are shy and fearful, and demonstrate an inability to care for others.

Low self-esteem or perceiving oneself as a person of low regard is generally associated with high degrees of loneliness or social alienation.[76] The adolescent who feels worthless, unattractive, unpopular, or stupid, may have difficulty in initiating as well as maintaining relationships. In contrast, high self-esteem assists in forming close personal relationships which, in turn, reinforces that self-esteem, with the end result being a decrease in loneliness.[77]

Related to low self-esteem is a lack of self-confidence. Young people lacking self-confidence tend to screen out activities where they might

---

75. Natale, *Loneliness and Spiritual Growth*, 86–87.
76. See, for example, Tim Brennan, "Adolescent Loneliness: Linking Epidemiology and Theory to Prevention," in *Suicide and Depression Among Adolescents and Young Adults*, ed., Gerald Klerman (Washington: American Psychiatric Press, 1986), 201; Strommen, *Five Cries of Youth*, 24.
77. Collins, *Christian Counseling*, 96.

fail. They generally will not try out for the school play, work on an important committee, or join in a spontaneous game of volleyball or softball because of a fear of failure. Adolescents who suffer from self-contempt may retreat into the world of imagination where they dream of themselves as worthy, or they may put up a false front to convince others that they are worthy. Both responses tend to separate the teenager from others.[78]

One way to be sensitive to youth who lack healthy self-esteem and confidence is by making sure recreational activities are noncompetitive and cooperative in nature. In cooperative games, youth play with one another rather than against each other; consequently, these games help eliminate fear and feelings of rejection. Young people who are nurtured on activities that stress cooperation, acceptance, and success have a greater opportunity for developing healthy self-concepts and self-confidence than do games and activities that guarantee failure and rejection for many.[79] Some cooperative recreational activities were described earlier in this chapter.

Shyness and fear of social risk-taking can also hinder the initiation and development of relationships. Interestingly, one researcher found the relationship between shyness and loneliness to be significantly higher for boys than girls.[80] In addition to the insecurity of reaching out to others, shy teenagers often erect barriers to keep others out because of fear of intimacy, fear of being known, fear of rejection, or fear of being hurt.[81] These youth need to be taught how to build and maintain friendships, nurture relationships, and effectively communicate with others. Skills that will assist the teenager in relational and communication skills include listening and attending, conversation, and self-disclosure, all of which were described earlier in the chapter.

Teenagers who have an inability to care, or even demonstrate hostility toward others, may also find they are restricted in the initiation, maintenance, and development of social and intimate relationships. Selfishness and lack of interest in other people have also been found to be characteristics of lonely adolescents.[82] Involving youth in inner-

78. Strommen, *Five Cries of Youth,* 22–23.
79. Terry Orlick, *The Cooperative Sports and Games Book* (New York: Pantheon, 1978), 3–5.
80. Brennan, "Adolescent Loneliness," 202.
81. Collins, *Christian Counseling,* 97.
82. Brennan, "Adolescent Loneliness," 202.

city or third-world ministry is one way to develop a heart or compassion for other people. A mission trip to a country such as Haiti, the poorest nation in the Western hemisphere, can be effective in creating a sense of compassion and concern in an otherwise uncaring youth.[83]

Cultural Causes: Some commentators suggest our contemporary society itself may very well be a significant contributor to loneliness. Rapid social changes in recent history have isolated people from close meaningful contact with each other and have made loneliness increasingly widespread.

With the great migration from rural communities to the city that has taken place in the twentieth century, we can sense the dislocation and loneliness that has come with it. In 1900 over 70 percent of all persons in United States lived on farms and in rural communities. By 1975 it was just the reverse.[84] Psychologists suggest that although cities crowd people together physically, there are several factors about large urban configurations that seem to create isolation, anxiety, and loneliness.[85] As people have moved closer together, there has been a tendency to withdraw from others. A fear of strangers or crime often leads to suspicion and avoidance, while crowding appears to increase feelings of stress, anxiety, and hostility toward others.

The technological-urban society of the contemporary world has a number of characteristics conducive to loneliness. Samuel Natale suggests that the rapid increase in technological and scientific changes have left young people deprived of a sense of belonging and community.[86] Psychologist Craig Ellison cites television as a technological advancement that promotes loneliness in at least two ways. First, the content of television often promotes aggressiveness and violence, behaviors which hardly promote intimacy and relationships. Second, the addictive nature of television tends to break down communication and interaction among family members, as each member is locked into a fantasy world.

---

83. Two nondenominational organization that are succesful in engaging teenagers in cross-cultural ministry opportunities are Teen Missions, 885 East Hall Road, Merritt Island, Fla. 32953 and Group Workcamps, Box 481, Loveland, Colo. 80539, (303) 669-3836. Roman Catholic youth can contact Catholic Relief Services (212) 838-4700 for information regarding opportunities for involvement in the developing world.

84. Edgar Jackson, *Understanding Loneliness* (Philadelphia: Fortress, 1980), 24.

85. For example see Jackson, *Understanding Loneliness,* 24; Ellison, *Loneliness,* 81; Collins, *Christian Counseling,* 95.

86. Natale, *Loneliness and Spiritual Growth,* 78.

When television rules the household, there tend to be fewer family walks and discussions, and less playing together. Even when family members watch television together, there is relatively little discussion of the programs.[87]

Inextricably related to technology is mobility, in that better transportation, the development of large corporations, and opportunities for advancement have required increased movement. Families today move so much that adolescents have little chance to form meaningful and long-lasting friendships and relationships with those of their own age. Consequently, argues Natale, for many youth, adolescence consists of a series of relationships which have been broken or never secured.[88]

In this impersonal, technologically heightened world where people communicate through computers and microchips, modems, electrical impulses, cellular phones and facsimile transmitters, teenagers need an emotionally warm environment where they can receive love, friendship, understanding, care, and touch. A scene from the popular situation comedy "Cheers" helps illustrate this. An overweight gentleman in a rumpled overcoat enters the bar to a welcome chorus of his name, "Norm!" He walks to his seat at the end of the bar where he is at home with his friends who accept and know him. The theme song of the show says, "Sometimes you want to go where everybody knows your name. And they're always glad you came. . . ." Youth workers who want to meet the emotional, psychological, and spiritual needs of today's lonely and disenfranchised adolescents are encouraged to build a strong youth religious education program that promotes Christian community. Today's teenagers, as much as anybody else, want a place they can go where everybody knows their name.

Social Causes: It has been stressed earlier that one of the significant changes taking place during the adolescent years is the distancing from parents and movement toward peers and friends as significant others. The development of this peer and friendship network is an essential part of healthy development as peer groups provide emotional security, empathy and friendship. Strommen found that a significant issue for lonely youth is having or not having friends. Most lonely adolescents in his study (87 percent) said that outside of their families they really

---

87. Ellison, *Loneliness,* 68–73.
88. Natale, *Loneliness and Spiritual Growth,* 81.

belonged to no particular group, and were bothered by the lack of friends at school.[89]

Clearly, one of the deepest needs of human beings is the need to belong and be accepted. Rejection by peers has a terrible impact on an adolescent's sense of loneliness. One of the reasons adolescents are rejected is that they are not skilled in the activities that count in the eyes of their peers, such as athletics or music. Another reason is appearance. Those who are less beautiful or handsome, or have some sort of physical "defect" may have difficulty being accepted. Other adolescents may be rejected because their value system differs from that of the majority.[90]

Wayne Rice, in his book on community building, *Up Close and Personal,* tells the story of Dolores, a teenage girl. As a sophomore in high school, Dolores was short, overweight, and wore clothes that were not in style. For these reasons, she had few friends and endured life as a loner. For a short time, Dolores tried attending a church youth group but quit because the youth group rejected her for the same reasons she was rejected at school. She found that there was no difference for her between the youth group environment and the church environment.[91] The church youth group must be a place where teenagers who, like Dolores, normally feel lonely, isolated, and rejected, can experience inclusion and acceptance—a place where scholastic abilities, appearance, or athletic prowess do not matter. This is what Christian community is all about!

Spiritual Causes: Even if a teenager's interpersonal relationships are secure and generally satisfactory, that individual may still experience a sense of loneliness or alienation. Centuries ago the great church father Augustine wrote, "You have made us for yourself, O Lord, and our hearts can never rest until they rest in you." In the twentieth century, existential writers like Jean-Paul Sartre and Albert Camus have written poignantly concerning the anxiety, anguish, alienation, and loneliness that occupy a life without God.

There is a loneliness or sense of isolation that is spiritual in nature and comes to the individual who is separated from God or senses that life has no meaning or purpose. Life without God, Craig Ellison reminds us, is

89. Strommen, *Five Cries of Youth,* 24.
90. Ellison, *Loneliness,* 96–98.
91. Rice, *Up Close and Personal,* 11–12.

impersonal and irrational, with no lasting intimacy. Ultimate intimacy, he goes on to say, depends upon finding, knowing, and sharing God.[92] Lloyd Ogilvie, in his collection of devotional reflections says, "We shall be lonely, in spite of the people around us, until we experience friendship with God."[93] This *existential* loneliness often comes because sin has alienated an individual not only from God also but from others. When God is ignored and sin is unconfessed, loneliness is likely to persist.[94] There is a sense of despair and alienation among youth who lack a faith, observes Merton Strommen.[95]

Perhaps no recent generation of youth is more alienated from God or senses a more profound despair than today's young people. Gallup polls find that while 95 percent of adolescents in United States believe in God, fewer than one third have ever personally experienced the presence of God.[96] In one large denomination it was reported that 63 percent of the youth felt some degree of apartness from God and man; one-half of this group gave evidence that it was an acute issue.[97] In the ecumenical sample used by Merton Strommen for *Five Cries of Youth,* 43 percent of the responding youth strongly wished they could find a deep faith in God, and the same proportion said they were "much bothered" because they did not feel close enough to Christ.[98]

Today's generation of teenagers is a part of the age bracket tagged with the title "Generation X." Also known as "Baby Busters," this population is made up of people born between 1965 and 1983, and is characterized by sociologists and religious leaders as being distinctly different from preceding generations in many areas of life.[99] Nowhere is this difference more evident than in the area of religious faith and practice. George Barna observes that while many contemporary youth still believe in one all-powerful God who created the world and rules it today, Eastern

---

92. Ellison, *Loneliness,* 212.

93. Lloyd John Ogilvie, *God's Best for My Life* (Eugene, Oreg.: Harvest House, 1981), n.p.

94. Collins, *Christian Counseling,* 98.

95. Strommen, *Five Cries of Youth,* 147.

96. *The Religious Life of Young Americans,* 23, 28.

97. Strommen, *Five Cries of Youth,* 145–46.

98. Ibid.

99. Sociologists are not in agreement as to what the age boundaries are for Generation X. The years 1965 to 1983 are cited by George Barna, *The Invisible Generation: Baby Busters* (Glendale, Calif.: Barna Research Group, 1992), 19.

views and New Age philosophies have made significant inroads among this generation.[100]

Kevin Ford describes many of today's young people as ambivalent toward religion, not rejecting it as much as neglecting it. He goes on to suggest, however, that for those teenagers who are seeking religion as an answer to this existential loneliness and life's tough questions, they are looking for a practical kind of faith that will make a difference in their everyday lives and communities. They tend not to be concerned about denominational affiliation, formal liturgies and traditions, or hard-nosed doctrinal stands on nonessential issues such as mode of baptism, and petty rules, and attitudes about life-style and dress.[101]

How do adult youth workers assist alienated and ambivalent adolescents in establishing an intimate relationship with God through Jesus Christ? Reaching today's youth with the Gospel message of hope and reconciliation means abandoning, for the most part, a preachy, confrontative approach that may have worked in the past. This strategy needs to be replaced with a personal, process-oriented approach. It is what Ford calls "incarnational evangelism," and means becoming incarnate or being figuratively born into a teenager's world. He describes a five-step process in this approach to evangelism.[102]

First, do what adolescents do. Rather than inviting unchurched youth to a Bible study, worship meeting, or conference, build relationships with them by taking part in activities that they enjoy doing, such as going to the beach, skiing, watching a movie, or attending a sporting event.

Second, enjoy and accept them as they are. The adult youth religious educator will be most effective in sharing the hope of the Gospel with teenagers when the presentation is natural and unprogrammed. Adolescents tend to be suspicious, perhaps cynical, of adults who want to get close to them. However, when teenagers sense that an adult youth worker is genuinely accepting and caring, they generally respond.

Third, affirm that which is good in their interests and values. There are many points where the values and interests of the youth religious educator can intersect with those of an alienated yet seeking teenager.

---

100. George Barna, *Generation Next* (Ventura, Calif.: Regal, 1995), 74.

101. Kevin Ford, *Jesus For a New Generation* (Downers Grove, Ill.: InterVarsity, 1995), 133–39.

102. Ibid., 200–202.

It is usually easy to find common interest in areas such as sports, hobbies, or music. However, the youth worker might also establish philosophical commonality such as an acceptance of the existence of the supernatural or an emphasis on responsible care and management of the environment.

Fourth, share the Gospel message of hope and reconciliation in their terms. Jesus was a master at "contextualizing," or telling His story in terms that the listener could best relate to. For example, when conversing with the Samaritan woman who came to get water from the well, Jesus told her about a "living water" (John 4:1–26). When an adolescent refers to getting high on drugs or alcohol, the youth worker might talk about a "better high" one can receive through a relationship with Jesus Christ.

Finally, invite them to establish a relationship with God. This is no time, as Merton Strommen suggests, for a hard sell of the Gospel. Rather, it is an occasion for enabling alienated teenagers to reflect on their relationship with God, their lonesomeness for God, and even their desire to flee from Him. They need the freedom to discuss their rebellion and proneness to go it alone; they also need to be encouraged to remain open to God's voice and to take advantage of times when they can be heard. Finally, says Strommen, youth need to understand that Christianity is a relationship with a personal and caring God, and when that relationship is secured the emptiness of a lonely life disappears.[103]

DATING RELATIONSHIPS

One day, the 1920s story goes, a young man asked a city girl if he might call on her. We know nothing else about the man or the girl—only that, when he arrived, she had her hat on. Not much of a story to us, but any American born before 1910 would have gotten the punch line. 'She had her hat on': those five words were rich in meaning to early twentieth century Americans. The hat signaled that she expected to leave the house. He came on a 'call,' expecting to be received in her family's parlor, to talk, to meet her mother, perhaps to have some refreshments or to listen to her play the piano. She expected a 'date,' to be taken 'out' somewhere and

---

103. Strommen, *Five Cries of Youth*, 155.

entertained. He ended up spending four weeks' savings fulfilling her expectations.[104]

Beth L. Bailey, *From Front Porch to Back Seat*

In the early twentieth century, a style of courtship that we today call *dating* was introduced to the American culture. What was to eventually become an institution of the youth subculture in United States began to supplant the old courting system of *calling*. According to the calling system, a gentleman would pay a visit to the home of a young lady where he might be served something to eat and drink, and the couple would engage in polite conversation.

Dating moved the courting patterns from the parlor to the streets and public forum. The urban setting with its restaurants, theaters, and sporting events, provided young people with opportunities for new kinds of freedom to engage in close opposite-sex companionship without adult supervision. Furthermore, there was a reversal in gender roles as to who was the initiator in the courting experience. Whereas in the old style of courting the girl or young lady (or perhaps the mother) invited the gentleman to call, an invitation to go on a date came from the young man.[105]

By 1925 dating had become a universal custom in the United States and has been described as an American invention. In most societies or cultures throughout history, mate selection was a decision made solely by parents.[106] In a few societies the parents still decide whom the children will marry while the children are yet infants or even before they are born.[107] In these situations the bride and groom often meet for the first time at the wedding; thus, there is no need for dating as a part of the mate selection process. In Canada and the United States, however, dating is firmly entrenched in the youth subculture as an institution. Many teenagers, though not all, begin this activity in early adolescence.

What is dating? A simple definition suggests simply that when a boy and a girl plan to meet alone or in a group at a specified place and

---

104. Beth L. Bailey, *From Front Porch to Back Seat* (Baltimore, Md.: The Johns Hopkins University Press, 1988).

105. Ibid., 13–21.

106. Jack O. Balswick and Judith K. Balswick, *The Family* (Grand Rapids, Mich.: Baker, 1991), 55.

107. Robert B. Taylor, *Introduction to Cultural Anthropology* (Boston: Allyn and Bacon, 1974), 294.

time, a date has been arranged.[108] Another definition describes dating as activity that allows opposite sexes to interact socially with nonfamilial age-mates.[109]

Kinds of Dating

Dating activity falls into several categories, some of which are casual, steady, group, and double-dating. In casual dating the purpose is to provide entertainment and opportunity for acquaintance. Couples are relatively uninvolved emotionally, and conversation for the most part is superficial.

In steady dating, or "going steady," partners date each other exclusively and are more emotionally involved. Going steady still may mean different things to different people. For some teenagers the relationship may be very serious, perhaps approaching marriage; for others it simply means an exclusive arrangement between the two. Many youth, especially those in early adolescence, date in groups, while others participate in double-dating. Double-dating occurs when two couples engage in an activity together, usually attendance at a movie or athletic event.[110]

Functions of Dating

Dating serves a number of purposes in the youth subculture including social activity, status achievement, socialization, and marriage mate selection.

Social Activity: In many instances adolescent social dating is nothing more than an outlet for social enjoyment, recreation, and entertainment. Teenagers often go out on dates simply to have fun and to have companionship at social functions. Youth group social activities are ideal opportunities for teenagers to experience the enjoyment of dating without the pressures of getting physical or serious. This kind of atmosphere presents a healthy alternative to the tight dating patterns found in other adolescent circles such as school, where lack of dating may lead to reduced acceptance by peers. The community aspect of the youth group should be broad enough to include those involved in various kinds of dating relationships and those who are not.

Socialization: Dating serves as a form of socialization. In this sense dating gives adolescents an opportunity to better understand themselves

---

108. Gerald Adams and Thomas Gullotta, *Adolescent Life Experiences* (Pacific Grove, Calif.: Brooks/Cole Publishing, 1989), 285.
109. Guerney and Arthur, "Adolescent Social Relationships," 97.
110. Ibid., 98–99.

as well as members of the opposite sex. It gives a young person an opportunity to try out and learn about his or her own feelings and personality while discovering the personalities of members of the opposite sex. It allows young people to discover emotions such as anger, jealousy, love, and patience.

Status Achievement: Dating also may be a means of status achievement. Being seen with a popular or attractive boy or girl, a star football player, or a cheerleader may bring prestige to an individual and raise his or her status within the peer group. However, Christian young people should be encouraged not to date for status or to allow physical appearance to be the center of the relationship.

Mate Selection: Finally, dating plays a significant role in the mate selection process. Dating is often viewed as a form of courtship, with marriage as the ultimate goal. Teenagers find out what kind of person they get along with or do not get along with, what kinds of relationships are satisfying and what kinds are not. Dating is also seen as preparation for future marital and family roles.[111]

Dating and Sexual Activity

While not necessarily in conflict with the norms and values of most parents, adolescent dating does bring with it some parental concern. Parents may be concerned that their adolescent children not begin dating at too early an age—and for good reason. One study found a clear correlation between the age at which a girl's first date occurs and the likelihood of sexual intercourse before high school graduation. In other words, the younger a girl began dating, the more likely she was to have had sex before graduating.[112] Another study of evangelical Protestant youth found that those who began dating at age 13 or before were far less satisfied with their moral behavior than those who began dating at age 16 or after.[113]

Given the liberal view of sexuality in contemporary culture, one might expect sexual activity to be an accepted and integral part of adolescent

---

111. Summarized from Robert Winch, *The Modern Family* (New York: Holt, Rinehart, and Winston, 1971), 530–32; Guerney and Arthur, "Adolescent Social Relationships," 97.

112. B. Miller, J. McCoy, and T. Olson, "Dating Age and Stage as Correlates of Adolescent Sexual Attitudes and Behavior," in *Journal of Adolescent Research* 1, (1986), 361–371.

113. Roy Zuck and Gene Getz, *Christian Youth—An In-depth Study* (Chicago: Moody, 1968), 159.

dating. This is indeed the case. The Project Teen Canada discovered 11 percent of the teenage population to have engaged in sexual relations on the first date. Another 42 percent agreed that intercourse is appropriate after a few dates.[114] Since early dating appears to lead too soon to an inappropriate intimacy, there is good reason, as Bonnidell Clouse suggests, to keep teenagers in groups and provide chaperones as much as possible.[115]

Readiness for Dating

When is a good time to allow adolescents to date? This is a question parents frequently ask. There is no "right" age, although 16 seems to be an acceptable age for permitting either a daughter or son to begin normal dating—that is, to go to an activity or event without a chaperone. Before the teenager's sixteenth birthday, parents might allow him or her to go on occasional dates such as homecoming or a church banquet. Younger adolescents may occasionally be permitted to go on group or double dates. Another consideration is the maturity and responsibility level of the individual. Rather than setting an arbitrary age limit at which dating can begin, parents might work out a plan with each son or daughter.

CONCLUSION

This chapter has explored the expansive world of adolescent social relationships. The social role changes that occur in adolescence have a profound impact on the teenager as well as his or her parents. Adolescence inevitably introduces significant change and upheaval in the typical family. Parents must learn how to relinquish power and autonomy to the teenager. In turn, the adolescent must learn how to cope and function in an ever-expanding world of relationships.

While this period of social transition may create a certain amount of emotional pain and anxiety for most teenagers, parents and youth alike can be assured that in most instances the struggle to achieve maturity in social relationships is followed by a state of relative quietness and stability.

---

114. Bibby and Posterski, *The Emerging Generation,* 75–77.
115. Bonnidell Clouse, "Adolescent Moral Development and Sexuality," in *Handbook of Youth Ministry,* eds., Donald Ratcliff and James A. Davies (Birmingham, Ala.: Religious Education Press, 1991), 204.

5

Adolescence and the Institutions of School, Work, and Church

To understand the lives of adolescents and what it means to be adolescent, one must know where and how they spend their time. Mihaly Csikszentmihalyi and Reed Larson suggest the paths of teenagers pass through three main domains: home, school, and public life. The home is the most pervasive context of adolescents' lives, claiming over 40 percent of their time. However, school can also be seen as a setting where significant socializing takes place, as youth are constantly exposed to the pervasive influence of peer relationships. For a number of teenagers, work consumes a significant portion of their day and for many more the church and church-related activities constitute a vital dimension of their lives.[1]

ADOLESCENTS AND SCHOOL

School is a way of life for most teenagers today. Almost a third of the week-day schedules of teenagers is consumed by the various dimensions of the educational setting: formal classrooms, the cafeteria, halls, and extracurricular activities.[2]

---

1. Mihaly Csikszentmihalyi and Reed Larson, *Being Adolescent* (New York: Basic Books, 1984), 57–59.
2. Ibid., 60.

While in 1900 only one out of ten 14- to 17-year-olds were in school, in the 1990s nine of ten in this age bracket attend.[3] For many teenagers, however, the experience is not always pleasurable. For a great number of adolescents, school is faced with little enthusiasm or enjoyment, and for many it is a source of strain and drudgery, especially as they grow older.[4] Nonetheless, school is recognized by adolescents as a crucial part of their lives, illustrated in part by the high percentage of adolescents who actually remain in school. Bibby and Posterski asked Canadian secondary students how the government should arrange priorities, and found education to rank in the number one position.[5]

The education and school experience for American and Canadian teenagers is a good news–bad news situation. In the United States, elementary, secondary, and higher schooling is considered a basic right for every American citizen. In Canada the attitude is much the same, and over the years both countries have prided themselves in their efforts to make a quality education available for every individual.

The bad news is that the public school systems are under considerable strain and are plagued by a plethora of problems. In 1983 the National Commission on Excellence in Education reported to the United States public on the status of public or government sponsored schooling in this country. The publication, called *A Nation At Risk,* included some dire warnings: "We report to the American people that while we can take justifiable pride in what our schools and colleges have historically accomplished and contributed to the United States and the well being of its people, the educational foundations of our society are presently being eroded by a rising tide of mediocrity that threatens our very future as a nation and a people."[6]

Furthermore, secondary students have new forces to contend with— violence and victimization are a growing part of public schools in every part of the nation. The discipline problems public school teachers are faced with in the 1990s bear no resemblance to the issues they had to

---

3. Nancy Busch-Rossnagel, "Adolescence and Education," in Richard M. Lerner and Nancy L. Galambos, eds., *Experiencing Adolescents* (New York: Garland, 1984), 283.

4. See Peter Benson. Dorothy Williams, and Arthur Johnson, *The Quicksilver Years,* (San Francisco: Harper & Row, 1987), 14–15; Reginald W. Bibby and Donald C. Posterski, *Teen Trends,* (Toronto, Ont.: Stoddart, 1992), 223.

5. Bibby and Posterski, *Teen Trends,* 224.

6. National Commission on Educational Excellence, *A Nation at Risk* (Washington, D.C.: The Commission, 1983), 5.

Figure 5.1
School Problems Rated by Teachers

Late 1940s	Late 1980s
Talking out of turn	Drug Abuse
Chewing gum	Alcohol abuse
Making noise	Pregnancy
Running in the halls	Suicide
Cutting in line	Rape
Dress-code violations	Robbery
Littering	Assault

deal with four decades ago. Compare the answers given by teachers in the late 1940s and late 1980s, when they were asked what the top disciplinary problems were.[7]

Mediocre Grades and Low Achievement Test Scores

One of the major concerns of many people is that the academic performance of American students has been gradually declining. The National Commission on Educational Excellence asserted that "If an unfriendly foreign power had attempted to impose on America the mediocre educational performance that exists today, we might well have viewed it as an act of war. . . . We have even squandered the gains in student achievement made in the wake of the Sputnik challenge. Moreover, we have dismantled essential support systems which helped make those gains possible. We have, in effect, been committing an act of unthinking, unilateral educational disarmament."[8] Among the indicators of the conditions of the American public school education system were the following:

• "International comparisons of student achievement . . . reveal that on 19 academic tests American students were never first or second and, in comparison with other industrialized nations, were last seven times.

• Some 23 million American adults are functionally illiterate by the simplest tests of everyday reading, writing, and comprehension.

7. Thomas Toch, "Violence in Schools," *U.S. News and World Report,* November 8, 1993, 34.
8. National Commission on Educational Excellence, *A Nation at Risk*, 5.

• About 13 percent of all 17-year-olds in the United States can be considered functionally illiterate. Functional illiteracy among minority youth may run as high as 40 percent. . . .

• Many 17-year-olds do not possess the 'higher order' intellectual skills we should expect of them. Nearly 40 percent cannot draw inferences from written material; only one-fifth can write a persuasive essay; and only one-third can solve a mathematics problem requiring several steps."[9]

By the 1990s, in spite of attempts at reforming the public educational system, test scores for American students remain low and do not compare favorably with those of other industrialized countries. Parents and experts alike continue to be frustrated with the products of our public high schools. Obviously, the problem has not occurred overnight but rather has been transpiring for decades.

High School Dropouts

The term "dropout" refers to anyone who leaves high school without a diploma, and is usually interpreted as a student's inability or unwillingness to learn.[10] Compared to the 1920s and 1930s, when most students left after the eighth grade, the percentage of students who graduate from high school is high.[11] High school dropout rates declined by more than 15 percent during the 1980s, so that in 1990 a little more than one in ten of the nation's youth between 16 and 19 dropped out of school.[12] This lower dropout rate is one encouraging trend in education, although the number of students who quit school prematurely is still cause for concern.

The incidence of dropout is not consistent across the country, differing among communities and counties, socioeconomic classes, and racial and ethnic groups. Counties with the highest proportion of teenagers who are not in school and do not have a diploma are in the South—especially severe in the predominantly white Appalachian counties.[13] High dropout

---

9. Ibid., 8–9.

10. Hans Sebald, *Adolescence,* (Englewood Cliffs, N.J.: Prentice-Hall, 1984), 164.

11. Busch-Rossnagel, "Adolescence and Education," 300.

12. Carrie Teegardin, "Dropout Capital of Georgia," in *The Atlanta Constitution,* June 8, 1993, E1.

13. Ibid., E6. The top two counties are in the Midwest and have a high population of Amish who refuse to send their children to high school.

rates also occur in urban high schools that draw from neighborhoods composed predominantly of families from lower socioeconomic classes and minority groups. The lowest rates of dropout are found in the middle-class suburbs.[14]

There are a number of characteristics of dropouts, most of which probably overlap various socioeconomic and minority groups:[15]
• Their marks tend to be well below average.
• They have failed at least one school grade.
• They tend to display behavior problems which require discipline.
• They tend to change schools frequently.
• They seldom participate in extracurricular activities.
• Parents often have lower levels of education and occupation.
• Families tend to be characterized by lack of communication, no personal satisfaction with each other's company, a low level of happiness in the home, and nonacceptance of one another as total persons.
• They tend to have low self-esteem.

Not all dropouts exhibit lower academic ability. Some average or above-average students drop out of school because they feel the requirements of high school are stifling or not challenging enough. They may sense that school and the available curriculum are not effectively equipping them for life in the real world.[16]

Furthermore, the public school system is geared to a large degree to young people who are going on to college or university. Many high schools provide relatively little in the way of preparation for adolescents who are not considering higher education. David Elkind calls this group of teenagers the *forgotten half,* because there is so little provided for them in the way of vocational training.[17] For these teenagers, there is a lack of relevance between the school's curriculum and the circumstances of their lives. The option of dropping out of school and getting a job may appear somewhat more attractive than staying in school and studying courses in which they are not interested. Other variables related to school dropout include poverty, broken homes, abuse at the hands of family members,

---

14. Sebald, *Adolescence,* 165.
15. Summarized from Busch-Rossnagel, "Adolescence and Education," 301–302.
16. Ibid., 301.
17. David Elkind, *A Sympathetic Understanding of the Child,* 3d ed. (Boston, Mass.: Allyn and Bacon, 1994), 206.

negative influence of peers, learning disabilities, and lack of interest in school work.[18]

What are the consequences of dropping out of high school before graduation? It is likely that the dropout will have low lifetime earnings and a greater possibility of being unemployed. Furthermore, research studies indicate that lower schooling attainment is related to poverty, divorce, and early death.[19]

How can the youth worker help the dropout or potential dropout? Here is an opportunity for the youth religious educator to do informal counseling with the intent of helping the teenager realize the necessity of completing high school. It may also mean helping the dropout explore the alternatives of getting a diploma. A regular return to high school may not always be possible because of age differences or a lapse in time. Other means to graduation include the attendance of night courses, taking correspondence courses, or attending special schools designed for school returnees.

Violence in Schools

Until recently, schools were relatively immune from the violence and crime that has spread throughout American society. This is no longer the situation on most public secondary school campuses. In a setting that should provide a haven of security second only to the home, public schools and schoolyards now often resemble a battleground. Gun violence is on the rise in schools all over America—in big cities, small towns, inner cities, suburbs, and rural areas. Inner-city schools have added "drive-by-shooting" drills to traditional fire drills. Some campuses are fenced in, are equipped with metal detectors, have locker searches and student shakedowns, or employ uniformed security officers.[20]

The following striking statistics underscore the violence perpetrated in public schools in the 1990s.[21]

• More than 3 million crimes a year are committed near or in the 85,000 public schools.

• Nine percent of eighth grade students carry a gun, knife or club to school each day.

---

18. Sebald, *Adolescence,* 166–75.
19. Busch-Rossnagel, "Adolescence and Education," 303.
20. Thomas Toch, "Violence in Schools," 32.
21. Ibid.

• An estimated 270,000 guns go to school each day.
• In the New York City public schools in 1992, there were 5,761 violent crimes. This number was up 16 percent from the previous year.
• Forty-three percent of rural principals, 54 percent of suburban principals, and 54 percent of those in urban schools said violence has increased in their schools in the past five years.
• Approximately 69 percent of teenagers in a Gallup poll say classroom disturbances are a fairly large concern. Another 58 percent say fighting in schools is a problem and 28 percent agree that the possession of weapons in school is an issue.[22]

Among the tragic casualties in the fall of 1993 were the following:
• "A 15-year-old girl at suburban Lake Brantley High School near Orlando Florida, Fla., allegedly gashed a classmate repeatedly. . . .
• A ninth grader was killed and a 10th grader wounded when another student allegedly opened fire in the crowded cafeteria of Atlanta's Harper High School. . . .
• A 15-year-old was shot at Los Angeles's Dorsey High School while waiting in line for a permit to transfer into the school. . . .
• A 14-year-old student at rural South Iredell High School, north of Charlotte, NC, was arrested for shooting a classmate on the sidewalk in the back and chest as school was dismissed. . . .
• A 17-year-old was gunned down at Downers Grove South High School near Chicago after a football game, where he had served as his school's mascot, a hornet. He was in a car when a Hinsdale South High School student, 15, walked over, purportedly put a gun to his head and pulled the trigger."[23]

In Canada, violence in the public school environment is increasing as well. One in three teenagers feel that violence is a "very serious" problem in their schools. When Canadian teenagers were asked about violence at school, 45 percent said they knew someone who had been physically attacked at school.[24]

School violence has detrimental effects on adolescents. With students literally fearing for their lives, learning is next to impossible in some schools. The ever-present threat of fights, stabbings, or shootings leaves

---

22. George Gallup, *Growing Up Scared in America* (Princeton, N.J.: The George H. Gallup International Institute, 1995), 3.
23. Quoted from Toch, "Violence in Schools," 32.
24. Bibby and Posterski, *Teen Trends,* 228.

many students more concerned with mere survival than with science or history. Mental-health experts are concerned about the psychological impact that all the real-life violence in schools may have on adolescents. One researcher suggests the possibility of an epidemic of post traumatic stress syndrome, which will significantly hinder normal development.[25] Furthermore, school violence is numbing in that it signals to teenagers that violence is normal. In addition, violence increases the fear of becoming victims, which in turn makes adolescents likely to interpret the intentions of others as threatening, perhaps causing them to resort to violence themselves.[26] One overall result is a shocking increase in juvenile violence and crime, and the loss of human lives.

To what can this new and frightening code of school conduct be attributed? Sociologists point to several sources. Some authorities suggest it is the result of a hopelessness of poverty. While it may be true that poverty, often intensified by discrimination, contributes to violence, it must be recognized that the rise in school violence is seen in all socioeconomic areas. Other specialists agree that the breakdown of the American family is a major contributor. One source says that 70 percent of juvenile court cases involve children from single-parent families.[27]

Many young people are surrounded by violence. Real-life shootings are a way of life for a number of youth, and for nearly all children and teenagers, television brings murders and violent acts into the living room. This exposure to so much violence has a numbing effect on young people and unambiguously communicates that violence is normal. The ready availability of guns has escalated conflict into a deadly affair. According to one survey, 35 percent of inner-city youths carry guns, and 70 percent said family members owned guns. In one suburban school, 18 percent of the students owned handguns.[28]

THE ADOLESCENT AND THE WORKPLACE

The nature of adolescence and the adolescent life-style has undergone dramatic transformation since the 1950s, and one of the areas of most significant change has been the workplace. In growing numbers,

---

25. Tom Morganthau, "It's Not Just New York . . . ," in *Newsweek,* March 9, 1992, 29.
26. Toch, "Violence in Schools," 34.
27. Ibid.
28. Ibid.

adolescents have entered the world of work, holding down jobs that consume a significant portion of their time and energy after school, on school nights, and on weekends. The large, adolescent part-time labor force that helps staff fast-food restaurants, all night corner stores and gas stations, retail stores, factories, and motels, has become a familiar part of the North American social landscape.

This pattern of full-time students engaged in part-time work exists in distinct contrast to patterns in other parts of the world. In some European countries, for example, young adolescents enter into a work apprentice program in conjunction with their school education. In many other countries of the Western World, it is uncommon for adolescents to participate vigorously in the work force while attending school. In the United States, adolescents have been a part of the labor force in the past. However, young people who work today have motivations for employment that are very different from the motivations of the youth of earlier years, and the work they perform differs significantly in nature and kind.[29]

Historical Patterns of Adolescent Employment in the United States

Historically, the practice and pattern of working youth in the United States have gone through three stages or phases: up to the twentieth century, the early twentieth century, and 1945 to the present.

Phase One: Up to the Twentieth Century: Until the beginning of the twentieth century, it was common for almost all youth and, indeed, many children to enter the labor force in a full-time capacity. Up to this point in time, less than 10 percent of the nation's 14- to 17-year-olds attended school.[30]

Several factors contributed to this pattern of youth employment. First, society expected that children work, and labor was seen as an integral part of the socialization process.

Second, it was often necessary for young people to work. The money they earned, or the services they provided—for example, work on the family farm—was often essential to the survival of the family.

---

29. Ellen Greenberger and Laurence Steinberg, *When Teen-agers Work* (New York: Basic Books, 1986), 3–4.

30. Fred Vondracek and John Schulenberg, "Adolescence and Careers," in Richard M. Lerner and Nancy L. Galambos, eds., *Experiencing Adolescents,* (New York: Garland, 1984), 331.

A third reason for child and youth labor was to prepare them for their future occupation. This would take place in two ways. Often, children followed their parents in the choice of occupation; thus, working with their parents served as on-the-job training. Youth also trained as apprentices; boys would often begin their training as early as 12 years of age.

Fourth, child and youth labor was predominant because formal school was optional, and often considered unnecessary for most occupations. Finally, there was a sufficient number of job opportunities available for young people, making it an easy choice to enter into the work force.[31]

Phase Two: Early Twentieth Century: A second phase of adolescents in the work force spanned the first part of the twentieth century to about 1940–1945. During this period opportunities for full-time employment for adolescents gradually declined so that only 9 percent of the 14- to 17-year-olds were identified by the United States Census as employed.[32] Rarely were school and work combined. In 1940 only 5 percent of the males and 2 percent of the females in the 16- to 17-year age bracket worked and went to school.[33]

One contributing factor to the major change in the youth employment situation was the steady rise in secondary education, the high school. Secondary education essentially released young people from employment. A second reason was the recognition of adolescence as a distinct stage of life. With the emergence of adolescence came the attitude that young people were not adults and that healthy emotional and psychological development required a period of time to prepare for adulthood roles and responsibilities, including work.[34]

A third contributor to the decline of youth in the work force was the Great Depression of the 1930s, which left most adolescents jobless. This was followed by improved technology and automation, especially after World War II, which decreased the need for cheap labor and simultaneously increased the number of jobs requiring high school and college diplomas. Thus, a new pattern emerged—school instead of work.[35]

---

31. Ibid., 330–31.
32. Cited in Greenberger and Steinberg, *When Teenagers Work,* 14.
33. Vondracek and Schulenberg, "Adolescence and Careers," 332.
34. Ibid.
35. Vondracek and Schulenberg, "Adolescence and Careers," 332; Greenberger and Steinberg, *When Teenagers Work,* 13.

Phase Three: 1945 to Present: Between 1945 and the end of the twentieth century, a third phase of youth employment emerged. If the first phase found young people almost exclusively in the work force, and the second saw youth almost exclusively in school, the most recent trend sees adolescents combining school and part-time work.[36] According to the U.S. Bureau of the Census, 41.1 percent of the male and 39.3 percent of the female 16- to 17-year-olds were employed either parttime or fulltime in 1992.[37] As we view employment among in-school adolescents, it is important to realize that the above statistics may not clearly depict the student employment situation. The proportion of students who have at least some paid work experience is much higher, since many teenagers frequently move in and out of the work force. It is estimated that as many as 80 percent of in-school adolescents will receive formal work experience before they graduate from high school.[38]

Given the high rate of part-time work among students, it is important to consider some of the factors contributing to this pattern. First, there is the cultural assumption that part-time working experience is helpful in making the transition into the full-time labor force. Thus, teenagers are often strongly encouraged by parents and other adults to seek out part-time employment.

A second factor concerns the surge of interest in youth employment issues in the 1960s and 1970s. Government legislation and education practices took aim at improving opportunities for youth employment, and encouraged the combination of schooling and part-time work experience. Enactments such as the 1964 Economic Opportunity Act and the Youth Employment Act of 1977 provided billions of dollars for the development of a variety of youth employment programs. From the perspective of education, panels such as the Work-Education Consortium (1978) stressed the importance of combining school and work experience.[39]

Another major factor contributing to the rise of adolescent part-time employment has been the increase of the low-paying service sector of the economy (distribution as opposed to production; for example, fast-food

---

36. Ibid., *When Teenagers Work,* 14 ff.
37. U.S. Bureau of the Census, *Statistical Abstract of the United States: 1993,* (113th edition.) Washington, D.C.: U.S. Government Printing Office, 1993, 393.
38. Vondracek and Schulenberg, "Adolescence and Careers," 333.
39. Ibid., 333–34.

restaurants, clothing stores, 24-hour convenience stores and gasoline stations). These types of jobs are usually characterized by low wages, part-time hours, irregular shifts, minimal fringe benefits, nighttime and weekend hours, and little opportunity for promotion. While these are generally considered poor jobs for adults, they are good, or at least acceptable, for adolescents who also attend school.[40]

Finally, it is argued that lowered expectations in the school system make it possible for students to work at a job with minimal consequences to grades. Greenberger and Steinberg argue that students have been allowed to shape academic programs for themselves that are unchallenging, and schools have become so undemanding that teenagers are able to invest considerable hours in the work place without hindering their performance at school.[41]

Why Do Teenagers Work?

Adolescents seek employment for a variety of reasons. One influencing factor is related to simple economics. The expense of being a teenager has risen steeply in recent years. While the cost of adolescent "essentials" such as gasoline, movies, and compact discs has gone up, the money available from parents (allowances) has not increased accordingly.

Coupled with increasing costs of adolescent "staples" is the unfortunate fact that teenagers have become more materialistic, or as Greenberger and Steinberg put it, they have developed over time an inflated desire for the acquisition of luxury goods. Expensive designer clothes, brand name sports shoes, nice cars, electronic equipment such as headphones and CD players are just a few items teenagers deem necessary. With a limit to what parents can afford or are willing to buy for their adolescent children, teenagers are forced to earn their own spending money.[42]

Of course, not all teenagers work for immediate gratification or selfish gain. Some seek employment to gain experience in the occupational field they find attractive, or simply because they are bored. In some cases teenagers are forced to work to help supplement the family income.

---

40. Greenberger and Steinberg, *When Teenagers Work,* 24–27, and Csikszentmihalyi and Larson, *Being Adolescent,* 64.
41. Greenberger and Steinberg, *When Teenagers Work,* 191.
42. Ibid., 28–29.

Arguments in Favor of Youth Employment

Adolescent employment is often extolled as an ideal opportunity for young people to develop and mature in various aspects of life. One of the strongest arguments in favor of youth employment is that it promotes personal responsibility. Greenberger and Steinberg found evidence for change in adolescents' level of responsibility in three spheres. First, girls who work gain a greater sense of self-reliance than those who do not (in contrast, working may produce the opposite effect on boys). Second, working enhances teenagers' view of themselves in terms of having good work habits. Finally, and most significantly, working leads to increased financial autonomy.[43]

A second argument in favor of student employment is that it can enable the adolescent to become better acquainted with the world of work and other practical matters, such as the handling of money. This argument, however, does not take into consideration the fact that work available to teenagers is usually menial and is often undertaken with little genuine commitment and motivation.[44] Furthermore, it is argued that most teenagers learn relatively little about the responsible handling of money. The majority of adolescents save none or very little of the money they earn through working and spend it largely on themselves.[45]

A third argument for student employment is that work uses the adolescent's time and energy in a productive manner, for which the individual is financially compensated. Furthermore, employment can help the teenager in the process of attaining autonomy and self-identity.

Finally, for some adolescents, part-time work provides an opportunity to gain experience in the occupational field that he or she desires to pursue. While some adolescents successfully seek and find jobs that will provide them with firsthand experience in their anticipated choice of vocation, experts counter this argument with the suggestion that most adolescents do not seek employment to gain experience in a chosen vocational field. Furthermore, the majority of the part-time jobs available to teenagers are menial and routine, and contribute relatively little to the shaping of one's future vocation.[46]

---

43. Ibid., 105.
44. Csikszentmihalyi and Larson, *Being Adolescent,* 92.
45. Greenberger and Steinberg, *When Teenagers Work,* 106.
46. Csikszentmihalyi and Larson, *Being Adolescent,* 93, and Vondracek and Schulenberg, "Adolescence and Careers," 343.

Drawbacks to Youth Employment

While there are identifiable arguments in favor of engaging adolescents in the labor force, there may be extensive costs incurred. Noted child psychologist David Elkind in *The Hurried Child*[47] and *All Grown Up and No Place to Go*[48] argues that moving young people into a quasi-adulthood brings about stressful consequences. While Elkind does not specifically refer to student employment as a contributing factor to stress, at least one bit of research supports the notion that employment can have negative stressful consequences for the working student. Ellen Greenberger and Laurence Steinberg found that working a great deal during the school year related to higher rates of drug and alcohol use, higher delinquency rates, poorer grades, and absence from school.[49]

Second, most part-time jobs involve highly repetitive and routine activities with few opportunities for creativity and decision making. Thus, they nurture boredom and cynicism toward gainful employment rather than fostering a positive attitude.

A third argument against student employment is that there is decreased time with family and family activities, as well as less time available for friends and church activities. For the youth worker this can create some serious difficulties. Some youth ministries struggle because a majority of the potential youth-group attendees are consumed with school and work. This leaves them little time for involvement in youth activities. Furthermore, work schedules of different youth vary, making it difficult, if not impossible, to find a slot of time satisfactory for everyone.

Adult youth workers must be flexible and creative if they are going to have a significant impact on teenagers who work. One tactic the youth worker can take is visiting youth at their places of employment, perhaps over the lunch hour or coffee break. While this may be a cumbersome and time-consuming approach to youth ministry, it is personal. For a generation of youth who highly value friendships and relationships, this could prove to be a fruitful endeavor.

A second approach might be to replace weekly large-group activities with a variety of small groups that meet at different times and on different days. It is considerably easier to accommodate smaller groups of four

47. David Elkind, *The Hurried Child* (Reading, Mass.: Addison-Wesley, 1981).
48. David Elkind, *All Grown Up and No Place to Go* (Reading, Mass.: Addison-Wesley, 1984).
49. Greenberger and Steinberg, *When Teenagers Work*, 187.

or five youth in finding a convenient meeting time and place than it is for a larger number of adolescents.

Helping Adolescents Make A Decision About Employment

Should adolescents be encouraged to work while in school? Essentially two alternative points of view must be considered. One view suggests that work is good and profitable for a teenager, while another argues that work interferes with healthy adolescent development and may in fact be detrimental to personal growth. The fact is that to hold exclusively to one or the other is probably unwise. Whether an adolescent should engage in part-time employment or not depends on the situation and the nature of the individual. In helping young people to make the decision to work or not, the following questions should be considered:

• Will the job build and enhance commitment to work, and promote responsibility and competence?

• To what degree will the employment interfere with school? In no study has working been shown to have a positive effect on one's grade point average.[50]

• Will the job interfere with family and peer relationships, church and youth group involvement, or personal well-being?

• Will the job contribute, even minimally, to future career goals? For example, a young person aspiring to be a mechanic might get a job at a service station so as to receive mechanical experience. Unfortunately, most jobs available to adolescents are not of the type that serve to prepare one for full time vocation.

• Is the student capable of handling money through savings and responsible spending, or will he or she spend earnings selfishly or foolishly?

THE CHURCH AND RELIGIOUS LIFE OF TEENAGERS

The church is another institution that has traditionally played an important role in the lives of young people. There is considerable concern however, that adolescent interest in the church and religion is rapidly declining. The evidence suggests that at least in America, the church is failing to interest and retain the adolescent segment of the population.

---

50. Ibid., 118.

The Role of the Church in the Lives of Teenagers

For teenagers in the United States and Canada, religion and the church play a moderate role. According to one study, just one-third of the adolescent population (34 percent) claim that religion is an important dimension of their everyday activities, while 44 percent feel it is somewhat important. This is compared to 53 percent of the adults who feel religion is important to them. Girls (38 percent) are more likely than boys (30 percent) to see religion as very important in their lives.[51]

Similar results were identified by the Gallup poll, which discovered that less than half of America's adolescents (43 percent) believe it is very important to have a deep religious faith. On a list of nine personal values, religious faith ranked only eighth. According to the study, teenagers gave greater importance to having personal peace and happiness, being well educated, helping people in the community, getting married, and having children.[52]

Regular attendance at a church or synagogue, suggests Kenneth Hyde, is a strong indicator of personal religious commitment.[53] If this is the case, how religiously committed are young people in the United States? According to a Gallup poll, 48 percent of the teenagers surveyed said they had attended a religious service the previous week, down from a high of 57 percent in 1989.[54] Forty-one percent of the youth interviewed attended Sunday school or Bible study classes, while 36 percent were active in a church youth group.[55]

The Barna Report found that 47 percent of the teenagers researched attended church services every week. Another 22 percent went two or three times a month. Thirty-three percent attended church once a month or not at all.[56]

Studies of Canadian youth indicate that they are even less interested in religion and church involvement than their American counterparts. In 1984 only 23 percent of Canadian teenagers said they "very often"

---

51. *Today's Teens,* (Glendale, Calif.: The Barna Research Group, 1991), 34.

52. George Gallup and Robert Bezilla, *The Religious Life of Young Americans* (Princeton, N.J.: George Gallup International Institute, 1992), 11.

53. Kenneth Hyde, "Adolescents and Religion," in Donald Ratcliff and James A. Davies, eds., *Handbook of Youth Ministry* (Birmingham, Ala.: Religious Education Press, 1991), 120.

54. Gallup and Bezilla, *The Religious Life of Young Americans,* 38.

55. Ibid., 32–33.

56. *Today's Teens,* 34.

attended religious services.[57] By 1991, just 18 percent of the 15- to 19-year-olds indicated they were attending religious services—a decrease of 5 percent in just seven years.[58]

The diminishing role of church and religion in the lives of contemporary youth is measured in other ways as well. The following findings from empirical research underscore this tendency.

• When seeking help or encouragement, only 6 percent of adolescents surveyed would go to ministers or priests. Clergy ranked far below friends (72 percent), mothers (54 percent), fathers (38 percent), and teachers and school counselors (13 percent) as a source of help. On a more positive side, 29 percent of the respondents indicated clergy have a lot of influence on them.[59]

• Friends, home, school, music, and television are rated ahead of religion as factors adolescents believe have the greatest influence on their generation. Only 13 percent of the teenagers interviewed feel that religion holds a great deal of influence in their lives.[60]

• Only one youth in four expressed a high degree of confidence in organized religion—lower than that recorded by the adult population.[61]

• When asked if religion can answer specific problems, teenagers were usually evenly divided on whether religion could or could not. The problems and percent of adolescents who felt religion could answer were as follows: drugs and alcohol (58 percent), sexual issues (55 percent), marriage and divorce (54 percent), government morality (45 percent), and world problems (45 percent).[62]

• In 1991, only 5 percent of Canadian youth indicated they received "a great deal" or "quite a bit" of enjoyment from religious groups, down from 24 percent in 1984.[63]

• Only 1 percent of Canadian teenagers indicated they would turn to religious leaders for counsel on the subject of sex, and only 2 percent would turn to a minister or priest about right or wrong.[64]

---

57. Reginald W. Bibby and Donald C. Posterski, *The Emerging Generation* (Toronto, Ont.: Irwin, 1985), 121.

58. Bibby and Posterski, *Teen Trends,* 50.

59. *Today's Teens,* 22.

60. Gallup and Bezilla, *The Religious Life of Young Americans,* 11.

61. Ibid.

62. Ibid., 62.

63. Bibby and Posterski, *Teen Trends,* 51.

64. Ibid., 248.

Hyde says regular church attendance as a mark of commitment is even more powerful when it is accompanied by the habit of private personal prayer.[65] Most teenagers pray but not necessarily on a consistent basis. According to the Gallup poll, 42 percent of the teenagers surveyed said they prayed frequently. For 49 percent, however, it is only an occasional or rare practice and 8 percent never pray.[66]

The statistics raise concerns on both sides of the Canada—United States border. Authors of the Barna Report of young people in the United States ask the critical question "Are we witnessing the emergence of a new generation that is decidedly turning its back on religion as an important force in their lives?"[67] Gallup and Bezilla conclude that many youth are turned off by churches and organized religion, and that churches are failing to play a central role in the religious lives of many youth.[68]

Canadian sociologist Reginald Bibby concludes, "Organized religion is in serious trouble with young people."[69] Fellow Canadian and co-author Donald Posterski sums up the situation in Canada by saying, "The majority of young people in Canada are sending a sobering message to those who value organized religion. Attendance continues to decline and participation in youth groups is low. Relatively few teenagers place much value on religious involvement. In the minds of the vast majority of young people, religion is something marginal to everyday life."[70]

George Barna is not so pessimistic. Perhaps it is a matter of seeing the glass half empty, as the aforementioned analysts do, or half full. Barna argues that many teenagers are spiritually inclined and are open to giving the local church or parish with which they are involved an opportunity to prove its worth. He goes on to suggest that the attendance and participation figures of adolescents indicate amazingly high levels of religious activity. The bad news, however, is that having given the church a fair chance at convincing them to stay, large numbers of youth choose to end their interaction with the church once they have the freedom to do so.[71]

---

65. Kenneth Hyde, "Adolescents and Religion," 120.
66. Gallup and Bezilla, *The Religious Life of Young Americans*, 38.
67. *Today's Teens*, 34.
68. Gallup and Bezilla, *The Religious Life of Young Americans*, 11.
69. Bibby and Posterski, *Teen Trends*, 50.
70. Ibid., 247.
71. George Barna, *Generation Next* (Ventura, Calif.: Regal, 1995), 85–87.

Factors Related to Youth Involvement in church-related Activities

What types of teenagers are most likely to be involved in church-related activities such as worship service, Sunday school class, catechism, youth group, or Bible study? Several factors help characterize the participants of church-related activities.

Family Configuration: One important determinant of who participates in religious programs is family configuration. Youth who have both parents living at home are more likely to be involved in church activities than teenagers from single-parent families.[72] One reason adolescents from single-parent homes are less active in church-related activities is that the single parent is consumed with surviving in a less than ideal family situation. Emotional problems associated with separation or divorce may override other concerns the parent may have. Consequently, single parents often have relative little time or energy left to make sure their adolescents are attending religious activities.

How can the youth religious educator encourage greater participation of teenagers from single-parent homes? One strategy is to take special care in assuring that adolescents from these homes are informed of youth ministry activities. A special phone call or personal reminder from an adult worker or member of the youth group would be helpful. Furthermore, youth religious educators can take some pressure off single parents by providing transportation for their teenagers to youth group functions and other church-related activities.

Parents' Attendance: Parental religious practice is another major predictor of adolescent religiousness and attendance to church-related activities. In their study of Catholic adolescents, Antanas Suziedelis and Raymond Potvin found parental modeling to have a pronounced effect on church attendance and religiousness of adolescent children, more so for girls than boys.[73] Fern Willits and Donald Crider's study of Protestant and Catholic youth indicated that the parents' attendance correlated substantially with church attendance of both sons and daughters.[74] Dean

---

72. *Today's Teens,* 41.

73. Antanas Suziedelis and Raymond H. Potvin, "Sex Differences in Factors Affecting Religiousness Among Catholic Adolescents," in *Journal for the Scientific Study of Religion* 20, (March 1982), 38–51).

74. Fern K. Willits and Donald M. Crider, "Church Attendance and Traditional Religious Beliefs in Adolescence and Young Adulthood: A Panel Study," in *Review of Religious Research* 31 (September 1989), 68–81.

Hoge and Gregory Petrillo of the Boys Town Center for the Study of Youth Development interviewed Roman Catholic, Southern Baptist, and United Methodist youth and likewise found that parents have a strong influence on their children's church attendance and youth program participation.[75]

The research clearly indicates that commitment to participation in church and other religious activities is sometimes better caught than taught. It must be entrenched deeply in the minds of parents that they serve as significant role models for their teenagers' own religious practices.

Size of Church: Teenagers who are affiliated with large or moderate sized congregations are more likely to engage themselves in religious activities than those involved in smaller congregations.[76] Why are smaller churches and parishes failing to interest and attract teenagers to their activities and programs? Perhaps it is because the programs in smaller churches have so few members that the programs are limited in quality and resources and consequently are not appealing to youth. It is also possible that the lay volunteers are not truly qualified to be working with today's adolescents.[77] What can smaller congregations do upon realizing they are not effective in attracting and reaching the teenagers in their congregation?

• Several small churches could band together, using their combined numbers and resources to develop a more exciting and impacting youth ministry.

• The church might invite a parachurch organization such as Youth for Christ or Young Life to cooperate in working with their teenagers.[78]

• The church should be committed to make youth religious education a priority by sending adult volunteer workers to one or more of the

---

75. Dean R. Hoge and Gregory H. Petrillo, "Youth and the Church," in *Religious Education* 74, (May-June 1979), 305–13.

76. Eugene C. Roehlkepartain and Peter L. Benson, *Youth in Protestant Churches* (Minneapolis, Minn.: Search Institute, 1993), 72–73; *Today's Teens,* 41.

77. *Today's Teens,* 54.

78. Young Life is an independent organization that forms clubs of high school students. The mailing address for Young Life is Box 520, Colorado Springs, Colo., 80901; the phone number is (719) 473-4262. Youth For Christ is a nondenominational rganization that also works with junior and senior high school students. The mailing address for Youth for Christ is Box 419, Wheaton, Ill., 60189. Their phone number is (312) 668-6600.

numerous national and regional training seminars or conferences available in the United States and Canada.[79]

Academic Standing: Adolescents who are among the best students
academically seem to be most likely to engage in religious activity.[80]
The challenge goes out to youth religious educators to reach the below-
average students, a group that the Barna Research Group suggests
feels rejected or ignored by the church. How can youth programs help
integrate them into the full life of the church? One way to impact
youth who are below average academically is by offering a tutoring
program. Tutoring will not only assist these teenagers in their education
process but will also help them attain personal confidence and a stronger
self-image.[81]

Age: One of the most important predictors of participation in church
and church programs is age. Older teenagers are less likely to take part in
church-related activities than younger adolescents. Eugene Roehlkepartain and Peter Benson of Search Institute report an 11 percent drop in
attendance to religious programs after the seventh and eighth school
years.[82] The Barna Report found that the oldest teenagers are consistently less likely than younger adolescents to take part in religious
activities.[83] A dramatic downward curve of church participation was
found in Canadian teenagers. The attendance of teenagers who go to
church "very often" drops by nearly 50 percent between ages 15 and 19.
Thirty percent of the 15-year-olds attend church regularly, 25 percent
of the 17-year-olds are regular attenders, but only 16 percent of the
19-year-olds continue to participate in organized church life.[84]

This downward swing in participation that comes with an increase
in age is a matter of concern for youth religious educators. Why do

---

79. Youth Specialties is a nondenominational organization that offers youth ministry
seminars across Canada and the United States. For information write National Resource
Seminar, Youth Specialties, 1224 Greenfield Drive, El Cajon, Calif., 92021 or call them
at (619)440-2333. Sonlife provides a variety of seminars, mostly related to developing a
long-range strategy for doing youth ministry. Their address is 526 North Main, Elburn,
Ill., 60119, and their phone number is 1-800-770-4769.

80. *Today's Teens,* 41; Gallup and Bezilla, *The Religious Life of Young Americans,* 11.

81. *Today's Teens,* 54.

82. Roehlkepartain and Benson, *Youth in Protestant Churches,* 72.

83. *Today's Teens,* 41.

84. Donald C. Posterski, *Friendship: A Window On Ministry to Youth* (Scarborough,
Ont: Project Teen Canada, 1985), 28.

many religiously involved youth drop out of the church as they increase in age? One could simply argue that disinterest in church and religion is a predictable dimension of growing up, part of going through the turbulent adolescent years. Barna argues that teenagers have always had a penchant for rejecting activities that adults revere or deem important.[85]

One analyst, however, insists that the inflexibility of many churches on theological and life style issues causes many older adolescents to depart from the church. Many teenagers contend that they are given insufficient latitude to subject their faith to intense and deep scrutiny. Sensing they have been given a "take it or leave it" ultimatum, many youth choose to move in different directions, seeking different spiritual dimensions to examine, or rejecting religion altogether.[86] By providing a safe context for youth to ask questions and explore answers to difficult questions, the wise and sensitive youth religious educator will reduce the possibility of adolescents under his or her spiritual care leaving the church.

Gender: Most research studies on gender differences indicate that females are slightly more active in religious activities than males at every age.[87] In their study of teenagers who are a part of mainline denominations in the United States, Roehlkepartain and Benson discovered this to be true. They found a greater percentage of girls (74 percent) than boys (67 percent) attended worship services at least once a week; more girls (43 percent) than boys (25 percent) volunteered for three or more hours of work in the church in the past month; a greater percentage of girls (35 percent) than boys (29 percent) participated in nonchurch religious programs for three or more hours in the past month; and 71 percent of the girls compared to 66 percent of the boys were involved for three or more hours in church programs other than the worship service in the last month.[88]

---

85. Barna, *Generation Next,* 86.
86. Ibid., 93–94.
87. See Michael Argyle and Benjamin Beit-Hallahmi, *The Social Psychology of Religion* (London, Eng.: Routledge & Kegan Paul, 1975), 71–79; Hapt M. Nelson and Raymond H. Potvin, "Gender and Regional Differences in the Religiosity of Protestant Adolescences," in *Review of Religious Research* 22, (March 1981), 268–85; Antanas Suziedelis and Raymond H. Potvin, "Sex Differences in Factors Affecting Religiousness Among Catholic Adolescents," 38–51; Hyde, "Adolescents and Religion," 121.
88. Roehlkepartain and Benson, *Youth in Protestant Churches,* 73.

A study of Southern Baptist youth also revealed that females were more likely to participate in religious activities than their male counterparts.[89] On the other hand, a national Gallup poll of American teenagers found little difference between males and females in their church and religious education attendance patterns.[90]

While the research literature identifies females as generally more religious than men, much less empirical work has been done to explain these differences. One possible explanation, however, is posited by Suziedelis and Potvin. Based on their exploration of Catholic adolescents, they determined that certain aspects of the stereotypic male role such as aggressiveness, strength, and toughness are not compatible with particular dimensions of religiousness.[91] Thus adolescent males tend to be less attracted to religious activities than do adolescent females.

The youth religious education program of a church might be made more attractive to boys by including male-oriented activities. Outdoor and wilderness activities such as camping, backpacking, white-water rafting, or rappelling can be used to challenge the male psyche and competitive spirit. Competitive sports such as basketball, tennis, ultimate Frisbee, or soccer will also be appealing to many (though not all) teenage males.

Reasons for Participation of Youth in church-related Activities

Another way to understand the profile of attendees of church-related activities is through an investigation of their reasons for participation. A Gallup poll asked teenagers why they usually engage in church youth groups and found the following reasons:[92]

• To help with their problems and worries (43 percent).
• To gain a better understanding of their religion (50 percent).
• To have a good time with people of their own age (35 percent).
• Because their parents wanted them to go (13 percent).

---

89. Nelson and Potvin, "Gender and Regional Differences in the Religiosity of Protestant Adolescents," 268–85.

90. Gallup and Bezilla, *The Religious Life of Young Americans,* 33, 41.

91. Suziedelis and Potvin, "Sex Differences in Factors Affecting Religiousness Among Catholic Adolescents," 38–51.

92. Gallup and Bezilla, *The Religious Life of Young Americans,* 32.

One of the major contributions to the empirical study and understanding of religious belief and practice is Gordon Alllport's Religious Orientation Scale. Allport was interested in the motivational forces behind religious behavior, and suggested there were two bipolar religious types—the intrinsically motivated and the extrinsically motivated. *Intrinsic* persons were described as those who are motivated to live their religion, while *extrinsic* people were characterized as ones who tend to use their religion for their own ends. Essentially, Allport was contrasting a mature religion with an immature religion.

Further research caused Allport and Michael Ross to include two additional orientations in their typology. The *indiscriminately proreligious* were described as individuals who seem to demonstrate both intrinsic and extrinsic motivations for religious involvement. Finally, they identified the *indiscriminately nonreligious,* those who do not show a strong tendency to be motivated either intrinsically or extrinsically toward involvement in religious or church-related activities.[93]

Ken Garland employed Allport's questionnaire items to investigate motives for participation and view of religion of high school youth who attend Conservative Baptist churches in Southern California. As a result of his empirical research, Garland was able to identify four profiles of religious youth.

Intrinsically Oriented Youth: Intrinsically oriented adolescents (34 percent) view religion as being good or important for reasons arising from within. These young people identified spiritual growth and giving honor to God as primary reasons for participating in church and youth religious education activities. To a lesser degree, they participate in order to serve others, learn about their own identity, and develop meaningful friendships with other people.

Extrinsically Oriented Youth: Adolescents who are extrinsically oriented (32 percent) feel religion is good for them and offers them various advantages in life. For example, these teenagers feel they will get along better with their parents if they please them by participating in church and youth group activities. Although their primary motives for attending youth activities—spiritual growth and honoring God—are the same as for the intrinsically oriented youth, they participate for

---

93. Gordon W. Allport and J. Michael Ross, "Personal Religious Orientation and Prejudice," in *Journal of Personality and Social Psychology* 5, (April 1967), 432–43.

these reasons because they believe God will reward them accordingly for their actions.

Indiscriminately Proreligious Youth: About 19 percent of the adolescents in this study are highly motivated to participate in church activities but unable to distinguish between intrinsic and extrinsic values regarding church and religion. In other words, they are motivated both intrinsically and extrinsically. Primary motivations for these youth were identity formation and learning for the sake of learning.

Indiscriminately Antireligious: A fourth group (15 percent) includes teenagers who maintain some religious attachments in their life but do so primarily to satisfy parental demands or to be with their friends. Their feelings about religion are that it is too restrictive or legalistic. In spite of their negative feelings about the church and religion, these young people participate regularly in church and youth religious education activities. Interestingly, their primary motives are also spiritual growth and honoring God. Perhaps their underlying motivation is that they can "score some points" with God, or eventually feel more positive about religion. Other reasons these young people give for attending youth-related activities are social contact and identity formation. These young people generally do not feel very good about their life and are often unhappy.

In addition to the profiles of youth attendees to church-related youth activities, Garland identified eight motivational factors for teenagers participating in church and church-related youth group activities. In descending order of importance to the youth, the motives are briefly described below.

Spiritual growth. This factor identifies a desire to grow closer to God in a personal relationship.

Honor to God. This indicates a desire to obey and honor God, or not to make him angry.

Service to others. This factor indicates a desire to better serve God and others.

Social contact. This factor describes a desire to make new friends and acquaintances, or to get closer to current friends and acquaintances.

Identity formation. This factor indicates a desire to find out who he or she is in relationship to God and others.

Cognitive interest. This indicates a desire to learn new things simply for the sake of learning.

Integration with life. This factor describes a desire to learn how the individual's faith relates to other dimensions of life.

Escape. This factor describes a desire to get away from unpleasant relationships or undesirable aspects of life.[94]

Several observations can be drawn from the participation studies. First, youth ministries that put significant efforts into entertaining young people with social activities and recreation are failing to meet the needs and interests of a large portion of their group. The young people in Garland's survey indicated that they participated primarily to know God better and to grow spiritually. Likewise, the Gallup poll discovered that adolescents attend church youth group activities for serious reasons. Hoge and Petrillo observed that youth group leaders who stressed teaching the Bible, helping spiritual development, and personal relationships with God in their youth programs had slightly higher levels of participation than those who stressed less doctrinal or theological objectives.[95]

On the other hand, many teenagers complain that they do not enjoy church-related activities. Youth ministries must not forfeit making learning fun, and should integrate appropriate measures of recreation and social activities. The youth religious educator can find out why teenagers participate in their youth group activities by administering a survey questionnaire.

Contrary to what many youth workers might assume, research studies indicate that teenagers attend youth activities because they want to— even those identified as antireligious. Very few participate only because of parental pressure. Youth religious educators might ask themselves the question, Would my youth ministry be any different if I assumed young people attended youth activities because they wanted to?

CONCLUSION

The life of a teenager is multifaceted. The contexts in which the adolescent experiences life is divided primarily between the home (see chapter 3), school, work, and church. After the home, school takes up the largest block of time in the life of a teenager. While youth readily

---

94. Ken Garland, "Why Kids Really Come to Your Meetings," in *Youthworker*, (Winter, 1992), 75–79.

95. Dean Hoge and Gregory Petrillo, "Youth and the Church," 305–13.

admit that school is a critical dimension of preparing for adulthood, it is often faced with little enthusiasm or enjoyment.

For as many as 80 percent of in-school adolescents, the work experience, whether part- or full-time, will be a part of their preparation for young adulthood. For some teenagers, work will provide an opportunity to gain valuable experience in the occupational field of pursuit. On the other hand, many of the jobs secondary students hold down will be menial and routine, contributing relatively little to the shaping of their future vocations.

The church continues to play a significant role in the lives of teenagers. There is considerable concern, however, that in the United States and Canada, traditional religious institutions are failing to interest and retain the adolescent segment of the population. Many youth will depart from organized religion for a period of time, although many of these dropouts will renew their relationship with the church in their middle or late twenties.

6

The Maze of Teenage Sexuality

One of the central issues facing adolescents is sexuality, something that consumes their thoughts as they worry about their behavior and anticipate their sexual development. *The National Sunday School Association's Youth Survey* asked 3,000 teenagers what kind of help they would like to receive from their churches. Help for sexual problems ranked first among twenty-one items.[1] In a survey of Canadian teenagers, four in ten admitted that they think about sex "very often," while three in ten admitted it to be an area that concerns them "a great deal" or "quite a bit."[2] Furthermore, numerous empirical research studies indicate that sexual activity in adolescence is an increasingly common event. Teenagers are freer than ever before to engage in premarital sex. This chapter will explore the many facts and issues related to teenage sexuality including sexual behavior, teenage pregnancy, abortion, sexually transmitted diseases, (STDs), homosexuality, masturbation, and sexual abuse.

SEXUAL BEHAVIORS AND ATTITUDES

Some of the most startling and alarming statistics concerning adolescents are related to their sexual habits, values, and attitudes. Per-

---

1. Cited in Josh McDowell and Dick Day, *Why Wait?* (San Bernardino: Here's Life, 1987), 19.
2. Reginald W. Bibby and Donald C. Posterski, *The Emerging Generation* (Toronto: Irwin, 1985), 75.

missive sexual activity among youth, while never rare, is becoming increasingly commonplace. The consequences, however, for engaging in illicit sex can be devastating. Most teenagers are not psychologically mature enough to engage in sexual activity without suffering painful results from their experiences. And while adolescents are physically capable of bearing children, they are generally neither emotionally nor economically capable of raising them. Of course, one of the most potentially harmful consequences of premarital sexual activity is the acquiring of a sexually transmitted disease. Because sexuality presents so many dilemmas and harmful effects to adolescents, Christian youth religious educators and parents alike are greatly concerned about the moral behavior of the teenagers they are involved with.

Premarital Sexual Intercourse

Contemporary adolescents live in a world in which premarital sexual intercourse is no longer seen as a moral issue or as an activity reserved for marriage only. The pervasive attitude of young people seems to be that sex is a personal right or choice and is associated more with a standard of permissiveness. An 18-year-old from Washington D.C. says, "In high school, everyone assumes you've already done it. The emphasis moves from 'Are you doing it?' to 'How are you doing it?' "[3] A 15-year-old from New York says, "Nobody cares anymore whether or not you're a virgin."[4] "For me, as long as it's in a caring relationship, as long as you're making love and not just having sex, it's OK," says an 17-year-old youth from the Atlanta area.[5] The research statistics related to adolescent sexual behavior confirm these attitudes. According to the national United States school-based *Youth Risk Behavior Survey* of the Centers for Disease Control (CDC), 76 percent of boys and 67 percent of girls in the United States have had sex by age 18. The study also reveals that of all students in the ninth through twelfth school years, 54.2 percent reported ever having sexual intercourse. Males were more likely than females to have had sexual intercourse (60.8 percent to 48 percent respectively). Black youth were

3. Kim Painter, "Fewer Kids Save Sex For Adulthood," in *USA Today,* March 5, 1991, 1D.

4. Lena Williams, "U.S. Teens Increasingly View Sex as a Personal Right, Experts Say," in *The Atlanta Journal and Constitution,* February 27, 1989, C4.

5. David Pendered, "Sex: Teens More Open, Active," in *The Atlanta Journal and Constitution,* January 13, 1991, D1.

significantly more likely to ever have had sexual intercourse than either white or Hispanic teenagers (72.3 percent, 51.6 percent, and 53.4 percent respectively).[6] In Canada, close to 50 percent of the teenage females in one empirical study admitted to being sexually active, while 62 percent of the males acknowledged their sexual activity.[7] Approximately 87 percent of Canadian teenagers approve of premarital sex when people love each other.[8]

Adolescents in America are engaging in sexual intercourse at younger and younger ages. According to the Centers for Disease Control, about one third (33.5 percent) of male students and one-fifth (20 percent) of female students initiated sexual intercourse before the age of 15; this is compared to one in 22 (4.5 percent) a generation ago.[9] Most research indicates that the average age for first having sexual intercourse is 15 for girls and 14 for boys.[10]

Adolescents have always been troubled by sexual temptations and preoccupied with sexual thoughts and concerns. But the behavior of adolescents has changed dramatically, and in the words of Tony Campolo, the sexual revolution among American youth is "awesome to behold."[11] Why the dramatic change in teenage sexual behaviors? One researcher suggests that young people are simply finishing what was started in the 1960s.[12] Adolescents are reflecting or adhering to the overpermissive sex norms of society at large, including those of their parents.

Researchers indicate that multiple factors are in play in influencing the premarital sexual behavior of teenagers. These influences include parental modeling, parent-teen relationships, family structures, peers, religions, and media.

---

6. Centers for Disease Control, "Sexual Behavior Among High School Students—United States, 1990," in *Morbidity And Mortality Weekly Report* 40, (January 1992), 885–88.

7. Reginald W. Bibby and Donald C. Posterski, *Teen Trends* (Toronto: Stoddart, 1992), 39.

8. Ibid.

9. Centers for Disease Control, "Selected Behaviors That Increase Risk for HIV Infection Among High School Students—United States, 1990" in *Morbidity And Mortality Weekly Report* 41, (April 1992), 231.

10. McDowell and Day, *Why Wait?*, 22.

11. Tony Campolo, "Christian Ethics in the Sexual Wilderness," in *Youthworker* 1, (Winter 1985), 13.

12. Cited by Williams, "U.S. Teens Increasingly View Sex as a Personal Right, Experts Say," 4C.

The Effect of Parental Modeling: As indicated above, one of the variables in the relationship between family configuration and adolescent sexual activity is the effect of behaviors and attitudes modeled by parents, especially mothers. While most parents would not likely want their young, unmarried child to be sexually active, many find themselves in personal conflict as they often endorse and model ideas such as individual choice and freedom to select one's life-style. Thus many teenagers feel they have evidence of adult hypocrisy, such as the Virginia high school student who rightly argues, "When my mother has a date Friday night and he is in the kitchen eating breakfast Saturday morning, how can she preach about premarital sex?"[13]

David Elkind notes that adolescents simply follow the lead set by adults. When adults did not engage in extramarital or premarital sex, neither did adolescents. Now that many adults view premarital sex as socially acceptable, so do teenagers.[14] A number of empirical studies support this notion. Results of one research study indicated that the mothers' dating behavior was positively related with their sons' early sexual behaviors (heavy petting and sexual intercourse).[15]

Another empirical study of parental influences on adolescents' sexual behavior revealed that believing one's mother had experienced intercourse prior to marriage predicted more sexual activity on behalf of the teenage children. The researchers concluded that the mother's premarital experience may have served as a model to be imitated.[16] Newcomer and Udry discovered that the more sexually active the mother was before marriage, the more likely the adolescent child was to engage in premarital sexual intercourse. However, this relationship was weaker for sons than for daughters.[17] Finally, a national study of 15- and 16-year-olds revealed that those adolescent females whose parents expressed and

13. Ibid.

14. David Elkind, *A Sympathetic Understanding of the Child,* 3d ed. (Boston: Allyn and Bacon, 1994), 194.

15. Les B. Whitbeck, Ronald L. Simons, and Meei-Ying Kao, "The Effects of Divorced Mothers' Dating Behaviors and Sexual Attitudes and Behaviors of Their Adolescent Children," in *Journal of Marriage and the Family* 56, (August 1994), 615–21.

16. Mel Hovell, et al., "Family Influences on Latino and Anglo Adolescents' Sexual Behavior," in *Journal of Marriage and the Family* 56, (November 1994), 973–86.

17. Susan F. Newcomer and J. Richard Udry, "Mothers' Influence on the Sexual Behavior of Their Teenage Children," in *Journal of Marriage and the Family* 46, (May 1984), 477–85.

modeled traditional attitudes about marriage and family life were only half as likely to report having sex as those with less conservative parents (9 percent as compared to 20 percent).[18]

The old adage *some lessons are better caught than taught* certainly rings true when it comes to teaching life-style practices and behaviors to adolescents. The onus is on parents to model a life-style that evidences purity and wholeness in the realm of sexual behavior. Single mothers or fathers who may be going out with someone themselves must be especially careful in their dating relationships. Teenagers are more likely to imitate the dating and sexual practices of a mother or father, rather than to follow the rules and guidelines set forth by the parents.

The Effect of Parent-Adolescent Relationships and Communication on Adolescent Sexual Behavior: The effect of parent-youth relationships on the sexual behavior of adolescents has been well documented. The *Teen Sex Survey* of Josh McDowell Ministries reveals that sexual contact (fondling breasts, fondling genitals, and/or having sexual intercourse) was much less likely among teenagers who had a close relationship with their father. The researchers also found that youth who perceived that their parents spent a lot of time with them were less likely than others to report having engaged in sexual contact. They concluded, however, that spending time in conversation with their adolescent children was not enough to persuade teenagers against engaging in premature sexual activity. While building relationships is important, even more critical is taking advantage of that forum to lead adolescents into knowing how to resist sexual pressure.[19]

In a national study of 15- and 16-year-olds, the researchers divided the subjects into two subgroups: 1) those whose parents expressed traditional values about marriage and family life, and 2) those who trans-mitted more permissive values. Among daughters of traditional parents, a mere 3 percent of those who discussed sex with either parent reported being sexually active, compared with 20 percent of the daughters who did not discuss sex with either parent. Interestingly, among daughters

---

18. Kristin A. Moore, James L. Peterson, and Frank F. Furstenberg, "Parental Attitudes and the Occurrence of Early Sexual Activity," in *Journal of Marriage and the Family* 48, (November 1986), 777–82.

19. *Teen Sex Survey in the Evangelical Church* (Dallas, Tex.: Josh McDowell Ministry, 1987), 5–8. The participating denominations included: The Church of the Nazarene, Evangelical Covenant Church, Church of God—Cleveland, Free Methodist Church, Lutheran Church—Missouri Synod, Grace Brethren Church, The Wesleyan Church, and The Salvation Army.

whose parents expressed more liberal attitudes, discussion of sex with parents was unrelated to behavior. Discussing sex with sons had no positive impact on sexual behavior of subjects in either group.[20]

In another study of factors associated with sexual risk-taking behaviors among adolescents, Tom Luster and Stephen Small measured the influence of family characteristics on three groups: *high-risk, low-risk,* and *abstainers.* High-risk adolescents were those who had more than one sexual partner and rarely or never used contraception. Low-risk teenagers were those who had only one partner and always used contraception. Abstainers were those adolescents who practiced sexual abstinence. When the three groups were compared, the results indicated that abstainers were 1) more closely monitored by their parents (for example parents knew the whereabouts of their teenage children), and 2) received more support from parents (parents were there when adolescents needed them), than either high-risk and low-risk males and females.[21]

The research underscores the significance of healthy relationships between parents and youth, as well as the importance of communication concerning sexual matters. Unfortunately, studies also indicate that too little communication between adolescents and their parents is devoted to sexuality.[22] How can the youth religious education program assist parents in talking to their teenagers about sexual matters? One possibility is to offer a seminar or class on "Talking to Your Teenager About Sexuality." If the youth worker does not feel comfortable or adequate in addressing this topic to parents, he or she might have an expert (for example, a medical doctor, nurse, pastor, or counselor) teach the class or seminar. The church or youth religious education program should also make available books or curriculum that parents would find helpful in discussing sexual issues with their adolescent children.[23]

---

20. Moore, Peterson, and Furstenberg, "Parental Attitudes and the Occurrence of Early Sexual Activity," 777–82.

21. Tom Luster and Stephen A. Small, "Factors Associated with Sexual Risk-Taking Behaviors Among Adolescents," in *Journal of Marriage and the Family* 56, (August 1994), 622–32.

22. *Teen Sex Survey in the Evangelical Church,* 5; Moore, Peterson, and Furstenberg, "Parental Attitudes and the Occurrence of Early Sexual Activity," 777–82; Robert Sorensen, *Adolescent Sexuality in Contemporary America* (New York: World Publishing, 1972), 367.

23. Concordia Publishing House publishes a series of six books titled *Learning About Sex.* Each book in the series is graded in vocabulary and the amount of information it

The Effect of Family Structure on Adolescent Sexual Behavior: Clearly, the structure or configuration of the family has a strong effect on the premarital sexual behavior of adolescents, daughters in particular. Kinnaird and Gerrard found that daughters from divorced or reconstituted families were more likely not only to engage in premarital sexual activity, but to have begun sexual intercourse at younger ages than daughters from intact two-parent families. While only 53.3 percent of the subjects from intact families reported that they had engaged in premarital sexual activity, 70 percent of the divorced group and 80 percent of the reconstituted group reported that they were sexually experienced. In addition, among the daughters from divorced families, 57.1 percent of the sexually experienced teenage girls had their first intercourse by age 16. In contrast, 33.3 percent of the girls from reconstituted families and only 18.8 percent of those from intact families had their first intercourse by the age of 16.[24]

Newcomer and Udry reported that the state of being in a mother-only household predicted subsequent sexual activity of daughters, though not of sons.[25] Likewise, Miller and Bingham found daughters from single-parent families more likely to have engaged in sexual intercourse than those from intact families.[26] A Search Institute study of both boys and girls revealed that 52.9 percent of the youth ages 14 to 17 from single-parent homes had sexual intercourse two times or more; this compared to 34.5 percent of those from two-parent families who indicated having sex twice or more.[27]

What reasons can be given for more permissive attitudes and sexual behavior patterns of teenagers, especially daughters, from single-parent

---

provides from age 3 to late adolescence. They answer questions that persons at each age level typically ask. Another helpful source is Ann Cannon, *Sexuality: God's Gift* (Nashville, Tenn.: Family Touch Press, 1993).

24. Keri L. Kinnaird and Meg Gerrard, "Premarital Sexual Behavior and Attitudes Toward Marriage and Divorce Among Young Women As a Function of Their Mothers' Marital Status," in *Journal of Marriage and the Family* 48, (November 1986), 757–65.

25. Susan F. Newcomer and J. Richard Udry, "Parental Marital Status Effects on Adolescent Sexual Behavior," in *Journal of Marriage and the Family* 49, (May 1987), 235–40.

26. Brent C. Miller and C. Raymond Bingham, "Family Configuration in Relation to the Sexual Behavior of Female Adolescents," in *Journal of Marriage and the Family* 51, (May 1989), 499–506.

27. Peter L. Benson and Eugene C. Benson, *Youth in Single-Parent Families: Risk and Resiliency* (Minneapolis, Minn.: Search Institute, 1993), 17.

divorced households? A number of plausible explanations emerge from the related literature:

• Father-absent girls are deprived of the father's important teaching related to sexual behavior.[28]

• Families with inferior interpersonal relationships, poor communication, and weak problem-solving skills, characteristics often found in broken or single-parent households, may inadvertently cause young people to look to peers for nurturing relationships and love.[29]

• A single parent is unable to monitor or supervise teenage activities as effectively as two parents are. Single mothers are more likely to work full time than are mothers in two-parent households.[30]

• Divorced mothers are less religious and have more sexually permissive attitudes than do continuously married mothers.[31]

• Single mothers may be dating and may also be sexually active, thus modeling habits that overwhelm their attempts to control their children's sexual behavior.[32]

• Single parents are beset and preoccupied with problems and burdens that interfere with the supervision and teaching of their teenage children. Experiencing divorce represents a set of circumstances that is characterized by emotional turmoil, preoccupation with the marital problem, removal of one parent from the home, financial problems, and shifting responsibilities. In general, family life is in disarray. In such adverse conditions parents may lose control of their adolescent children's behavior.

Chapter 3 addressed the importance of building strong intact families. The need for functional two-parent homes is underscored once again in terms of the effect family structure has on adolescent sexual behavior. At every level or in virtually every domain of church ministry, efforts must be made to strengthen the family. Unfortunately, in contemporary

---

28. Mollie S. Smart and Russel C. Smart, *Adolescents: Development and Relationships,* 2nd ed. (New York: Macmillan, 1978), 113.

29. J. Jeffries McWhirter, et al., *At-Risk Youth: A Comprehensive Response* (Pacific Grove, Calif.: Brooks/Cole, 1993), 141.

30. Miller and Bingham, "Family Configuration in Relation to the Sexual Behavior of Female Adolescents, 499–506.

31. Ibid.

32. Mel Hovell et al., "Family Influences on Latino and Anglo Adolescents' Sexual Behavior," in *Journal of Marriage and the Family* 56, (November 1994), 973–86.

society many teenagers come from homes in which marriages are no longer intact.

The responsibility for building strong marriages and healthy families primarily lies outside of the domain of youth ministry (such as premarital and marital counseling, or marriage enrichment). However, there are some strategies youth programs can engage in to assist single parents and their adolescent children in handling the stress and pressures of life that contribute to inappropriate sexual behavior. For example, a support group might be formed for single parents of teenagers. In these groups, parents could be encouraged to talk about issues such as dating habits or pressures they experience in dating relationships. Support groups would also give single parents who are dating an opportunity to be accountable to others for their behaviors and practices.

While every adolescent needs contact from caring and responsive adults, the need is acute for teenagers from single-parent homes. Mark DeVries, in his book *Family-Based Youth Ministry,* says more than anything else, these youth need roots into an extended Christian family that will be there for them. This caring community can be created by doing several things:[33]
• Keep an accurate list of these adolescents' names, addresses and phone numbers, so that we do not allow them to "fall through the cracks" of a traditional youth program, as so many teenagers from broken homes do.
• Create a strategy whereby these youth are contacted on a regular basis. Since youth from single-parent homes may not have the support and help teenagers from intact families have to be involved in youth activities, it may take much more effort on behalf of the youth workers to reach them.
• Have youth leaders sit with youth during worship services.
• Invite a teenager to an all-church fellowship event, such as a dinner or concert.
• Have adult youth workers invite teenagers from single-parent households to serve with them in local or out-of-town service or mission projects.
• Design publicity for programs and youth events in such a way that adolescents from single-parent families get a personal invitation or reminder about the activity.

---

33. Mark DeVries, *Family-Based Youth Ministry* (Downers Grove, Ill.: InterVarsity, 1994), 111–12.

The Influence of Peers on Sexual Behavior: Peer group influence can affect adolescent behaviors, as has been documented in previous chapters. Without strong family support and healthy parent-child interaction, teenagers are especially susceptible to peer influence. Consequently other teenagers become the primary factor in the decision of whether to engage in illicit sexual activity or not.[34]

The empirical research of Robert Sorenson found peers to have an influence on the sexual activity of adolescents. Sixty-two percent of the adolescents in his study agreed with the statement "When it comes to sex, a lot of young people these days do the things they do because everyone else is doing it." This response seems to indicate that many teenagers use sex in order to gain acceptance in the eyes of others.[35]

However, when specifically asked of themselves whether their sexual behavior is influenced by others, 72 percent of the boys and 79 percent of the girls agreed that "so far as sex is concerned, what other young people do doesn't have any influence on what I myself do." Age variance among boys makes a significant difference in the tendency to conform. Younger boys have a much greater tendency to conform to their peers in areas of sexual behavior than do older boys and most girls.[36]

Sorenson suggests that strong pressure to conform is usually exercised by the boy in an attempt to persuade the girl to have sex. Otherwise, in most instances the influence of conformity is exerted by example rather than by enticement or argument.[37]

The Effect of Religion on Adolescent Sexual Behavior: What influence does religion or religious activity have on the sexual behavior of adolescents? While most empirical research indicates that religion or religious orientation does have some positive influence on the sexual behavior and attitudes of teenagers, it does not have the enormous impact that concerned Christian parents and youth religious educators would hope for or expect. The often cited research study *Teen Sex Survey in the Evangelical Church,* reported that 43 percent of the responding church youth said they had experienced sexual intercourse by their 18th birthday; 35 percent of the 17-year-olds, and 26 percent of the 16-year-olds admitted to having premarital sex.[38] Eugene Roehlkepartain

---

34. McWhirter et al., *At-Risk Youth,* 142.
35. Robert Sorensen, *Adolescent Sexuality in Contemporary America,* 53.
36. Ibid.
37. Ibid.
38. Ibid., 3.

and Peter Benson of Search Institute studied adolescents who were members of five Protestant mainline denominations and found that 31 percent of the subjects had intercourse by eleventh and twelfth grades (approximately ages 16 and 17).[39] By comparison, according to the earlier mentioned CDC national study of 16- to 18-year-olds in the United States, approximately 54 percent have had sexual intercourse.[40]

In an empirical study of religious participation and adolescent behavior, Arland Thornton and Donald Camburn determined that adolescents who attend church frequently and who value religion in their lives are less experienced sexually and have less permissive attitudes toward sex. In other words, the acceptance of sexual intercourse is lower among those with high involvement in religious institutions. However, when they broke the respondents into religious affiliation categories (Catholic, fundamentalist Protestants and Baptists, nonfundamentalist Protestants, Jews, and those with no religious preference), they found little difference in sexual behaviors and attitudes. The researchers concluded that religious participation is more important in determining sexual behavior and attitudes than is religious affiliation.[41]

According to an empirical study of teenage girls who were reared by single parents, religiosity, a rating of the importance of religion to the respondent, was found to have a strong influence on sexual behavior. In other words, the more important religion was to the adolescent, the less likely that individual would be to engage in premarital sexual intercourse.[42]

Timothy Woodroof investigated the relationship between religiosity and adolescent sexual behavior of 477 freshmen attending eight colleges affiliated with the Churches of Christ. He found a significant inverse relationship between the level of religious behavior (church attendance) and the level of premarital sexual activity. When respondents were grouped into those attending three times weekly and those attending

39. Eugene C. Roehlkepartain and Peter L. Benson, *Youth in Protestant Churches* (Minneapolis, Minn.: Search Institute, 1993), 102–3.

40. Centers for Disease Control, "Sexual Behavior Among High School Students— United States, 1990," 885–88.

41. Arland Thorton and Donald Camburn, "Religious Participation and Adolescent Sexual Behavior and Attitudes," in *Journal of Marriage and the Family* 51, (August 1989), 641–53.

42. Miller and Bingham, "Family Configuration in Relation to the Sexual Behavior of Female Adolescents," 499–506.

twice a week or less, Woodroof found that those who attended three times weekly were less sexually active than those attending twice a week or less. Viewed another way, 80 percent of those who attended church three times a week or more claimed to still be virgins, compared to 60 percent for those attending once or twice a week, and 37 percent for those who attended church less than once a week.[43]

Similarly, Roehlkepartain and Benson found a difference in the incidence of sexual behavior between teenagers of selected Protestant churches who were *highly active* in the church and those who were *inactive*.[44] While 32 percent of the inactive youth admitted to having had sexual intercourse at least once, only 12 percent of the active youth reported ever having had sex.[45]

While empirical research clearly indicates that participation in religious activity has some positive influence on sexual behavior and attitudes of teenagers, it is naive for Christian parents and youth religious educators to think that many of their youth are not engaging in some form of premarital sexual activity. In fact it can be determined that the sexual patterns of churched teenagers are not excessively different from those of the American and Canadian youth population at large. It can be concluded, however, that the more active teenagers are in church-related activities, the less likely the possibility is of their engaging in premarital sexual intercourse.

The Influence of the Media: Through mass media, young people are exposed to a variety of ideologies, life-styles and value systems that promote a freewheeling, overpermissive approach to sex. While basic values and norms are influenced primarily by parents and peers, one research report reveals that the media ranks third in influencing teenager behavior.[46] And the media indeed places a high priority on portraying illicit sexual behavior in a favorable light. Television represents one example. One research study estimates that the average person watches

---

43. J. Timothy Woodroof, "Premarital Sexual Behavior and Religious Adolescents," in *Journal for the Scientific Study of Religion* 24, (4 1984), 343–66.

44. *Highly active* adolescents were classified as those who said they attended worship services once a week or more, spent six or more hours in programs and events in the past month, and six or more hours doing volunteer work in the church in the last month. *Inactive* youth were on membership rolls but attended services only a few times a year or not at all.

45. Roehlkepartain and Benson, *Youth in Protestant Churches,* 102–3.

46. McDowell and Day, *Why Wait?,* 40.

approximately 9,230 sex acts a year on television—81 percent of this sexual activity is outside the commitment of marriage.[47] One review found that on prime time television, sexual intercourse is eleven times more likely to occur between unmarried couples than between husband and wife.[48] Neil Postman observes, "In its quest for new and sensational ventures to hold its audience, TV must tap every existing taboo in the culture: homosexuality, incest, divorce, promiscuity, corruption, adultery, and terrible displays of violence and sadism. As a consequence, these former taboos have become as familiar to the young as they are to adults."[49]

Advertising, whether in magazines or on TV, uses sex as a primary ingredient for selling. One study determined that women are often portrayed in swimsuits, underwear, or see-through clothing in a state of semi-undress or with considerable body exposure. The unclothed female body is displayed, to some degree, in about one in four advertisements.[50] Contemporary advertising uses sex to sell everything from soft drinks, to jeans, to cars, to underarm deodorant, and one of the biggest markets is the 20 million teenagers who have over $75 billion, annually, at their disposal.[51]

Another media monster that sends an undesirable message of sex and sexuality is popular music. For many years, rock music has been synonymous with illicit sex, and thus it continues in the 1990s. In much of contemporary pop and rock, argues Reynolds Ekstrom, sex is imaged as a means for immediate gratification, women are portrayed as mere objects of desire, and relationships are depicted as temporary, little-consequence affairs.[52] Titles of popular rock and pop songs alone are

---

47. Ibid.

48. Barbara Hansen and Carol Knopes, "Prime Time Tuning Out Varied Cultures," in *USA Today,* July 6, 1993, 1A–2A.

49. The comments are made by Neil Postman, in an interview for *U.S. News and World Report* in 1981. While the statement was made in the 1980s, it holds just as true for today as it did then. The interview was reproduced in Fredric Rissover and David Birch, eds., *Mass Media and the Popular Arts* (New York: McGraw-Hill, 1983), 278.

50. Edvin Ewry, "The Presentation of Gender in Advertising," in Arthur Berger, editor, *Media USA* (New York: Longman, 1988), 439.

51. Reynolds R. Ekstrom, "Consumerism and Youth," in Reynolds R. Ekstrom, editor, *Media and Culture* (New Rochelle, NY: Don Bosco Multimedia, 1992), 135.

52. Reynolds R. Ekstrom, "Media and Culture and the Rock of Ages: A Self-Help Guide for Pastoral Ministers," in Reynolds R. Ekstrom, ed., *Media and Culture* (New Rochelle, N.Y.: Don Bosco Multimedia, 1992), 91.

strong indicators of the nature of the message: "Me So Horny," "Living in Sin," "Girl U For Me," and "Show Me Love" are some examples. Now, of course, MTV (Music Television) provides the viewer with combined visual and audio messages, so that if the lyrical message happens to elude the teenager, it will be sure to be received through imagery. In the 1990s it is estimated that at any one time during prime time hours, about 345,000 people are tuned in to the MTV network. MTV finds about 70 percent of its regular viewers are under 25 and their target audience is made up of the 14- to 24-year-olds.[53]

According to the Teen Sex Survey, two of the primary sources of information about sex for churched youth are media: movies and television. This means the media are providing sexual training for a large proportion of youth.[54]

Encouraging Abstinence: While research studies demonstrate that a significant number of teenagers are sexually active, there are indications that a growing number of adolescents are choosing abstinence and chastity over engaging in premarital sexual intercourse. Across the United States, teenagers are hearing the message of abstinence from church, community, and school leaders.[55] For many adolescents, seeing how premarital sex has ruined the lives of others by sexually transmitted diseases or pregnancies has caused them to pledge virginity until marriage or at least drastically change their behaviors. Other teenagers are committing to sexual abstinence because of religious beliefs and values that teach that God made sex for marriage.

Many churches and parachurch organizations are following the lead of the Southern Baptist Convention and their "True Love Waits" program. Concerned that teenagers who practiced abstinence were feeling that they were a small minority and that even many adults fully expected them to be sexually active, leaders developed a national campaign involving local churches and ministries. According to the program, teenagers and college students, after hearing Bible studies, messages, or talks on sexual purity, are encouraged to sign covenant or pledge cards saying they will abstain from sex until they are married. Those who are currently sexually

---

53. Ibid., 78.

54. *Teen Sex Survey in the Evangelical Church,* 5.

55. For example, see Kim Painter, "Some Data, Good News for Relationships," in *USA Today,* October 5, 1994, 2A; Jeanne Wright, "A Push for Chastity: For Some Teens, Sex Can Wait," in *USA Today,* March 22, 1994, 4D.

active are encouraged to make a new beginning and sign a covenant to future abstinence as well.[56] The immensity of "True Love Waits" was evidenced in the summer of 1994 when some 200,000 adolescents had their pledge cards displayed on a three-block stretch of the National Mall in Washington, DC. A Christian rock concert and prayer vigil followed the public display of commitment to abstinence.[57]

While discussions or talks on sexual purity are important in relaying important information to teenagers, such instruction is not usually adequate. The message of sexual purity must be fortified by using additional teaching techniques. For example, one youth service featured a couple in a skit portraying the consequences of sexual sin. The actors took turns role-playing a person's conscience, future mates, children, boyfriend/girlfriend, family, and God. Following the role-playing, the teenagers in the audience, with their parents standing alongside, placed signed covenant cards on the altar to signify their vow of chastity to God.[58]

Some additional ways to teach abstinence before marriage are identified as follows:

• Use the object lesson whereby you have in your hands two roses, a white one and a pink one. Give the pink rose to the adolescents, each of whom picks off a petal. After twelve adolescents have picked off all the petals, the rose is bare. Remind them that teenagers who engage in premarital sexual experiences are like the pink rose. Just like the rose lost its beauty when its petals were picked off, so the adolescent has sacrificed wholeness and purity when he or she has engaged in premarital sex. Contrast this to the still-intact white rose, which signifies the purity of abstinence.

• Pair teenagers up with adults or other mature youth who will hold them responsible for their sexual behavior by meeting regularly and establishing a relationship of prayer, encouragement, and accountability.

• Use panel discussions to introduce and address issues of sexuality

---

56. For further information about "True Love Waits," call 800-LUVWAIT. Kits that include study materials and ideas for youth services are available for interested churches and youth groups.

57. Tom Morton, "Assessing True Love Waits," in *Youthworker* 11, (Fall 1994), 54–60.

58. Patricia Bolen, "Abstinence Plan Grows Among Youth," in *Moody Monthly* (January 1994), 57.

and sexual behavior. Allow the teenagers to hear from married couples, doctors or nurses, church staff, an unwed mother, and/or an individual with AIDS.

• Show a video clip to introduce the topic of sexual purity[59] or use statistics from newspaper or magazine articles to illustrate a point such as the rates of teenage pregnancy or sexual activity, or the incidence of sexually transmitted diseases among adolescents.

Teenagers are getting mixed messages from society concerning premarital sexual behavior. Parents and youth workers may be telling teenagers to say no to illicit sex, but almost everything adolescents see and hear is saying "go for it!" Teenagers need to understand the wrongness of premarital sexual activity and the dangers and consequences of promiscuous behavior. Premarital sexual activity may bring physical consequences such as pregnancy and disease, as well as emotional pains of guilt, loneliness and depression.

Are highly visible programs such as "True Love Waits" having a significant impact on behavior? Certainly, signing covenants does not indicate whether or not youth will actually keep their pledges. In other words, there is no guarantee behavior will match attitudes. Indeed, there are no empirical measurements of the success of "True Love Waits," although similar programs have reported some effectiveness. There is further evidence that programs encouraging abstinence are less effective with teenagers who are already sexually active.[60] If abstinence-only programs are going to be effective in changing the behavior of adolescents, they should incorporate the following components:

• Skills to resist social and peer pressure.
• The support of fellow teenagers.
• The support and teaching of older teenagers and adults.
• Education about sexuality.[61]

---

59. Youth Specialties' *Edge TV* and Group Publishing's *Hot Talk-Starter Videos* are ideal for introducing and exploring sensitive topics such as sexuality.

60. The success of "Postponing Sexual Involvement," a program developed by Grady Memorial Hospital in Atlanta, is discussed by Tom Morton in "Assessing True Love Waits," 54–60. Abstinence-only programs are further addressed by Bonnidell Clouse, "Adolescent Moral Development and Sexuality," in Donald Ratcliff and James A. Davies, eds., *Handbook of Youth Ministry* (Birmingham, Ala.: Religious Education Press, 1991), 205–6.

61. Ibid.

Masturbation

Randy was a senior in high school. He did not have a steady girl-friend, though he dated once in a while. Randy was deeply troubled by his sexual fantasizing and thoughts and one day he gathered up the courage to talk about this to his youth pastor, in whom he placed much trust and confidence. After a series of sessions, however, Randy admitted that his real struggle was with masturbation. Once he got an erotic thought in his mind he had trouble getting rid of it until he relieved the tension through masturbation. Sometimes he could go a few days without masturbating; then there were days when he would masturbate two or three times. Randy experienced tremendous guilt and frustration over this compelling habit.

Clearly, the most frequently practiced sexual activity among adolescents is masturbation, the stimulation of one's own genitals to the point of orgasm without the participation of another person. Most young people masturbate during their adolescent years, although it is more popular among young boys than girls. One study found that more than 90 percent of males and 50 percent of females have masturbated to orgasm at some point in their lives.[62] Robert Sorensen, however, found that only 58 percent of all adolescent boys and 39 percent of all adolescent girls have masturbated at least once.[63] It is facetiously suggested that 99 percent of teenage boys admit to masturbating, and the other 1 percent are liars!

Masturbation is also one of the most widely discussed and controverted issues related to human sexuality. A hundred years ago masturbation was widely condemned, not only by Christians but by those in secular society as well. It was blamed for a number of physical and mental illnesses including loss of hair, heart stress, insanity, mental retardation, syphilis, and interference with the normal functioning of sexual intercourse.[64] However, there appears to be no medical or scientific evidence that masturbation is physically harmful in any such ways.[65]

---

62. J.D. Atwood and J. Gagnon, "Masturbatory Behavior in College Youth," *Journal of Sex Education and Therapy* 13, (1987), 35–42.

63. Sorensen, *Adolescent Sexuality in Contemporary America,* 129.

64. Jack O. Balswick and Judith K. Balswick, *The Family* (Grand Rapids, Mich.: Baker, 1991), 185; Les Parrot, *Helping the Struggling Adolescent* (Grand Rapids: Zondervan, 1993), 182.

65. Gary R. Collins, *Christian Counseling* , rev. ed. (Dallas, Tex.: Word, 1988), 261; John S. Feinberg and Paul D. Feinberg, *Ethics for a Brave New World* (Wheaton, Ill.: Crossway Books, 1993), 163.

On the other hand, for the teenager, masturbation is often accompanied by feelings of guilt, frustration, self-condemnation, and anger over its compulsiveness, although these disorders are not attributable to the practice alone. These feelings may exist partially as a result of the forbidding and condemning attitudes of society and various religions, even though these postures today are very different from those in years past.

While masturbation is widely practiced and hotly debated, the Bible is silent on the subject; this silence makes it difficult for some Christians to speak to the issue.[66] And where there is lack of clarity about an issue or practice, there is usually a variety of positions or views. Christians specializing in sex education and ethics generally hold to one of three positions, none of which is completely satisfactory.

The more restrictive position suggests that masturbation under any condition is sin. Jay Adams holds to this view and bases his position on four principles: 1) it is adultery of the heart, 2) the Bible does not present it as an option, 3) it is a perversion of the sexual act, and 4) we must not be mastered by anything.[67] The Roman Catholic Church has much to say on the subject of masturbation. Historically, the Church's hierarchical magisterium has taught that masturbation is a moral evil and forbids its practice. The Church prohibits masturbation because it is a deviation from the creation of new life through intercourse and thus violates the will of God.[68]

The permissive position holds that masturbation is healthy and morally permissible in all or most circumstances. Charlie Shedd, for example, calls masturbation "a gift of God," the wise provision of a wise God. To teenagers he says, "So long as masturbation is not humiliating; so long as it helps you to keep on the good side of sociable; so long as you

---

66. While the Bible does not speak directly to the issue of masturbation, there are those who attempt to present a biblical basis for their views on the subject. For example, James R. Johnson, "Toward a Biblical Approach to Masturbation," in *Journal of Psychology and Theology* 10, (Summer 1982), 137–46 suggests that biblical principles limit the practice of masturbation but do not preclude it. Clifford L. Penner, "A Reaction to Johnson's Biblical Approach to Masturbation," in *Journal of Psychology and Theology* 10, (Summer 1982), 147–49 however, argues that Johnson's conclusions are founded on his *interpretations* of the text rather than on the text itself.

67. Jay Adams, *The Christian Counselor's Manual* (Grand Rapids: Baker, 1973).

68. Michael D. Place, "Masturbation," in Richard P. McBrien, gen. ed., *The Harper-Collins Encyclopedia of Catholicism* (San Francisco, Calif.: HarperSanFrancisco, 1995), 841.

can accept it as a natural part of growing up; then you thank God for it and use it as a blessing!"[69]

Perhaps the most helpful and reasonable approach is the middle position which argues that masturbation can be a healthy way of releasing sexual tension and frustration, but has the potential to be morally unhealthy and inappropriate as well. This is the view of Herbert Miles who, in his book, has sections titled "When is Masturbation Sinful?" and "When is Masturbation Not Sinful?" In answer to the first question, he suggests it is sinful when: 1) one's sole motive is sheer biological pleasure unrelated to anything else, 2) when it becomes a controlling, compulsive habit, 3) when the habit results in feelings of inferiority and guilt, and 4) when the individual accompanies the activity with viewing pornography or sensual pictures, and fantasizes having sex relations with the woman depicted. In this case the boy is involved in lust and is guilty of adultery of the heart (Matthew 5:28).[70]

When, then, is it not sinful? He says, "When masturbation is practiced on a limited basis for the sole purpose of self-control, when it is guided by basic Christian principles, and has no evil results, it is an acceptable act. It is not lust. It should not be followed by guilt feelings."[71] This middle position will not be a satisfactory response to many people; on the other hand, any view taken will draw a certain amount of criticism.

The following observations will be helpful to share in small, same-sex youth groups:[72]

• Masturbation is very common.
• It is of no harm physically and is not the cause of any mental illnesses.
• It can be harmful if it becomes compulsive, excessive, or accompanied by lust. It can produce guilt, self-centeredness, and low self-esteem.
• Masturbation is never mentioned in the Bible, and we should be careful not to make strong arguments from silence. God does not affirm or condemn it in scripture.
• Masturbation can be helpful in relieving tensions, and is a substitute for sexual intercourse apart from marriage.
• Masturbation is rarely stopped simply by a determination to quit.

69. Charlie Shedd, *The Stork is Dead* (Waco, Tex.: Word, 1968), 73.
70. J. Herbert Miles, *Sexual Understanding Before Marriage* (Grand Rapids, Mich.: Zondervan, 1971), 145–46.
71. Ibid., 147.
72. Summarized from Collins, *Christian Counseling,* 261–62.

• Masturbation can be reduced by prayer, allowing the Holy Spirit to control one's thoughts, being accountable to another person, avoiding sexually arousing materials (certain movies, television shows, magazines, or novels), resisting the urge to dwell on sexual fantasies, and simply by keeping busy.

Adolescent Homosexuality

With the onset of puberty, Rob began to realize some differences between himself and the other guys. While other males his age began to develop fascinations for girls, he was preoccupied with other guys. Even in his earlier childhood, he recalls, he was different—always on the fringe, never one of the gang. In early adolescence Rob realized he was looking at boys because he was gay, and his romantic dream was to save himself for marriage to another man.[73]

For a very small percentage of adolescents, the sexual experience includes homosexual acts or feelings. Homosexuality is defined as a condition whereby an individual prefers sexual involvement with members of the same sex. When referring specifically to a female who has same-sex preference, the term "lesbian" is used; "gay" is a word often used to describe a male homosexual.

Homosexuals cannot be stereotyped. They come from all socioeconomic backgrounds, all age groups, and they possess a variety of interests. All effeminate males are not homosexual, and some masculine, athletic types engage in sexual activity with members of the same sex. Parents and youth religious educators should be cognizant of the fact that homosexuals are found in churches and youth groups, as well as in the unchurched community.[74]

It is difficult to determine precisely how many adolescent homosexuals currently exist or if that number is growing. Some teenagers have engaged in at least one homosexual experience. Nonetheless, since the adolescent years are a time of identity seeking and exploration, most of these teenagers have had no subsequent homosexual relationships. While gays and lesbians are very vocal, Robert Sorensen found that only 9 percent of all adolescents in his survey reported ever having one

---

73. Adapted from Ed Hurst, *Overcoming Homosexuality* (Elgin, Ill.: David C. Cook, 1988), 7–8.
74. Ibid., 14–15.

or more homosexual experiences.[75] While youth workers may feel ill at ease and inadequate in addressing this thorny problem, it is highly probable that some of the adolescents in their groups are struggling with homosexuality.

Important Distinctions: The current debate on homosexuality demands that some critical distinctions be made, notably the differences between homosexual behavior, homosexual orientation, and the practice of homosexuality as a life-style. *Homosexual behavior* simply refers to engaging in sexual activity with a member of the same sex. In some cases these actions are forced upon an individual, in other situations they may be a unique, one-time occurrence, or experimentation. Thus, homosexual behavior does not necessarily indicate that an individual is a homosexual person.

Some individuals may be described as having a *homosexual orientation* or *disposition*. These persons may feel a sexual attraction toward members of the same sex but for one reason or another choose not to engage in homosexual behavior. It must be noted that nowhere in Scripture is an individual condemned simply for having homosexual tendencies or feelings.[76] However, when one dwells on homosexual thoughts and engages in fantasy, then thoughts become lust, and lust is sin.[77]

A *practicing homosexual* is one who engages in homosexual activity, at least periodically, over a long period of time. This willful practice or way of life is unambiguously condemned and forbidden by scripture (Lev. 18:22, 20:13; Rom. 1:26–27; I Cor. 6:9–11).[78]

---

75. Sorensen, *Adolescent Sexuality in Contemporary America,* 285.

76. Episcopal priest and seminary professor Philip E. Hughes, *Christian Ethics in Secular Society* (Grand Rapids: Baker, 1983), 175, argues that to be strongly tempted or disposed to engage in homosexual activity is not itself sin. The sin is in doing it, not in the temptation to do it. This view is not held by all Christians. Reformed ethicist Greg Bahnsen, *Homosexuality: A Biblical View* (Grand Rapids, Mich.: Baker, 1978), 63–84, argues that no distinction should be made between the outward homosexual act and the inward homosexual condition. He argues that homosexuality is immoral in any context, whether it be outward acts, desire, or inclination.

77. Collins, *Christian Counseling,* 282.

78. Feinberg and Feinberg, *Ethics for a Brave New World,* 189–201 and Hughes, *Christian Ethics in Secular Society,* 173–79 argue that certain scripture passages clearly condemn homosexual practice. There are a growing number of theologians and ethicists, however, who feel that the Bible does not condemn a loving sexual relationship between two homosexuals. For a review of those who would not judge homosexual acts as wrong,

The Ethic of Love: In effectively working with the adolescent who either struggles with homosexual thoughts or is practicing homosexuality, it is the responsibility of the youth minister or volunteer worker to first check his or her own attitude concerning homosexuals. If the youth religious educator retains a revulsion about them, jokes about them, condemns them, uncritically stereotypes them, or is unfamiliar with the complexity of homosexuality, then in all probability he or she will be ineffective in ministering to them. Jesus loved sinners and those who were tempted to sin. Youth religious educators who follow in his footsteps should do the same. If youth workers sense no inner compassion for overt homosexuals or for people with homosexual tendencies, then they must ask God to give them the compassion they lack.[79]

Loneliness and Acceptance: For the homosexual teenager the world can be an extremely lonely place. When young people discover that they have homosexual tendencies or feelings, they often experience a measure of terror and anxiety. Afraid to let other youth, teachers, or even their families know of their sexual tendencies, many homosexual adolescents live in fear of being exposed and exist in a world of social alienation. One man describes what it was like for him to grow up gay: "The only goal left to me in life was to hide anything that could identify me as gay. . . . I thought that anything I did might somehow reveal my homosexuality, and my morale sank even deeper. The more I tried to safeguard myself from the outside world, the more vulnerable I felt. I withdrew from everyone and slowly formed a shell around myself. Everyone could be a potential threat to me. I resembled a crustacean with no claws; I had my shell for protection, yet I would never do anything to hurt someone else. Sitting on a rock under thousands of pounds of pressure, surrounded by enemies, the most I could hope for was that no one would cause me more harm than my shell could endure."[80]

One might think that the church or youth program would be one place a teenager struggling with homosexuality might find relief from

---

see Charles E. Curran, "Homosexuality and Moral Theology: Methodological and Substantive Considerations," in Edward Batchelor, Jr., editor, *Homosexuality and Ethics* (New York: Pilgrim Press, 1980), 171–85. Letha Scanzoni and Virginia Mollenkott, *Is the Homosexual My Neighbor?* (San Francisco: Harper & Row, 1978) use a liberal interpretation of scripture to allow for certain forms of homosexual relationships.

79. Collins, *Christian Counseling,* 287.

80. Quoted in Myra Pollack Sadker and David Miller Sadker, *Teachers, Schools, and Society,* 3d ed. (New York: McGraw-Hill, 1994), 463.

his or her loneliness and sense of alienation. In reality, the church has been one of the least accepting institutions toward homosexuals. However, the watchword for churches, suggests David Field, should be acceptance. This does not imply an uncritical recognition of homosexual behavior as acceptable; it does mean that Christians should accept those with homosexual conditions as fellow sinners and love them as fellow sinners.[81]

The youth ministry program should provide an environment where young people with homosexual tendencies can talk about their problem and are treated in the same manner as any other individual who commits a sin. It is unfortunate that so many Christians react to homosexuals with condemnation and horror. Growing up in such an environment, adolescents learn to fear homosexuals and to suppress any gay tendencies within themselves. Instead of admitting and dealing with one's same-sex preferences, the struggling teenager keeps them hidden deep inside.[82]

When the struggling homosexual cannot get help and understanding from the church, youth group, or youth pastor, he or she may drift toward homosexual groups who *are* understanding, accepting, and loving. By its condemning and attitude of nonacceptance, therefore, the church sometimes inadvertently pushes people into situations in which overt homosexual behavior is encouraged.[83]

To the Homosexual Teenager: To the homosexual teenager it must be absolutely clear that homosexual behavior is wrong. In the case of sexual practice, the homosexual is in the same position as a straight person whose situation demands abstinence. Sexual self-control is important regardless of one's sexual orientation and can be nurtured through prayer and meditation, avoidance of sexually arousing situations or people, deliberate decisions to avoid sexual activity, and accountability to a friend or youth worker.

TEENAGE PREGNANCY

It's not a pretty picture. It's not a TV soap opera either. The reality of pregnancy outside of marriage is scary and lonely. To have

81. David Field, *The Homosexual Way—A Christian Option?* (Downers Grove, Ill.: InterVarsity, 1979), 41.
82. Collins, *Christian Counseling,* 287.
83. Ibid.

premarital sex was my choice one hot June night, forcing many decisions I thought I would never have to make. Those decisions radically changed my life.[84]

Problems related to teenage sexual activity are complex and wide-ranging. One of the most critical issues of adolescent sexual development and activity, however, is that of teenage pregnancy or "babies having babies." And one source says that the United States is in the midst of a teenage pregnancy epidemic that is unrivaled by any other industrialized nation.[85] The following statistics highlight the critical situation in America:[86]

• Approximately 1.1 million teenage girls become pregnant each year; about half carry the pregnancy to term.

• More than 3,000 teenage girls become pregnant every day; about 75 percent of these will be unintentional.

• Of girls under the age of 15, 125,000 become pregnant each year.

• About 24 percent of all girls will become pregnant before the age of 18. Compare this to a 1972 study which found that 10 percent of all American female adolescents reported having been pregnant at least once.[87]

• Four out of five teenagers who become pregnant are unmarried.[88]

The rising incidence in teenage pregnancies is due largely to the increased sexual activity of American youth. It was mentioned earlier in this chapter that teenagers in the United States are engaging in sexual intercourse at younger and younger ages. Moreover, for those youth who are sexually active, a good percentage of them use no form of contraception. According to a national survey of 15- to 19-year-olds, approximately 25 percent of the respondents who had sexual activity the three months prior to the survey failed to use contraception of any kind during the last sexual intercourse.[89] The pregnancy rate

---

84. Quoted from McDowell and Day, *Why Wait?*, 16.

85. Sadker and Sadker, *Teachers, Schools, and Society,* 450.

86. Except where stated otherwise, the following statistics are summarized from McWhirter et al., *At-Risk Youth,* 138.

87. Sorensen, *Adolescent Sexuality in Contemporary America,* 303.

88. Bonnidell Clouse, "Adolescent Moral Development and Sexuality," in Donald Ratcliff and James A. Davies, eds., *Handbook of Youth Ministry* (Birmingham, Ala.: Religious Education Press, 1991), 196.

89. Centers for Disease Control, "Sexual Behavior Among High School Students— United States, 1990," 885. For additional statistics and comments concerning adolescent

among American youth is much higher than the rate in most Western countries, yet sexual activity in these nations is comparable to levels in the United States. The reason for the high pregnancy rates among American teenagers appears to be because U.S. youth are reluctant to adopt contraception.[90]

The increase in teenage sexual activity and subsequent pregnancies might be traced to several additional factors: 1) a decline in the number of teenage marriages and an increased willingness to have a child outof wedlock,[91] 2) an increasingly early onset of puberty coupled with a rising mean age of marriage, which makes the time gap between physical maturity and marriage much greater,[92] 3) society's increasing acceptance and tolerance of premarital sex and pregnancy of unwed mothers, and 4) easy access to abortion.

Health, community, and public school officials who see teenage pregnancy and birth rates climb despite so called progressive programs and strategies are frustrated, perplexed, and groping for explanations. For example, a Colorado high school that became the first in the state to introduce a teenage parenting program, including an on-campus nursery and the handing out of condoms, found the birth rate to soar to 31 percent above the national average.[93]

Once a teenage girl becomes pregnant, she faces several options: 1) she could raise the child by herself, 2) she could marry the father, 3) she could get an abortion, 4) she could have the child raised or informally "adopted" by a family member, or 5) she could give the child up for adoption.

Single Parenthood: The choice to keep the child may appear to be an attractive option to the pregnant teenager. In fact 90 percent of white teens and 97 percent of African-American teenagers who carry their pregnancy to term keep their babies rather than give them up for adoption.[94] However, adolescent girls usually lack adequate financial

---

contraception practices, see Brent C. Miller and Kristin A. Moore, "Adolescent Sexual Behavior, Pregnancy, and Parenting: Research Through the 1980s," in *Journal of Marriage and the Family* 52, (November 1990), 1025–44.

90. Miller and Moore, "Adolescent Sexual Behavior, Pregnancy, and Parenting: Research Through the 1980s," 1025–44.

91. Ibid.

92. McWhirter et al., *At-Risk Youth,* 138.

93. Jana Mazanec, "Birth Rate Soars at Colorado School," in *USA Today,* May 19, 1992, 3A.

94. McWhirter et al., *At-Risk Youth,* 139.

and physical resources to care for their children and frequently do not have the financial, physical, or emotional support of the child's father. In some cases, they may be rejected or shunned by their own family. Additional drawbacks may include an inability to effectively nurture an infant, the loss of a normal social life, and the inability to complete secondary education. Many times the children of teenage pregnancies become parents themselves in twelve to sixteen years, thus repeating the cycle. Consequently it is not uncommon for a young woman to become a grandmother before reaching the age of 30. Furthermore, teenage girls often choose to keep or even intentionally have a child for the wrong reasons: to keep a boyfriend, to force a marriage, to gain attention, to have someone they can love and hold, or even to spite a parent.[95]

Marriage: Marriage may appear to be the socially correct thing to do, but parenthood for teenage couples also brings with it acute problems. Adolescent married mothers still experience many of the struggles and difficulties unwed mothers do. They experience the loss of normal adolescent social life, lost educational opportunities, and financial difficulties. Many teenage mothers lack parenting skills. Empirical research data indicate that adolescent parents are significantly more at risk for child abuse and neglect; infants of teenage parents have disproportionately high numbers of developmental problems.[96] Furthermore, the divorce rate for teenage marriages (most of which are associated with pregnancy) is extremely high.[97] Only 20 percent of teen pregnancies result in marriage.[98]

Abortion: Many unmarried adolescent girls who find themselves in the unfortunate situation of expecting a baby opt for abortion, the external intervention into the reproduction process with the intent of terminating pregnancy.[99] Among pregnant adolescents, approximately 42 percent choose to terminate the life of their child, amounting to about

---

95. For more extensive descriptions of the consequences for unmarried teenaged girls who keep their babies see McWhirter et al., *At-Risk Youth,* 143–45; Miller and Moore, "Adolescent Sexual Behavior, Pregnancy, and Parenting: Research Through the 1980s," 1025–44.

96. Louise Guerney and Joyce Arthur, "Adolescent Social Relationships," in Richard M. Lerner and Nancy L. Galambos, eds., *Experiencing Adolescents* (New York: Garland, 1984), 105.

97. Ibid., 104.

98. McWhirter et al., *At-Risk Youth,* 145.

99. This definition of abortion is given by Feinberg and Feinberg, *Ethics for a Brave New World,* 50.

400,000 teenage abortions a year.[100] Adolescents account for over 25 percent of all abortions carried out in the United States, giving this country one of the highest rates of teenage abortions among developed countries.[101]

While in some nations abortion is an accepted practice with little controversy, in countries such as the United States and Canada few ethical or social issues incite more public or personal debate and discord. While the issue is complex and the arguments are numerous, essentially two predominant views exist: pro-choice and pro-life. *Pro-choice* advocates, including many theologically liberal Christians, argue that it is a woman's paramount privilege to choose or control what to do with her body, including the abortion of fetuses.[102] *Pro-life* or anti-abortion proponents, including most conservative Protestants and many Roman Catholics, oppose the practice of destroying a fetus.[103]

Central to the abortion debate are the questions of the beginning of life and personhood. Pro-choice supporters, such as Beverly Harrison, argue that while the fetus is *a* form of life, it is not yet a "person." For those who advocate choice, birth is the critical developmental mark for conferring full human standing.[104] On the other hand, most individuals who hold to a pro-life position believe the fetus becomes a human life at conception.[105]

---

100. McWhirter et al., *At-Risk Youth,* 139; Miller and Moore, "Adolescent Sexual Behavior, Pregnancy, and Parenting: Research Through the 1980s," 1025–44.

101. McWhirter et al., *At-Risk Youth,* 139; U.S. Bureau of the Census, *Statistical Abstract of the United States: 1993* (113th ed.) Washington, D.C., 1993, 83.

102. For example, see Beverly Wildung Harrison, *Our Right to Choose* (Boston: Beacon, 1983).

103. Most pro-life advocates allow for abortion in special situations such as: 1) abortion to save a mother's life, and 2) abortion in the case of rape or incest. For example, see Feinberg and Feinberg, *Ethics for a Brave New World,* 73–79 and Norman L. Geisler, *Ethics: Alternatives and Issues* (Grand Rapids, Mich.: Zondervan, 1971), 220–26.

104. Harrison, *Our Right to Choose,* 217–19. Mary Anne Warren is quoted by Harrison as proposing the following criteria for personhood: 1) consciousness, 2) reasoning, 3) self-motivated activity, 4) the capacity to communicate, and 5) the presence of self-concepts and self-awareness. Harrison goes on to suggest that a fetus possesses none of these criteria of a normal "person."

105. Feinberg and Feinberg, *Ethics for a Brave New World,* 73–79. Baruch Brody, *Abortion and the Sanctity of Human Life: A Philosophical View* (Cambridge, Mass.: MIT Press, 1975), 80, identifies six alternatives as to when the fetus becomes life: the moment of conception; the time at which segmentation takes place; the time at which fetal brain activity commences; the time at which the mother feels movement of the

The debate over abortion is extremely sensitive, and emotions run high on both sides of the issue. Advocates in each camp accuse the others of being uncaring or insensitive. The reality is that there are caring and sensitive people in each group. Pro-choice people are interested in protecting the right to a girl's choice over what she does with her body as well as being concerned about bringing an unloved or unwanted child into the world. On the other hand pro-life or anti-abortion supporters affirm the unborn baby's right to life. If it is wrong to unjustly kill a person after birth, is it not just as wrong to take a life before birth?

It is my position that except in rare situations in which the baby must be sacrificed to save the mother's life, abortion is wrong. What about pregnancy resulting from the horrifying crimes of rape or incest? Christians who oppose abortion are divided on whether or not abortion should be permissible under such circumstances. Norman Geisler, for example, argues that in the instances of rape and incest there is no moral obligation placed upon a girl to carry through with her pregnancy.[106] John and Paul Feinberg, while genuinely sensitive and compassionate toward the victims of such crimes, offer several arguments against abortion even in cases of rape and incest: 1) it is never right to do evil to achieve good; 2) while rape and incest are acts of violence, so is abortion; 3) it is never right to commit murder to alleviate suffering; 4) both physical and psychological harm or pain may come to the mother who aborts.[107]

What about bringing any child into this world who is unwanted or will be unloved because of the situation in which it was conceived? Because a child is unwanted by its birth mother does not mean a child is altogether unwanted. Today there are a large number of couples who are unable to have children themselves and desperately wish to adopt. The youth religious educator, when working with a pregnant teenager, should encourage the girl to carry the baby to term and then make the baby available for a couple who very much want a child of their own.

How does the youth worker respond to the teenage girl in the youth group who has undergone an abortion? At this point the goal is not to condemn or instill guilt. Instead, the sensitive and compassionate

---

fetus; the time at which the fetus has a reasonable chance of surviving if born; and the moment of birth.

106. Geisler, *Ethics: Alternatives and Issues*, 222–23.

107. Feinberg and Feinberg, *Ethics for a Brave New World*, 77–79.

youth religious educator should try to help the girl experience God's forgiveness and assist her in working through the grief process that may follow an abortion.

Some girls may suffer what is called post-abortion syndrome (PAS), some form of negative psychological reaction to her abortion. In a collection of interviews by Linda Francke of women who had experienced abortion, approximately 70 percent expressed some type of negative feeling such as guilt, shame, anxiety, anger, and grief.[108]

According to another survey of women who had at least one abortion, 94 percent of the respondents reported they had experienced negative psychological effects attributable to their abortions. Approximately 20 percent said that they actually made at least one suicide attempt, and many others reported that they were unable to put the abortion out of their minds.[109] Most communities and cities have a pro-life crisis counseling center that provide support groups and counseling for girls who may be suffering from some form of post-abortion syndrome. The youth religious educator should be familiar with the assistance available in his or her area, so that referral can be made when the need arises.[110]

Adoption: Clearly the preferred response to teenage pregnancy by Christian adults of all persuasions is adoption. Interestingly though, releasing a child for adoption is the least popular choice for teenagers. Contemporary teenagers are far less likely to relinquish their baby to formal adoption than they were in the past. Less than 10 percent of the unwed pregnant girls who carry their child to term plan for adoption.

One reason a teenage girl might hesitate to choose an adoption plan for her baby is the misconception that a loving person would not allow her child to be given away. Perhaps she thinks others will view her as cold or uncaring. The youth worker can remind this girl that in some situations adoption can be a very caring, loving, and responsible decision.

---

108. Linda Bird Francke, *The Ambivalence of Abortion* (New York: Random, 1978), 3, 61, 74, 81, 84, 91, 99, 104.

109. The empirical study was done by an organization called Women Exploited by Abortion (WEBA) and reported in David C. Reardon, *Aborted Women: Silent No More* (Westchester, Ill.: Crossway, 1987), 22–23. WEBA is an organization made up solely of women who have had an abortion.,

110. Local chapters of WEBA offer post-abortion counseling, help, and support to women and girls who have experienced abortion. WEBA may be listed in the phone directory, or can be located through a local or state right-to-life organization. The address for the national U.S. headquarters is Box 267, Schoolcraft, Mich. 49087.

Adoption can be a traumatic experience for a young girl. Releasing a baby for adoption marks the end of one of life's most intimate relationships. After carrying a child for nine months, giving birth, and then relinquishing the child to strangers will most likely be extremely difficult. It is then that the girl may experience postpartum depression. The challenge to the youth worker during these vulnerable times is to be available to the girl, especially during the hospital stay and the weeks following her discharge. Visits, flowers, cards, or anything else that lets the teenager know she is being thought of by the youth worker and her peers will be helpful.[111]

Some adolescent mothers, particularly those younger girls in whom abstract and hypothetical reasoning are not fully developed, will benefit from structured individual or small group contact with peers who have chosen to release their baby through adoption, those who have kept their child, or adoptees. Often young adolescents have a difficult time perceiving the reality of the difficulty of rearing a child. They consider only the innocent-looking, helpless infant and cannot fathom relinquishing the child. They have difficulty imagining the difficult and frustrating times they may have ahead should they choose to keep their infant. Group experiences with other teenagers who have relinquished or parented a baby can help girls see the reality of parenting beyond infancy. These experiences can also give them the opportunity to talk to adoptees about their perceptions of being adopted and the feelings they have about their birth mothers.[112]

Finally, the youth religious educator can assist the girl in the adoption process by putting her in touch with a credible adoption agency. In the United States each state licenses public or private agencies to serve as adoption agencies. Public agencies are usually subsidiaries of the state and may be called the state welfare program or child welfare department. Private adoption agencies are typically nonprofit organizations, often operated by churches or denominations. The agency serves as an intermediary or middleman between the mother and the adopting parents. In private and public agencies the procedure is essentially the same. The birth mother signs legal documents relinquishing the rights to her child

---

111. For additional insights in assisting an unwed teenage mother through adoption see the manual by Cheryl Kreykes Brandsen, *A Case for Adoption* (Grand Rapids, Mich.: Bethany Christian Services, 1985).

112. Ibid., 39.

in favor of the agency. The agency then places the child with the parents who have been selected for the adoption.[113]

SEXUALLY TRANSMITTED DISEASES

Premarital sexual activity brings with it the possibility of contracting one or more sexually transmitted diseases (STDs). Over 2.5 million American teenagers contract STDs annually, and the rates of these diseases among adolescents are escalating.[114] More startling is the fact that teenagers have more STDs than any other group in the United States. One source suggests 75 percent of the cases occur among young people ages 15–24.[115] Another similarly reports the rate of STDs in the 16- to 20-year-old age group to be three times that of the general population.[116]

In 1981, approximately 20 STDs were identified; in 1993 there were around 60, with a new disease apparently being discovered every nine months.[117] For each of these diseases there are physical and often emotional consequences. The physical consequences of sexually transmitted diseases vary, but most are irreversible. Some sexual diseases can be cured and in some cases the severity of symptoms can be reduced, but other diseases such as genital herpes and AIDS are incurable.

With STDs comes a variety of symptomatic occurrences. For example, the symptoms of genital herpes for both sexes include blisters and open sores in the area of sexual organs. Males with gonorrhea experience a pus-like discharge, while for females, untreated gonorrhea can cause irreversible infertility.[118]

Chlamydia causes a penis discharge in males, while in females it brings about vaginal itching, abdominal pain, and bleeding. Syphilis

---

113. Douglas R. Donnelly, *A Guide to Adoption* (n.c.: Focus on the Family, 1987), 5. Bethany Christian Services is a national Christian organization that serves as an adopting agency. The address of the US national office is 901 Eastern Avenue, NE, Grand Rapids, Mich. 49503–1295. Their phone number is 1-800-238-4369.

114. McWhirter et al., *At-Risk Youth,* 145; John Ankerberg and John Weldon, *The Myth of Safe Sex* (Chicago: Moody, 1993), 56.

115. Evan Pattishall, "Health Issues in Adolescence," in Richard M. Lerner and Nancy L. Galambos, eds., *Experiencing Adolescents* (New York: Garland, 1984), 209.

116. Ankerberg and Weldon, *The Myth of Safe Sex*, 56.

117. Ibid., 53.

118. Alan E. Nourse, *Herpes* (New York: Franklin Watts, 1985), 72.

is a potentially severe, sexually transmitted disease that may, if left untreated, produce a variety of debilitating conditions including damage to the heart, the brain, or the spinal cord, and even premature death.[119]

Most tragic is the fact that, with sexually transmitted diseases, the consequences of the parents' sins are often passed on to the next generation. Babies of sexually infected mothers may be born with serious abnormalities including hearing loss, mental retardation and learning disabilities, blindness, and heads abnormally small or large. Some infants will be born prematurely, and many babies will experience death before or shortly after birth. Children born with AIDS are becoming increasingly common, and most children diagnosed with AIDS die within six months of birth.[120]

The suffering and pain that comes with STDs is not limited to the physical. A teenager who has contracted a sexually transmitted disease is likely to experience emotional trauma as well, including depression, embarrassment, and guilt. In some instances the diseased youth will suffer social isolation and loneliness.

It might be helpful to summarize several critical points about sexually transmitted diseases. No discussion of premarital sex with adolescents would be complete without emphasizing these important facts:[121]

• Unless there is a sudden and significant change in society's permissive attitude toward sexuality, casual and premarital sex are likely to continue.

• One of the very real dangers of casual sex is that members of both genders may acquire a sexually transmitted disease.

• STDs are infectious diseases, spread by sexual intercourse, and should be treated by a physician like any other infectious disease.

• Any male or female who develops a puslike discharge from the penis or vagina, or blisters or open sores in the area of sexual organs, should visit a physician and have tests made.

• Any teenager who has sexual intercourse with multiple partners should be examined by a medical doctor at regular intervals, so that infectious sexual diseases may be detected and treated.

---

119. Derek Llewellyn-Jones, *Herpes, AIDS and Other Sexually Transmitted Diseases* (London: Faber and Faber, 1985), 90–106.

120. The above comments are summarized from McDowell and Day, *Why Wait?*, 203–15, and Ankerberg and Weldon, *The Myth of Safe Sex*, 54–63. For more exhaustive descriptions of the consequences of STD's, the reader is referred to these two sources.

121. Llewellyn-Jones, *Herpes, AIDS and Other Sexually Transmitted Diseases*, 17–18.

Upon discovering that an adolescent has acquired an STD or may have been exposed to an STD, the youth religious educator should refer that person to a physician immediately. As was mentioned earlier, serious danger results from failure to medically treat sexually transmitted diseases. Teenagers who test positive must also tell anyone with whom they have had sexual intercourse.

THE PLIGHT OF AIDS

"Everybody knows that pestilence has a way of recurring in the world, yet somehow we find it hard to believe that one can crash down on our heads from a blue sky. There have been as many plagues as there have been wars in history, yet always these plagues and these wars take us by surprise. A pestilence isn't a thing made to man's measure, therefore, we tell ourselves that these pestilences are nothing but a bogey of the mind, a bad dream that will pass away. But, it doesn't pass away, and from one bad dream to another, it is the men who pass away." (Albert Camus, "The Plague")[122]

Since ancient times humankind has been ravaged by plagues or communicable diseases as devastating and destructive as war itself. In the 1980s an epidemic began to spread throughout the world that has the potential to become as deadly as the bubonic plague or Black Death that marked the end of the Middle Ages—*acquired immunodeficiency syndrome,* commonly known as AIDS. In fact, AIDS has already taken more American lives than did the Vietnam War. The first cases of AIDS were reported in the United States in 1981; by 1993 more than 300,000 individuals had developed AIDS and over 200,000 had died from the disease.[123] The global statistical projections for the year 2000 are 30 million adults and 10 million children infected with the *human immunodeficiency virus* (HIV), the virus that actually causes AIDS.[124]

Gay men account for the majority of AIDS cases, although injecting drug users are at high risk as well. Cases due to heterosexual contact have been increasing, and many children are contracting the deadly disease

---

122. Albert Camus, *The Plague* (New York: Vintage, 1948).

123. *Surgeon General's Report to the American Public on HIV Infection and AIDS* (Rockville, Md.: Centers for Disease Control and Prevention, n.d.), 1.

124. Henry P. Bellutta, "AIDS," in David Levinson, editor, *Encyclopedia of Marriage and the Family, Vol. 1* (New York: Simon & Schuster Macmillan, 1995), 27–31.

through infected mothers. Other people have contracted the disease through blood transfusions and the receipt of blood clotting factors. AIDS always results in death, usually in a slow, painful, and traumatic manner.

AIDS is actually caused by the *human immunodeficiency virus* (HIV) which enters the blood and infects certain cells. Once these cells begin to die, flulike symptoms appear. As the disease progresses, the conditions get more severe. In the final stage, the patient is diagnosed with full-blown AIDS and by this time is suffering from extreme tiredness, loss of weight, diarrhea, high temperatures, and sight loss. Thus, an individual could test HIV positive yet not have AIDS. The great majority of those who have HIV, however, will contract AIDS. Full AIDS can take nearly ten years to develop from initial contraction of HIV.[125] AIDS destroys the immune system, making the body easily susceptible to a large number of fatal diseases such as pneumonia, tuberculosis, or cancers, which it normally would be able to ward off.

AIDS is making frightening inroads into the adolescent population as the following statistics indicate:

• Through June 1995, a total of 2,284 AIDS cases among adolescents aged 13 to 19 years have been reported.[126]

• The number of AIDS cases among adolescents reported each year has increased from one case in 1981 to 417 cases in 1994.[127]

• In the 20- to 24-year-old age bracket, 18,000 cases have been reported by June 1995; more than 69,000 persons ages 25–29 have been reported with AIDS to the Centers for Disease Control and Prevention.[128] These figures are perhaps more indicative of the magnitude of the AIDS problem for teenagers because of the long incubation period. These young people clearly would have contracted the HIV virus in their adolescent years.

• Twenty percent, or one in five, of the AIDS patients are 20 to 29 years old (once again, they probably contracted HIV in their teens).[129]

---

125. McWhirter et al., *At-Risk Youth,* 145–46, and Ankerberg and Weldon, *The Myth of Safe Sex,* 66–67.
126. Centers For Disease Control and Prevention, *Facts About Adolescents and HIV/AIDS* (December 1995), fact sheet.
127. Ibid.
128. Ibid.
129. McWhirter et al., *At-Risk Youth,* 146; Centers for Disease Control, *HIV/AIDS Surveillance Report* (Atlanta: U.S. Department of Health and Human Services, Public Health Service, May, 1993), 11.

• In 1989 AIDS became the sixth leading cause of death among persons aged 15 to 24.[130]

According to the Centers for Disease Control (CDC), the breakdown of AIDS cases among adolescents (13–19 years) in the United States by exposure category is as follows: males who have sex with males (25 percent), those who inject drugs (13 percent), those who have heterosexual contact with HIV-risk partners (12 percent), males who have sex with males and inject drugs (4 percent), those who receive treatment for blood clotting (31 percent), and those who receive a blood transfusion (7 percent).[131] Among adolescents, HIV infection is more prevalent among males, but recent trends also point to a rise in diagnosis and infection among adolescent females. In 1987, 14 percent of the diagnosed cases of AIDS among adolescents were females; in 1994 that figure grew to 43 percent.[132]

While teenagers are very much aware of AIDS and the serious threat to life it brings, change in sexual behavior may be minimal. The Centers for Disease Control reports the percentage of students who received HIV instruction in school increased from 54 to 83 percent during 1989–1991. However, during that same period only slight declines occurred in the percentages of students who reported ever having sexual intercourse (59 percent to 54 percent), having two or more partners in a lifetime (40 percent to 35 percent), and having four or more sex partners during a lifetime (24 percent to 19 percent). This is not exactly a radical turnaround in sexual behaviors. Among those high school students who reported ever having had sexual intercourse, the percentage of those who said they used condoms did not change significantly from 1990 (46 percent) to 1991 (48 percent).[133] In Canada, approximately the same proportion of teenagers (about 55 percent) engaged in sexual intercourse in 1992 as in 1984.[134]

130. Centers for Disease Control, "Selected Behaviors That Increase Risk For HIV Infection Among High School Students—United States, 1990," in *Morbidity and Mortality Weekly Report* 41, (April 1992), 231.

131. Centers for Disease Control and Prevention, *Facts About Adolescents and HIV/AIDS* (February 1993), fact sheet.

132. Centers for Disease Control and Prevention, *Facts About Adolescents and HIV/AIDS* (December 1995), fact sheet.

133. Centers for Disease Control, "HIV Instruction and Selected HIV-Risk Behaviors Among High School Students—United States, 1989–1991," in *Morbidity And Mortality Weekly Report,* 41, (November 1992), 866–68.

134. Bibby and Posterski, *Teen Trends,* 47.

While AIDS awareness is not a problem with adolescents, it appears that the reality of AIDS is hardly causing teenagers to jump on the abstinence bandwagon; nor is it changing their behavior in the use of condoms. Young people tend to have the attitude that it could never happen to them, that they are somehow invulnerable to something as catastrophic and devastating as AIDS. Unfortunately some teenagers have trouble believing that they can become infected with HIV since they rarely see people their age who have AIDS. Because of the possible ten-year lag time between contracting the HIV virus and acquiring AIDS, patients may not show symptoms until they are in their twenties.

The chance of the youth religious educator encountering a teenager with full-blown AIDS will be quite slim. However the youth worker can help adolescents assess their risk for contracting AIDS. If teenagers answer yes to any of the following blunt questions, they could have the HIV infection.

1. Have you ever had unprotected anal, vaginal, or oral sex with a male or female who
   - you know was infected with AIDS?
   - injects or has injected drugs?
   - shared needles with an HIV-infected person?
   - had sex with someone who shared needles?
   - had multiple sex partners?

2. Have you ever used syringes or needles that were used by anyone before you?

3. Have you ever given or received sex for money or drugs?

4. Have you had sex with someone who had a blood transfusion or received clotting factors between 1978 and 1985?

If the adolescents answer yes to any of the above questions, they should be referred to a doctor or health clinic where they can talk about the situation, get more information, and decide if testing for HIV needs to be done. Another option for the teenagers who are looking for counseling and testing for HIV is the community health center or public clinic. Some sites will do a test free of charge; others will charge a fee.[135]

---

135. To find a testing site near you call the CDC National AIDS Hotline (1-800-342-2437). For further information concerning AIDS, write CDC National AIDS Clearinghouse, Box 6003, Rockville, Md., 20849–6003.

Youth religious educators must do all they can to make adolescents aware of AIDS and its deadly consequences. Teenagers must be presented with the data related to these diseases, and warned of the dangers and irreversible consequences that may accompany sexual activity. They must be persuaded that the only truly effective means of preventing HIV infection is refraining from sexual intercourse until marriage, and then limiting sexual activity to a monogamous husband-wife relationship.

"What about safe sex?" some teenagers may argue. The only genuinely safe sex is abstinence before marriage and monogamy within marriage. The Centers for Disease Control says, "Although the risk for HIV infection is decreased by correct use of condoms and reduction of the number of sex partners, these approaches do not completely eliminate the risk."[136] Ankerberg and Weldon add that the only solution to STDs such as AIDS is a radical change in sexual attitudes and behavior. To risk infertility, lifelong pain and suffering, cancer and other diseases, or even death is absurd. To teach our own youth and children that safe sex is the solution seems almost criminal.[137] Even the CDC states its first goal is to help decrease the proportion of highschool students who have initial intercourse.

Adolescents should be taught certain facts about AIDS. For example, it is important for them to know how this infectious disease is transmitted and how it is not. AIDS is transmitted through the exchange of body fluids, usually by sexual contact or needle sharing, and not through casual social contact. They should know that condoms are only about 90 percent effective in preventing the contracting of HIV.

Some effective ways to teach adolescents about the crisis of AIDS and its deadly consequences include the following:
• Have someone with AIDS come and talk with the youth group about the tragic consequences of this disease. Be sure this person endorses sexual abstinence before marriage as the only truly form of safe sex.
• Have someone from the medical profession talk with the youth group about AIDS. Be sure opportunity is given for a time of questions and answers.
• Have a panel discussion on AIDS. Possibilities for panel members include a pastor, a medical doctor, an AIDS patient, and/or a parent or sibling of someone with AIDS.

---

136. Centers for Disease Control, "Selected Behaviors," 239.
137. Ankerberg and Weldon, *The Myth of Safe Sex*, 63.

- Use current statistics or a video clip as a starter for a discussion on AIDS.[138]
- Have youth group members visit an AIDS patient in his or her home or in the hospital. Encourage the youth to consider this visit as an opportunity to minister and reach out to someone who is suffering a slow and agonizing death. Following the visit, spend some time debriefing. Talk about topics such as the physical and emotional consequences of AIDS, the importance of abstinence from premarital sex, and the response Christians should have to AIDS and those suffering from the disease.[139]

ADOLESCENT SEX OFFENDERS

The sexual revolution begun in the 1960s has wrought more disturbing trends than were previously imagined. One trend that has been identified by experts is the sexual abuse of children by other children and adolescents. In 1989 *The Atlanta Constitution,* one of the leading newspapers in the United States, ran a startling report titled "New Sex Abuse Trend: Kids Attacking Kids." In the article the following hideous crimes were described:

- "A 6-year-old Atlanta girl was at home playing video games when she was dragged into a bedroom and raped. Her alleged assailant: a 13-year-old neighborhood boy.
- In a middle-class suburb of northeast Atlanta, a 14-year-old girl was asleep in her bed recently when she was attacked, beaten and raped. The rapist was her 17-year old brother.
- An Atlanta woman learned that her 4-year-old son had gonorrhea, a sexually transmitted disease. Police eventually identified the boy's molester as his baby-sitter's grandson—a 12-year-old boy who admitted he had both anal and oral sex with the child."[140]

---

138. Group Publishing offers a series of videos called *Hot Talk Starters.* Video No. 6 includes a segment on AIDS.

139. The Centers for Disease Control National AIDS Clearinghouse provides an excellent source describing educational sources and materials on HIV and AIDS. The publication lists books, brochures, manuals, posters, study guides, teaching aids, and videos. Many of the sources promote abstinence as the best choice for adolescents deciding whether or not to engage in sexual intercourse. The clearinghouse number is 800–458-5231.

140. Jane Hansen and Sandra McIntosh, "New Sex Abuse Trend: Kids Attacking Kids," in *The Atlanta Constitution,* October 15, 1989, A1 and A18.

One expert in juvenile crime says, "We always look at the kids being the victims. Now we're looking at kids victimizing other kids." The following national U.S. statistics bear this out:[141]
• More than 50 percent of young boys and as many as 20 percent of girls who are sexually abused are molested by teenagers.
• Sixty to 80 percent of adult sexual offenders say they committed their first sex offense as teenagers.
• The average age of the first offense of all adult sexual offenders is about 13 years old.
• The rate of juveniles arrested for rape doubled from 20 per 100,000 to 40 per 100,000 in the past decade.

The most common trait among adolescent sexual abusers is that they themselves were the victims of similar abuse. Somewhere between 80 and 90 percent of those teenagers who have completed treatment for sex abuse crimes say they themselves were abused as children. Offenders come from a variety of socioeconomic backgrounds and cut across all religious, race, and class lines. There are, as one expert put it, just as many sons of senators who get into trouble for sexual crimes as there are sons of fathers in any other profession or occupation.[142]

It is crucial that adolescent sexual offenders are identified and dealt with so the cycle of child abuse and molestation is broken. It is naive for parents or youth religious educators to believe that if left alone, an adolescent will grow out of his or her deviant behavior. There is no such thing as a one-time child molester or rapist. Adolescent sex offenders average seven victims; adult offenders who committed their first sex offense as teenagers average 380 victims.[143] If a youth worker discovers that someone in the youth group is guilty of child abuse, molestation, or rape, it should be reported to the appropriate child protection agency in the community. While some states tend to lock up offenders, there are counseling centers nationwide designed to intensively treat adolescent sex abusers.

Date Rape
"Hurry right home from school and stay away from strangers," says a caring mother to her adolescent daughter. Most young girls know that

---

141. Ibid.
142. Ibid.
143. Ibid.

they must be wary of strangers, but what they may not be aware of is that they have more to fear from people they are acquainted with. Contrary to popular belief, most women and girls who are raped are not violated by a stranger. The majority of assailants are husbands, ex-husbands, friends, dates, boyfriends, or acquaintances of some sort. One survey of 7,000 college students nationwide found that one in seven (14 percent) reported being raped and 47 percent of these women were violated by dates or acquaintances.[144] In another study, 13 percent of the girls said physical force had been used to force them into kissing, petting, or intercourse.[145]

There is some discussion and debate as to what actually constitutes rape. Keith Olson defines rape as "gaining genital penetration of a woman without her consent by using force, fear, or deceit."[146] However, in regard to sexual intercourse on a date, it is often difficult to determine whether force was used or not. In other cases it is sometimes suggested that the girl may have invited sexual activity. Is it rape when the girl initially says yes to having sex and then changes her mind? Is the girl partially to blame if she dresses provocatively? Some males feel that they deserve sex if they have spent money on a girl, others insist that when a girl says no she really means yes or try again. A study of 11- to 14-year-olds in Rhode Island found that a fourth of the boys and a sixth of the girls said it was acceptable for a man to force a woman to kiss him or have sex with him if he had spent money on her.[147] While there is much debate as to when genital penetration is rape, the growing consensus of public opinion and the courts is that when a girl says no, it is rape.

Youth religious educators can offer guidelines to both adolescent males and females that will help lower the risk of date or acquaintance rape.[148]

----

144. The study was funded by the National Center for the Prevention and Control of Rape. The results are cited in Candace Walters, *Invisible Wounds* (Portland: Multnomah, 1987), 21.

145. Reported in James A. Davies, "Adolescent Subculture," in Donald Ratcliff and James A. Davies, eds., *Handbook of Youth Ministry* (Birmingham, Ala.: Religious Education Press, 1991), 14.

146. G. Keith Olson, *Counseling Teenagers* (Loveland, Colo.: Group, 1984), 442.

147. Cited in Nancy Gibbs, "When Is it Rape?" in *Time*, June 3, 1991, 54.

148. Adapted from Daniel Goleman, "When The Rapist is Not a Stranger," in *The New York Times*, August 29, 1989, 13.

For adolescent females:
• Avoid going out with anyone you do not trust or whose character you have reason to suspect.
• Assert your right to set limits and communicate these limits clearly and early. Say no when you mean no. One of the most effective tactics to avoid date rape is to make clear early in the encounter you are not interested in sex.
• Be assertive with a date who may be pressuring you. Passivity may be interpreted as permission.
• Be careful how you dress and act toward the opposite sex. Some males may take sexually provocative dress and flirting as an invitation to or desire for sex.
• Be careful to avoid any situation where you might be vulnerable.
For adolescent males:
• Be aware of negative peer pressure. Know that it is all right not to "score."
• Understand that when a girl says "no" she means "no"—not "maybe" or "try again". Rejection to sexual activity does not necessarily mean a rejection of you as a person.
• Realize that forced sex on a date meets the legal definition of rape. Know that such activity may lead to the girl reporting you to authorities.
• Know that this is a sexual sin perpetrated not only against the girl, but against God.

Girls who have been abused or raped by dates will need special counseling. They likely will need to deal with the emotional pain of being sexually assaulted and the guilt that often comes with being violated. Many youth religious educators may not feel comfortable or equipped to do such counseling, in which case referral should be made to a professional counselor.

CONCLUSION

There are no simple answers to the immense problems related to adolescent sexual activity. Empirical research indicates that the number of teenagers engaging in premarital intercourse will not decline significantly. Furthermore, adolescents will become sexually active at younger and younger ages. But as long as youth continue to engage in illicit sexual activity, they will risk the painful consequences from their experiences such as unwanted pregnancies or sexually transmitted diseases.

Nevertheless, the situation is not hopeless. Studies suggest that participation in religious activities has some positive influence on sexual behavior and attitudes of teenagers. Furthermore, there are indications that a growing number of youth are choosing abstinence and chastity over engaging in illicit sexual activity.

7

Addictive Behaviors: Eating Disorders and Substance Abuse

In contemporary society addictive behaviors occur in epidemic proportions and are a hazard to the well-being of people of all ages and backgrounds. In the United States and Canada millions of people are addicted to any number of behaviors or substances, including drugs, alcohol, gambling, tobacco, sex, and even work. Since the 1970s, clinicians, as well as the public, have become increasingly aware of addictive eating disorders, especially among teenage girls and young women.[1]

An addiction is described as any behavior or thinking that is habitual, repetitious, and is difficult or impossible to control. Usually, the addiction brings short-term pleasure, but there may be long term consequences to one's health, welfare, and psychological well-being.[2] This chapter will focus on the addictive eating disorders of anorexia nervosa and bulimia nervosa, as well as the use and abuse of alcohol and illicit drugs.

THE EATING DISORDERS OF ANOREXIA NERVOSA AND BULIMIA NERVOSA

On February 4, 1983, at the age of 32, pop singer Karen Carpenter suddenly died of heart failure. Further investigation revealed that she

---

1. Paul E. Garfinkle, "Classification and Diagnosis of Eating Disorders," in Kelly D. Brownell and Christopher G. Fairburn, eds., *Eating Disorders and Obesity* (New York: The Guilford Press, 1995), 125–34.
2. Gary R. Collins, *Christian Counseling,* rev. ed. (Dallas, Tex.: Word, 1988), 507.

had been struggling with an eating disorder called *anorexia nervosa* for twelve years, and medical experts concluded that this had contributed to her untimely death. Ms. Carpenter represents thousands of young people, especially females, who struggle with an eating disorder, as well as a small percentage whose compulsion tragically ends in death. At one time considered rare, the diagnosed incidences of the eating disorders anorexia nervosa and bulimia nervosa are increasing at a staggering rate. As many as 25 percent of today's teenagers, mostly girls, are affected by either anorexia nervosa or bulimia.[3]

Anorexia Nervosa

While *anorexia nervosa,* which literally means "nervous loss of appetite," is the better known of the two eating disorders, it is not as common. About 2 percent of the total population suffers from anorexia nervosa, about 90–95 percent of whom are adolescent females.[4] While the condition was first described in a medical journal in 1689, anorexia only became well known as a disorder in the 1970s and 1980s. The incidence of anorexic behavior is increasing among teenage populations.

Anorexia is essentially a self-inflicted starvation, whereby the individual compulsively refrains from eating in order to attain thinness. The victim continues to see herself as overweight, while in reality she is often abnormally thin. The following are characteristics of anorexia:[5]
• Refusal to maintain minimal normal body weight for age and height.
• An intense fear of becoming overweight or obese, which does not diminish with progression of weight loss.
• Disturbance in the way one's body weight or shape is experienced, such as feeling fat even when distinctly underweight.
• For postmenarcheal females, the loss of menstruation.

In addition, the anorexic adolescent generally suffers from physical side effects such as an intolerance to cold, excessive skin dryness, low blood pressure, chemical deficiencies, and heart problems. She may also manifest depressive symptoms such as depressed mood, social

---

3. Les Parrott, *Helping the Struggling Adolescent* (Grand Rapids, Mich.: Zondervan, 1993), 109.

4. Carol Lee Grant and Iris Goldstein Fodor, "Adolescent Attitudes Toward Body Image and Anorexic Behavior," *Adolescence* 21, (Summer 1986), 269–82.

5. The characteristics of anorexia nervosa are summarized from American Psychiatric Association, *Diagnostic and Statistical Manual of Mental Disorders,* 4th rev. ed. (Washington, D.C., 1987), 544–45.

withdrawal, insomnia, and irritability.[6] Extreme cases of anorexia may result in death, about half of which are caused by suicide.[7]

Bulimia Nervosa

Closely related to anorexia, is *bulimia nervosa*, which literally means "ox-hunger."[8] This is an eating disorder characterized by binge eating, followed immediately by purging through self-induced vomiting, laxative abuse, excessive exercise, and/or fasting. Although bulimia has only come to medical attention in recent years, it is the more common of the two eating disorders.[9] Surveys indicate that approximately 19 percent of female adolescents report bulimic symptoms.[10] The following are some primary criteria for the assessment of bulimia:[11]

• Recurring episodes of binge eating. An episode of binge eating is characterized 1) as a rapid consumption of a large amount of food in a short period of time (e.g., within a two-hour period); 2) a sense of lack of control over eating during that period (e.g., a feeling that one cannot stop eating or control what and how much one is eating).

• The practice of inducing vomiting, using laxatives, fasting, or vigorous exercising to prevent weight gain.

• An average of at least two binge episodes a week for at least three months.

• A persistent concern about weight and body shape.

Additional complications as a result of bulimia nervosa may include menstrual problems, dental problems,[12] and depression. Compared to anorexics, however, many bulimics enjoy reasonably good health and are generally within the normal weight range. Bulimics are typically ashamed of their eating disorder and prefer to binge on food when they

---

6. Ibid., 541.

7. W. Stewart Agras, *Eating Disorders: Management of Obesity, Bulimia, and Anorexia Nervosa* (New York: Pergamon, 1987), 15.

8. Brenda Parry-Jones and William Parry-Jones, "History of Bulimia and Bulimia Nervosa," in Brownell and Fairburn, eds., *Eating Disorders and Obesity,* 145–50.

9. Pierre J. V. Beumont, "The Clinical Presentation of Anorexia and Bulimia Nervosa," in in Brownell and Fairburn, eds., *Eating Disorders and Obesity,* 151–58.

10. Hans W. Hoek, "The Distribution of Eating Disorders," in Brownell and Fairburn, eds., *Eating Disorders and Obesity,* 207–11.

11. Adapted from *Diagnostic and Statistical Manual of Mental Disorders,* 4th rev. ed., 549.

12. Bulimics often experience dental problems because of the acids in the vomit. Dental problems may also occur because of the high sugar content in binging foods such as ice cream or cake.

are alone, or as inconspicuously as possible.[13] There is, however, a social element involved in that purging techniques are often learned from friends and through the media.[14]

Who Is Vulnerable to Eating Disorders?

Eating disorders are complex in nature, and it is difficult for most people to understand or appreciate why certain individuals are addicted to such behaviors. The body has built-in mechanisms that generally tell us when it is time to eat, and regular feeding is a normal and routine function. Nonetheless, many adolescents struggle with and suffer through eating disorders, often experiencing physical consequences as severe as death.

The causes related to eating disorders are complicated and no one factor leads to these illnesses. Rather, anorexia and bulimia are the result of the complex interaction of a number of cultural and psychological forces.

Gender: An overwhelming majority of adolescents suffering from these compulsive behaviors are females. In fact most studies indicate that about 90 percent of anorexics and bulimics are female.[15] What makes females so much more vulnerable to eating disorders? Contemporary Western society places a significantly greater amount of emphasis on dieting and slimness for girls and women than it does on boys and men. Beginning as early as the elementary school years, girls are more likely than boys to consider themselves in need of dieting or see themselves as being overweight.[16] In fact, many males are more concerned with putting on bulk and muscle than they are with losing weight and dieting. However, the importance of being attractive and feminine is conveyed to girls from an early age. Thinness is inextricably related to femininity and beauty; to achieve thinness girls engage in dieting and weight control, which, in turn, contributes to the development of eating disorders.[17] For males, self-worth and masculinity are defined more by power, intelligence, and occupational accomplishments than by body shape or weight.

---

13. Ibid., 546.

14. Agras, *Eating Disorders,* 3.

15. Arnold E. Andersen, "Eating Disorders in Males," in Brownell and Fairburn, eds., *Eating Disorders and Obesity,* 177–82.

16. Ibid., 177.

17. Ruth H. Strievel-Moore, "A Feminist Perspective on the Etiology of Eating Disorders," in Brownell and Fairburn, eds., *Eating Disorders and Obesity,* 224–29.

Males who may be more susceptible to eating disorders are those who participate in activities that require them to keep their weight down to a minimum. Wrestlers, for example, will do whatever it takes to "make weight," and then after matches engage in binge eating. Male ballet dancers, long-distance runners, and models may also resort to starvation to keep their weight down.

Age: The age of onset for both anorexia and bulimia is usually between 12 and 18 years and the disorders occur predominantly among adolescent girls and young women.[18] The incidence of eating disorders under the age of 14 is low, although children as young as 7 have been diagnosed with anorexia nervosa.[19] The onset of anorexia seldom occurs after age 40. Peer pressure to be slender, accompanied by the desire to look like the models in teenage glamour magazines no doubt encourages many adolescent girls to go on slimming diets, a few of which develop into anorexia or bulimia.

Social Class: Another major factor contributing to eating disorders is social class. Interestingly, anorexia and bulimia are almost nonexistent in economically disadvantaged countries. The disorders are most common in the industrialized countries such as the United States, Canada, Australia, Japan, New Zealand, South Africa, and the European nations.[20] Furthermore, eating disordered individuals come almost exclusively from middle and upper socioeconomic classes. It is possible that this is due, at least in part, to underreporting, especially in Third World countries. However, it is probable that eating disorders are indeed more prevalent in affluent societies where the economy is thriving. It is in these economically privileged societies and classes that women are more likely to be pressured to succeed in the workplace while looking attractive and thin at the same time.

How Eating Disorders Begin

A teenage girl does not start a diet with the intention of becoming emaciated or decide to control her weight by vomiting, using a laxative, or purging in any other manner. However for the adolescent who is to

---

18. Michele Siegel, Judith Brisman, and Margot Weishel, *Surviving an Eating Disorder* (New York: Harper & Row, 1988), 15, 24.

19. Rachel Bryant-Waugh and Bryan Lask, "Childhood-Onset Eating Disorders," in Brownell and Fairburn, eds., *Eating Disorders and Obesity,* 183–87.

20. *Diagnostic and Statistical Manual of Mental Disorders,* 4th rev. ed., 542, 548.

become controlled by an eating disorder, dieting and weight loss subtly take on a function that is both unplanned and unanticipated. What begins as an attempt to control one's appearance and weight ultimately becomes a behavior that is out of control. There are a number of reasons that precipitate the onset of an eating disorder in teenage girls.

Perfectionism: One common characteristic of anorexic adolescents is their propensity toward perfectionism. They are nearly always hard-working, conscientious, and dependable. They are often the model child, usually above average in their school performance, yet highly demanding and critical of themselves. They are continually trying to prove their competence.[21]

Low Self-Esteem: Bulimics and anorexics alike tend to be adolescents who do not feel secure about their self-worth. They tend not to have developed sufficient means of feeling worthy, competent, or effective.[22] The eating disordered teenager struggles to be perfect, yet feels she must strive to prove her competence to others as well as to herself.

Identity Problems: Adolescence is a period of great vulnerability to a variety of identity struggles. Some psychologists theorize that anorexia is a rejection of female sexuality and an attempt to remain a "little girl."[23] One hypothesis is that anorexic girls avoid many of the social consequences of adolescence by reducing their weight, expunging secondary sexual characteristics such as breast development, and reverting to a prepubertal role.[24]

For some adolescents, an eating disorder is the only way to assert the autonomy every teenager longs for: "I am an individual and I have control of my life." Being in control of their diet and eating habits, what they do to their bodies, and what they weigh may be a way of exercising and expressing their individuality.[25]

Family Pressures: The children of parents who espouse the notion that weight and physical appearance are critical to self-worth may be predisposed toward eating disorders. And if parents model excessive dieting and judge themselves harshly in terms of weight or shape, the children

21. Siegel, Brisman, and Weishel, *Surviving an Eating Disorder,* 15.
22. Ibid., 15, 24.
23. Parrott, *Helping The Struggling Adolescent,* 109.
24. Agras, *Eating Disorders,* 11.
25. Margo Maine, "Eating Disorders," in David Levinson, ed., *Encyclopedia of Marriage and the Family,* Vol. 1 (New York: Simon and Schuster Macmillan, 1995), 207–11.

are even more likely to apply these same standards to themselves. When parental approval is connected to appearance, the risk of incurring an eating disorder is high.[26] Eating-disordered teenagers often come from homes where standards are high, achievement is prized, attractiveness and slimness are seen as important, and dieting is praised.[27]

Social Influences: Clearly, the greatest barrage of messages teenage girls receive concerning body image, appearance, and the importance of slimness comes from society at large. The media and advertising agents target females, telling them to change their bodies or please others through their physical attractiveness. As young girls grow up, they are unfortunately sold on an ideal that few can realistically reach. However, this does not keep adolescent girls from trying, and a small percentage of them will inadvertently develop eating disorders.[28]

Seeking Help for the Eating-disordered Adolescent

There are at least two ways the youth religious educator can assist adolescents in overcoming eating disorders: by referring them to medical and/or psychological professionals, and by involving them in support groups.

Referral: The eating disorders of anorexia and bulimia represent psychological problems that are beyond the expertise of most youth religious educators. In most cases the intervention of medical and/or psychological professionals is necessary in order to make a significant difference in facilitating recovery and easing the burden the youth worker may be feeling in helping the individual get well. The various types of treatment that might be necessary for the eating-disordered adolescent include psychotherapy, and medical and/or nutritional help. In severe cases where an individual is in a life-endangering condition, hospitalization may be necessary.[29]

Support Groups: Whether or not an adolescent is in psychotherapy, a support or self-help group can be invaluable in helping an anorexic or bulimic teenager address the problem of an eating disorder and feel less isolated. A support group differs from a psychotherapy group in that it is not led by a therapist. Usually the leader or facilitator of a support

---

26. Ibid.
27. Collins, *Christian Counseling*, 512–13.
28. Maine, "Eating Disorders," 207–11.
29. Siegel, Brisman, and Weinshel, *Surviving an Eating Disorder*, 111–26.

group is an individual who has herself recovered from an eating disorder and is in the position of helping and inspiring others through her own experience.

Support groups can be structured in a variety of ways. In some groups a specific topic is addressed at each meeting, while in others there is no particular agenda. In some groups the session begins with a speaker and then participants break into smaller discussion groups to explore their feelings about the topic. Examples of topics that support groups might discuss are "How relationships are affected by eating disorders," and "What to do if you are hungry."[30]

There are several national or international organizations that exist for the purpose of helping families and victims of anorexia and bulimia.[31] The American Anorexia/Bulimia Association (AABA), with support groups in New Jersey, Philadelphia, Virginia, and Florida, has information packets on forming self-help support groups.

The National Association of Anorexia Nervosa and Associated Disorders (ANAD) has affiliated support groups in most of the United States, Canada, Germany, and Saudi Arabia. In addition they have a national hotline in the United States that provides counseling for victims and family members and can offer referral to therapists and support groups.

ALCOHOL CONSUMPTION AND ABUSE

Most people are not aware of how pervasive the problem of alcohol is on adolescents, since other illicit drugs often get much of the public attention. But, while in the United States the consumption of alcohol is illegal for the large majority of adolescents, experience with alcohol is almost universal among them; it is clearly the drug of choice for teenagers in the United States. A national survey of American secondary students indicates that 88 percent of 17-year-olds had consumed alcohol at some point in their life. More significant, perhaps, is the widespread

30. Ibid., 117–18.
31. National referral and support organizations for eating-disordered victims include the following: American Anorexia/Bulimia Association, 133 Cedar Lane, Teaneck, N.J., 07666, (201) 836-1880; National Association of Anorexia Nervosa and Associated Disorders, P.O. Box 7, Highland Park, Ill. 60035, (313) 831-3438; Anorexia Nervosa and Related Eating Disorders, P.O. Box 5112, Eugene, OR 97405, (503) 344-1144; The National Anorexia Aid Society, 5796 Karl Road, Columbus, OH 43229, (614) 436-1112.

occurrence of binge drinking, taking five or more drinks in a row. Thirteen percent of the 13-year-olds, 21 percent of the 15-year-olds, and 28 percent of the 17-year-olds reported taking five or more drinks in a row in the prior two-week period.[32]

A research study of Wisconsin adolescents reveals a similar incidence rate of alcohol consumption. Seventy-eight percent of the respondents between the ages of 12 and 17 had used alcohol at least once in their life. Fifty-five percent of the 12-year-olds and 94 percent of the 17-year-olds indicated they had consumed alcohol once or more in their lifetime. Rates for males and females were almost identical.

Some additional findings of the Wisconsin study included the following:
• Ten percent of the 12-year-olds reported at least one incidence of binge drinking.
• Thirty-seven percent, just over one-third, of the 17-year-olds reported binge drinking in the last two weeks.
• Thirty-seven percent of the 17-year-olds reported drinking 40 or more times in their lifetime.

Such statistics are alarming and identify teenage alcohol consumption as a national concern. Children are using alcohol at younger ages than ever before, and they are becoming problem drinkers sooner. In the 1940s and 1950s, teenagers took their first drink at ages 13 or 14; today they are starting at age 10 or younger.[33] Clearly, the number-one burden for today's youth is created by the consumption and abuse of alcohol.

According to an empirical study by the Search Institute, alcohol consumption is a problem for church youth as well. In this cross-denominational survey, it was found that 50 percent of the teenagers questioned had engaged in alcoholic consumption at least once in the past year, while 25 percent had used alcohol six or more times in the past year. More disconcerting is the fact that 28 percent had been on a drinking binge in the last year, and 17 percent had engaged in binge drinking at least three times in the past year. In spite of the popular image that boys are more likely to drink, rates of alcoholic consumption between

---

32. Lloyd D. Johnston, Patrick M. O'Malley, and Jerald G. Bachman, *National Survey Results on Drug Use From Monitoring the Future Study, 1975–1992, Vol. 1*(Rockville, Md.: National Institute on Drug Abuse, 1993), 12.

33. Ibid., 21.

males and females did not significantly differ.[34] These statistics should give youth religious educators and other church leaders great cause for concern, as teenagers in churches and youth groups are not immune from the use, abuse, and the resultant consequences of engaging in alcohol consumption.

Consequences of Alcohol Consumption

While many adolescents view alcohol as a relatively harmless substance, and some parents are relatively pleased that their teenage son or daughter "merely drinks and is not addicted to drugs," experts do not dispute the potentially dangerous effects of alcohol. Indeed, alcohol consumption is not without its perils and often deadly consequences.

Alcohol consumption at an early age is often an indicator of future drug or alcohol problems. One of the greatest risks in teenage alcohol drinking or the experimentation with alcohol is the possibility of becoming addicted to the drug. It is estimated that there could be over 4 million Americans under the age of 18, who are alcoholics or are addicted to the consumption of alcohol.[35] Astonishingly, this figures to be approximately one teenager in five.

Furthermore, alcohol is considered to be a "gateway" drug and often precedes the use of other drugs. One empirical survey of American adolescents found little or no drug consumption among those who had not consumed alcohol first.[36]

Empirical research studies also indicate that in the United States, alcohol is a contributing factor in 50 percent of traffic fatalities.[37] And the rates of vehicular deaths are consistently highest for persons between the ages 15 and 24, 60 percent higher than the rates for those age 25 to 44.[38]

---

34. Eugene Roelkepartain and Peter Benson, *Youth in Protestant Churches* (Minneapolis: Search Institute, 1993). The report is based on youth data from a Search Institute study on Christian Education. The study surveyed more than 11,000 adult and youth in five U.S. Protestant denominations: Evangelical Lutheran Church of America, Presbyterian Church (USA), United Church of Christ, and United Methodist Church.

35. Parrott, *Helping the Struggling Adolescent,* 93.

36. Cited in "Teen Alcohol Use Seen As America's No.1 Drug Problem," *National School Safety Center News Service,* February 1992.

37. James B. Jacobs, *Drunk Driving: An American Dilemma* (Chicago, Ill.: University of Chicago Press, 1989), 40; W. Wayne Worick and Warren E. Schaller, *Alcohol, Tobacco, and Drugs: Their Use and Abuse* (Englewood Cliffs, N.J.: Prentice-Hall, 1977), 51.

38. Jacobs, *Drunk Driving: An American Dilemma,* 17.

Intoxication is also positively correlated to the incidence of acquaintance or date rape. Researchers speculate that alcohol reduces the males' inhibition against violence, provides an excuse for sexual aggression, and reduces females' ability to resist unwanted sexual advances.[39]

One of the major causes of adolescent deaths is suicide. The suicide rate is almost 60 times higher for alcoholics than that of the general population, and about one-third of the suicides of the population as a whole are in some way related to alcohol. Either the person was an alcoholic, alcohol was mixed with barbiturates as the method of suicide, the person drank heavily to attain the courage to commit suicide, or the person committed suicide in a foggy state of mind due to excessive drinking.[40]

Why Do Adolescents Drink?

Adolescents give a variety of responses when asked this question. Most sources indicate that pressure from friends and peers has a powerful effect on one's use of alcohol. According to interview and statistical studies by Chris Lutes, some teenagers indicate that they drink because they want to and that blaming peer pressure is simply a feeble excuse. Nonetheless, 71 percent of the respondents admitted they would engage in drinking alcohol if their friends asked them.[41]

Apart from peer pressure, the most common reason teenagers give for drinking is pleasure or fun.[42] A 16-year-old girl from Washington says, "Teenagers drink because it is fun and very social."[43] Teenagers look forward to weekends so they can drink, party, and spend time with their friends. Others drink to escape—escape from pressures they are faced with, escape from boredom, and escape from depression. An 18-year-old female from Texas says, "Drinking helps you forget the problems and pressures of the world for a little while."[44] Additional

---

39. Deborah R. Richardson and Georgina S. Hammock, "Alcohol and Acquaintance Rape," in Andrea Parrot and Laurie Bechhofer, eds., *Acquaintance Rape: The Hidden Crime* (New York: John Wiley & Sons, 1991), 83–95.

40. Francine Klagsbrun, *Too Young to Die* (New York: Pocket Books, 1981), 69–70.

41. Chris Lutes, *What Teenagers Are Saying About Drugs and Alcohol* (Wheaton, Ill.: Tyndale, 1987), 49–51.

42. Ibid, 50.

43. Ibid, 48.

44. Ibid.

reasons adolescents give for consuming alcohol are to feel good, because they are upset, to experiment, or to relax.

While seldom given as a reason for drinking, the pressure of the advertising media must be considered as an influence. The advertising media target those in their late adolescence and early twenties. They not only portray drinking as a socially acceptable activity, but they glorify it by making it especially attractive to these young people. Beer advertisements depict handsome young men and beautiful women who appear to be living "the good life" with no serious life-related problems. Teenagers subtly connect athleticism, material success, physical beauty, fun, and a multitude of good friends with the consumption of their product. Rarely, if ever, do advertisers portray the negative consequences of excessive drinking—tragic traffic accidents, loss of jobs, sickness, family conflict, or crime, to name a few.

Recognizing Alcohol Abuse

It is important that the youth religious educator is competent in recognizing when adolescents are abusing alcohol. It is also necessary to remember, however, that the presence of one or two of the signs commonly associated with alcohol abuse does not necessarily indicate the teenager has problems with alcohol. On the other hand, if a teenager exhibits several of the following warning signs, it is possible he or she is using excessive amounts of alcohol. The signs may also indicate drug abuse.[45]

• Social withdrawal: spends significant amounts of time alone, avoids times of family interaction and fun.

• Deterioration in school performance: experiences a decline in school grades and consistently skips classes.

• Resistance to authority: becomes rebellious toward parents, school teachers, police, and others.

• Behavior problems: exhibits behavioral problems such as stealing or shoplifting, lying, or vandalism.

• Extreme mood swings: suffers extreme mood swings, including depression and suicidal gestures.

• Sexual promiscuity: engages in illicit sexual behaviors.

---

45. Summarized from Parrott, *Helping the Struggling Adolescent,* 94, and Rich Van Pelt, *Intensive Care* (Grand Rapids, Mich.: Zondervan, 1988), 190–91.

• Physical complaints: experiences unusual occurrences of illnesses such as colds, flu, headaches, and vomiting.
• Changes in relationships: forms a new circle of friends.
• Changes in eating habits: experiences an increase or decrease in eating habits, accompanied by significant weight gain or loss.
• Additional observable signs: exhibits obvious signs of being under the influence of alcohol such as slurred speech, staggering, and alcohol on the breath.

It is also important to distinguish between those adolescents who are perhaps just experimenting with the consumption of alcohol, regular users, and those who are addicted to or are abusing alcohol. Rich Van Pelt lists five stages in the adolescent's progression toward addiction:[46]

Stage 0. Exhibiting curiosity in a world where alcohol is readily available.

Stage 1. Learning about the mood swing: adolescents learn how easy it is to feel good with few, if any, consequences.

Stage 2. Seeking out the mood swing. Rather than using alcohol as an accompaniment to social events, the adolescent decides to get drunk as a goal and arranges to have his or her own supply of alcohol.

Stage 3. Being preoccupied with the mood swing. Getting drunk is the main goal of life. Students who drink daily may plan their days around trips to euphoria.

Stage 4. Feeling satisfied. The euphoria derived from alcohol consumption becomes harder to achieve; larger amounts are needed.

ILLICIT DRUG USE

As a high school student in Vermont, Patti (not her real name) was drinking every now and then with her friends. At 17 she went to a university to study medicine and by that time she was a weekend alcoholic. By the time she was 18, she was addicted to marijuana and over the next two years she experimented with cocaine. Eventually she completely immersed herself in the drug scene. Patti was not a child of poverty or an abused child from a

---

46. Adapted from Van Pelt, *Intensive Care,* 191. Van Pelt credits these stages to Dr. Larry Silver, former acting director of the National Institute of Mental Health.

broken home. She was from a good Christian home. Her father was an elder in the church, she was an honor student in high school, president of the student council, and president of the youth group in the church she attended regularly. If there were signs, her parents did not see them, because they could not imagine their daughter in that situation.[47]

• • •

Wendy is a blond-haired, blue-eyed, 2-year-old whose every breath is a struggle to live. She is underweight, cannot walk, talk or hold up her head. She is also blind and suffers from cerebral palsy; doctors say she is the product of a cocaine habit. Before Wendy was born, her 17-year-old mother lived a life of cocaine, parties, and jail. The teenage mother already had one miscarriage due to her drug habit. Instead of turning away from drugs, she continued to use cocaine and a variety of pills, and got pregnant again.[48]

While alcohol is the most widely used drug among teenagers, other illicit drugs continue to destroy young lives at an alarming rate. Since the social upheaval of the 1960s, illegal drug use has been spreading at epidemic proportions among teenagers. During the 1980s there was a sharp decline in the adolescent use of marijuana, cocaine, and other illegal drugs in the United States. But lest there be any doubt that there is a serious drug problem among teenagers, even without any serious resurgence of drug use among the youngest cohorts, the following national statistics of America's youth should be noted:[49]

• Forty-one percent of America's twelfth-grade students (17-year-olds) have tried an illicit drug; 25 percent have used an illicit drug other than marijuana.[50]

---

47. This profile is summarized from a story by Marcille Jordan, "College Student Discusses Her Experiences While on the 'Drug Scene,'" in *The Chieftain*, Toccoa, Georgia, March 20, 1990, 1B.

48. This profile is summarized from a story by Lesley Stedman and Lisa Stone, "Upstate Assesses Damage From Drug-baby Epidemic," in *Anderson Independent-Mail*, March 22, 1991, 1A.

49. Johnston, O'Malley, and Bachman, *National Survey Results on Drug Use, Vol. 1*, 21.

50. Use of "any illicit drug" includes marijuana, hallucingens, cocaine, heroin, or any use of other opiates, stimulants, barbituates, methaqualone, or tranquilizers not under doctor's orders.

• Thirty-three percent of the 17-year-olds reported the use of marijuana or hashish at some point during their lifetime. Apart from alcohol, marijuana is the drug of choice for most teenagers.
• Among eighth grade students (13- and 14-year-olds), more than one in every six (17 percent) have used inhalants, making this the most popular illicit drug for this age group.
• Marijuana has been tried by one in every nine (11 percent) 13- and 14-year-olds.

A similar study of secondary students in the Wisconsin public school system revealed the following statistics:[51]
• Lifetime marijuana or hashish use for 17-year-olds was 34 percent.
• Fourteen percent of the 17-year-olds had used marijuana in the last month. Eight percent had used the drug three times or more in the last month.
• Forty percent of the 17-year-olds reported the use of an illicit drug at least once in a lifetime.

Thus, despite a decline in the use of drugs from the 1970s and 1980s peak levels, it is true that America's adolescents demonstrate a level of involvement with illicit drugs that is greater than in any other industrialized country in the world. Even by long-term historical standards in the United States, these rates remain extremely high. And unlike teenagers in the 1950s and 1960s, today's youth are familiar with a wide range of substances they can use to alter consciousness and mood. Unfortunately, they will continue to have easy access to illegal drugs through highly elaborate supply systems. It is imperative then, that there are active counterforces in place to reduce current levels of use and to prevent the occurrence of any new epidemics.[52]

How do the habits of church youth compare with adolescents in the general population? One research study indicates that there is not a significant difference. According to a Search Institute report of church youth, one out of five (20 percent) 16- and 17-year-olds admitted to using marijuana in the past year. This rate is only slightly lower than the national rate of 22 percent. Three percent of the 16- and 17-year-olds had tried cocaine in the past year, a percentage identical to the national rate.[53]

---

51. *The Wisconsin Study: Alcohol and Other Drug Use* (Minneapolis, Minn.: Search Institute, 1991), 35–47.

52. Johnston, O'Malley, and Bachman, *National Survey Results on Drug Use, Vol. 1,* 20.

53. Roelkepartain and Benson, *Youth in Protestant Churches,* 102–3.

The study of church youth, however, did make an important distinction between teenagers who were highly active in church-related programs and those who were inactive. Inactive youth were four times as likely to use marijuana or cocaine than active youth. Once again the data suggests that church affiliation alone may not be sufficient to equip adolescents with the skills to resist the pressures of everyday living. Adolescents are less likely to engage in at-risk behavior such as drug use when they participate in effective religious education programs in their church.[54]

Types of Addictive Drugs

Most addictive drugs, whether legal or illegal, fall into one of seven categories: narcotics, barbiturates, tranquilizers, stimulants, hallucinogens, inhalants, and cannabis. Along with alcohol, they form the nucleus of the drug-abuse problem.[55]

• *Narcotics* depress the central nervous system causing stupor and insensibility. The most widely used narcotics are opium, morphine, codeine, and heroin. Addiction to these drugs, especially heroin, occurs over an abbreviated period of time.

• *Barbiturates,* also called "downers," depress the central nervous system but when abused are even more dangerous than heroin. They severely distort judgment, which can lead to an overdose.

• *Tranquilizers* are similar in effect to barbiturates in that they are depressants, and when abused, can create a barbiturate-like dependence. Some commonly abused tranquilizers include Valium, Librium, and Methaqualone.

• *Amphetamines,* also called "uppers," stimulate the central nervous system. The psychological effects of their use include hyperactivity, paranoia, and hallucinations. The most commonly abused amphetamine is methamphetamine or "speed."

• *Cocaine* is a dangerous and highly addictive stimulant. It creates an intense, though brief, state of euphoria when first taken, followed by severe depression. Addiction to cocaine occurs rapidly, and increased doses become necessary to achieve the "high." Cocaine has caused heart attacks in people as young as 19, as well as life-threatening damage to the

---

54. Ibid.
55. Modified from a pamphlet "Freedom From Addiction," by the Medical Association of Georgia, Atlanta, Georgia. See also Worick and Schaller, *Alcohol, Tobacco, and Drugs: Their Use and Abuse,* 115–25 for classification and description of illicit drugs.

heart, arteries, and brain. Sometimes cocaine hydrochloride is converted into a smokable form (free base). Cocaine can also be converted to a "rock" form known as crack.

• *Hallucinogens* have the ability to create vivid distortions of reality, and to create wild and sometimes terrifying experiences for the user. They induce a trancelike state, frequently with visual hallucinations. The most commonly abused hallucinogen is LSD, commonly called "acid."

• *Inhalants* can directly cause death or structural damage to the brain, spinal cord, and liver. They include airplane glue, gasoline, lighter fluid, and aerosol products.

• *Cannabis,* considered to be the least powerful drug, temporarily alters the user's mood and perception and produces a sense of well-being. Long-term use may cause mental confusion, damage to lung tissue, and create a psychological dependence. Examples of cannabis are marijuana (also know as pot, grass, or Acapulco gold) and hashish.

Consequences of Illicit Drug Use

The perils of illegal drug use are well documented, and in the United States drug abuse has become a national health crisis. Clearly, the deadliest consequence of a number of drug users is the contraction of AIDS. According to the Centers for Disease Control, 36 percent of the reported AIDS/HIV cases in the United States are associated with drug injection. The transfer of HIV-infected or contaminated blood occurs through the sharing of needles and syringes that are used for injecting drugs intravenously. The use of noninjected drugs such as "crack" cocaine can also place an individual at risk for HIV transmission, because these substances reduce inhibitions and lessen one's reluctance to engage in unsafe sex.[56]

There are additional physiological consequences related to drug use and abuse. Drug overdoses take the lives of a number of teenagers each year. Drugs such as cocaine, crack, and heroin used over a long period of time can cause severe impairment of internal organs and the nervous system.[57]

---

56. Centers For Disease Control and Prevention, *Facts About Adolescents and HIV/ AIDS* (December 1995), fact sheet.

57. J. Jeffries McWhirter et al., *At-Risk Youth: A Comprehensive Response* (Pacific Grove, Calif.: Brooks/Cole, 1993), p. 127.

Illicit drug use is also related to early sexual activity. According to an empirical research study by Rosenbaum and Kandel, the use of illicit drugs greatly increases the risk of early sexual activity for adolescent males and females. Furthermore, the younger the reported age at first consumption of drugs, the greater the risk for early sexual activity.[58]

PREVENTION OF SUBSTANCE ABUSE

There are three levels of intervention efforts available to youth religious educators in dealing with the prevention of substance use and abuse: primary, secondary, and tertiary. Each level involves activity at a different point in the consumption sequence.[59]

Primary Prevention

The level of prevention that affects the greatest number of adolescents is primary in nature because many adolescents (especially younger youth) have not yet experimented with alcohol or drugs. Primary prevention strategies include information giving, religious education that

Figure 7.1
Levels of Intervention

Prevention Type	Sequence	Types of Activities
Primary	Before use or abuse	Information, religious education, alternatives
Secondary	In the early stages of use or abuse	Crisis intervention, diagnosis, referral
Tertiary	Later, more frequent, and higher quantity of use and abuse	Detoxification, treatment programs

58. Emil Rosenblaum and Denise B. Kandel, "Early Onset of Adoescent Sex and Drug Use," in *Journal of Marriage and the Family* 52, (August 1990), 783–98.
59. The outline is adapted from Judith R. Vicary, "Adolescent Drug and Alcohol Use and Abuse," in Richard M. Lerner and Nancy L. Galambos, eds., *Experiencing Adolescents* (New York: Garland, 1984), 162.

encourages spiritual growth and faith development, and experiences and activities that provide an alternative to alcohol and drug consumption.

Joy Dryfoos suggests that most alcohol and drug prevention strategies and programs fall into one of five categories: 1) knowledge-oriented strategies, 2) affective strategies, 3) knowledge and affective strategies 4) social influence and life skills, and 5) alternative strategies.[60]

Knowledge Strategies: Knowledge only or information-based intervention strategies or techniques are based on the assumption that educating teenagers about alcohol and drugs will change attitudes that will, in turn, reduce consumption. However, according to the research done by Dryfoos, strategies that present information only demonstrate practically no effect on knowledge of substances, attitudes toward substances, skills in saying no to substance consumption, or behavioral change in regard to substance use.[61] Most information-based strategies are teacher-centered with limited group participation, and they often use ineffective scare tactics.[62]

Affective Strategies: Affective strategies are based on the assumption that psychological factors such as low self-esteem or inability to cope with stress put certain adolescents at greater risk of substance abuse. These strategies focus on the psychological issue (e.g., self esteem) with little or no mention of drugs or alcohol. Affective strategies used alone have only minimal effect on lowering substance use.

Knowledge and Affective Strategies: A number of strategies assume that behavior change will follow knowledge, attitude, and value change. Some techniques that combine information giving and affective content include the following:
• Take members of the youth group to an open meeting of a nearby rehabilitation program to listen to the stories of alcohol and drug addicts in treatment. Some clinics have evenings where the meeting is open to nonresidents.
• Use articles or television reports about lives of individuals negatively affected by drugs or alcohol to stimulate discussion about substance abuse.

---

60. Modified from Joy G. Dryfoos, *Adolescents at Risk* (New York: Oxford University Press, 1990), 153.
61. Ibid.
62. McWhirter et al., *At-Risk Youth: A Comprehensive Response,* 133.

• Have a recovering drug addict or alcoholic speak to the youth group about the negative consequences of substance use and abuse. Provide opportunity for members of the youth group to direct questions toward the guest speaker.

Social Influence and Life Skills Strategies: These strategies assume that peer pressure is the major factor in substance abuse; that focus on the peer group may be the most effective means to combat substance use; and that peer-taught programs appear to be more successful than adult-taught ones. A combination of approaches that include refusal skills and social or life skills are employed to prevent alcohol and drug consumption. These strategies include components such as:

• interpersonal resistance skills,
• abilities to cope with social pressures,
• problem solving and decision making skills,
• the ability to say no to drugs or alcohol,
• social skills for resisting peer pressure.

Of the five models, Dryfoos found this one to have the greatest effect in the intervention of teenage substance use and abuse.

Alternative Strategies: Another intervention approach that has proven to be somewhat effective is the creating and providing of alternatives to substance use. By their very nature, healthy youth group functions provide positive options to negative behaviors. However, an effort to include activities that encourage creativity will enable adolescents to realize a degree of accomplishment, pride in work, and a measure of personal satisfaction. Creative experiences include painting, drawing, molding pottery, singing, acting, playing a musical instrument, or writing.

Secondary Intervention

Despite the efforts and successes of primary prevention, there are many adolescents who become involved with substance abuse. Secondary efforts focus on reducing or intervening in this dysfunction. Churches and youth religious educators can offer a variety of services and ministries to accomplish that goal. Crisis hot lines, support groups, or drop-in centers are ways some churches assist adolescents who want to talk about drug-related problems.[63]

---

63. Vicary, "Adolescent Drug and Alcohol Use and Abuse," 170–72.

Since adolescents often respond positively to peer influence and group contexts, youth religious educators should encourage participation in recovery groups such as Alcoholics Anonymous (AA). Alcoholics Anonymous is a public organization that has benefited thousands of people, adolescents included. The goal of AA is to get individuals to recognize that alcoholism is a personal problem that each alcoholic must own up to and take responsibility for. Some churches have support or recovery programs that adapt the AA steps to recovery to fit their doctrine and religious beliefs.[64]

Support groups for parents of alcoholic teenagers are also available in the community through local churches, schools, and workplaces. One such group that is active throughout the United States is ToughLove. ToughLove is a support group for parents of adolescents who are addicted, abusive, uncontrollable, or in some way in trouble with the law or school. This organization holds workshops, publishes a newsletter and brochures, provides referrals to professionals, and offers ideas for helping adolescents cease their self-destructive behavior.[65]

Tertiary Prevention

The need for treatment for drug or alcohol abuse that extends beyond the skill of the youth religious educator is sometimes necessary for a smaller percentage of teenagers. Detoxification that is conducted under medical supervision is often the first step in treating a substance abuse problem. Usually detoxification takes place in a special hospital facility and is intended to stop a physiological dependence on a particular drug by eliminating it entirely from the individual's system. Rehabilitation counseling should accompany the detoxification process in enabling the adolescent to develop a positive, drug-free life-style.[66]

There are a number of residential programs in the United States and other countries that exist for the purpose of rehabilitating substance abusing adolescents. Usually these in-house recovery programs endeavor to help teenagers gain an understanding of their alcohol related problems and assist them in long-term recovery. The time spent in such a program

---

64. For more information write Alcoholics Anonymous, P.O. Box 459, Grand Central Annex, New York, N.Y. 10163 or call (212) 686-1100.

65. For further information write ToughLove, P.O. Box 1069, Doylestown, Pa. 18901. The telephone number is (215) 348-7090.

66. Vicary, "Adolescent Drug and Alcohol Use and Abuse," 172–73.

gives the adolescent an opportunity to develop personal recovery goals, to prepare for reentry into the community, to learn skills necessary for the prevention of a relapse, and to practice an abstinent life-style.[67]

One such organization is Teen Challenge, a Christian-oriented program that serves adolescents and young adults with alcohol and drug related problems. Teen Challenge has facilities in the United States as well as in a number of other countries.[68]

For teenagers in treatment, the youth religious educator can be involved in the following ways:[69]

• Continue to support the adolescent and the family through any rehabilitation or detoxification period. Visiting the teenager at the treatment facility is one way to demonstrate ongoing care and concern.

• Maintain support and contact with the adolescent after the period of rehabilitation. Relapses are a common occurrence, and emotional support is needed for ongoing progress. Visit the youth at his or her home, make a telephone call, drop a note of encouragement, invite the teenager into your home, or spend some time with the individual over a cup of coffee in a local restaurant.

• Involve the adolescent in activities that may lessen the attraction to drugs: go hiking, play tennis or racquetball, go fishing, attend a concert or sporting event together.

• Do not give up on a teenager who is recovering from a substance abuse problem. Be prepared to offer continued support in case of a relapse, and do not take a failure personally.

CONCLUSION

Two areas of addictive behavior have been addressed in this chapter: eating disorders and substance abuse. The eating disorders of anorexia nervosa and bulimia nervosa affect a small percentage of adolescents, mostly girls. Anorexia occurs when an individual compulsively refrains from eating in order to attain thinness. Bulimia, the more common of the two disorders, is characterized by binge eating followed immediately by

---

67. McWhirter et. al., *At-Risk Youth: A Comprehensive Response,* 121–32.

68. For additional information write Teen Challenge Training Center, National Office, P.O. Box 198, Rehrersburg, Pa. 19550, or call (717) 933-4181.

69. William J. Rowley, *Equipped to Care* (Wheaton, Ill.: Victor, 1990), 133.

purging. Adolescents who struggle with either anorexia or bulimia may suffer serious physical and emotional consequences.

No doubt the most pervasive problem among adolescents is substance use and abuse. While the consumption of alcohol is illegal for the large majority of teenagers, it is clearly the drug of choice for American youth. Almost 90 percent of 17-year-olds have consumed alcohol at some point in their life. While there has been a decline in illicit drug use from the 1970s and 1980s peak levels, American teenagers demonstrate a level of illicit drug involvement that is greater than any other industrialized country.

8

The Tragedy of Teenage Suicide

"I'm tired of it," shrieked distraught 15-year-old Brian Head just before he put a pistol to his head and pulled the trigger. Brian, an only child, was a smart teenager who worked as drama club stagehand. But he was shy, overweight, and the recipient of a considerable amount of cruel adolescent humor, taunting, and physical abuse. For several years Brian had put up with the teasing and tormenting from classmates, but the point came when he could take it no more, and in front of his fellow students, he violently took his own life.[1]

One of the tragedies of contemporary youth culture and adolescent behavior is the widespread incidence of suicide. At an escalating rate, teenagers are opting to take their own lives in response to the overwhelming pressures and struggles of daily living. Medical experts and sociological analysts are alarmed and troubled by the sharp increase in the rate of adolescent suicide. For example, Francine Klagsbrun, in her classic treatment of youth and suicide, describes teenage suicide as an epidemic that cannot be ignored or minimized.[2] Gerald Klerman, professor of psychiatry at Cornell University identifies the increase in

---

1. This story is summarized from Bill Hendrick, "Youth's Suicide Highlights its No. 3 Rank as Killer of Teens," *The Atlanta Constitution,* March 26, 1994, A1.
2. Francine Klagsbrun, *Too Young to Die,* 4th ed. (New York: Pocket Books, 1981), p. 9.

suicide attempts and deaths among adolescents as a serious mental health and national social problem.[3]

In the 1950s teenage suicide was given little attention. While adolescents occasionally took their own lives, these occurrences were generally seen as aberrations. In the 1990s, suicide is recognized as the third leading cause of death for teenagers in America.[4] And since many suicides are disguised or reported as accidents, it may in fact be the number-one killer of the 13- to 19-year-old age group. The problem of adolescent suicide takes on even greater proportions when suicide thoughts or unsuccessful suicide attempts are considered.

THE SCOPE OF ADOLESCENT SUICIDE

In the United States the rate of suicide for adolescents 15–19 years of age has quadrupled from 2.7 per 100,000 in 1950 to 10.8 in 1992.[5] Suicide moved from the fifth leading cause of death among the 15- to 19-year-old age group, to the third leading cause in 1992, claiming the lives of close to 4,000 youth annually.[6]

In a ten-year span between 1982 and 1992, the suicide rates for young persons between 15 and 19 increased by 24.1 percent from 8.7 per 100,000 to 10.8 per 100,000. The most substantial increase was found in young black males where the suicide rate more than doubled from 6.2 to 14.5 per 100,000. The highest rate of incidence is for white males (18.3 per 100,000) and more than five times as many males commit suicide as females.[7] For a more complete breakdown of suicide rates for gender and race, see Table 8.1.

------

3. Gerald L. Klerman, "Suicide, Depression, and Related Problems Among the Baby Boom Cohort," in Cynthia R. Pfeffer, ed., *Suicide Among Youth: Perspectives on Risk and Prevention* (Washington, D.C.: American Psychiatric Press, 1989), 63–81.

4. S. Patrick Kachur, Lloyd B. Potter, Stephen P. James, and Kenneth E. Powell, *Suicide in the United States 1980–1992* (Atlanta, Ga.: Centers for Disease Control and Prevention, 1995), 6.

5. Centers for Disease Control, "Attempted Suicide Among High School Students—United States, 1990," in *Morbidity and Mortality Weekly Report* 40, (1991), 633; S. Patrick Kachur et al., *Suicide in the United States 1980–1992*, 31.

6. Kachur, Potter, James, and Powell, *Suicide in the United States 1980–1992*, 6.

7. National Center for Health Statistics. *Vital Statistics Mortality Data, Underlying Cause of Death, 1982–1992* [machine-readable public-use data tapes], (Hyattsville, Md.: Centers for Disease Control and Prevention, 1993).

8. Compiled with data from National Center for Health Statistics. *Vital Statistics Mortality Data, Underlying Cause of Death, 1982–1992.*

Table 8.1
Suicide Deaths and Rates for Persons
15–19 Years of Age, per 100,000
for the Years 1982 and 1992[8]

	1982		1992		Percent of
	No.	Rate	No.	Rate	increase
All adolescents	1730	8.7	1847	10.8	24.1
Males	1422	14.1	1560	17.8	26.2
Females	308	3.2	287	3.5	9.4
White males	1297	15.5	1289	18.3	18.1
White females	276	3.4	242	3.7	8.8
Black males	91	6.2	198	14.5	133.9
Black females	22	1.5	25	1.9	26.7
Other males	34	12.2	73	17.4	42.6
Other females	10	3.9	20	5.0	28.2

Many nations experienced a rising rate in adolescent suicide in the 1970s and 1980s. This was especially true for Canada where the suicide rate for youth grew to become nearly as high as that of the elderly, normally the age bracket with the highest suicide rate. For example, in 1988 the suicide rate for men aged 74 or older was 30.6 per 100,000, compared to 26.9 per 100,000 for those aged 15–24. Furthermore, the suicide rate for Canadian youth is higher than it is for youth in the United States. By comparison, in 1988 the suicide rate for youths in the United States aged 15–24 was 21.9.[9]

The obvious question arises. Despite the many similarities between youth cultures in the two countries, why is the suicide rate for teenagers in Canada significantly higher than their American counterparts? While research is rather inconclusive, Leenaars and Lester offer two plausible explanations. One hypothesis is that the declining religiosity and religious affiliation among Canadian youth are linked to suicide attempts and ideation. A second suggestion is that Canadian adolescents, especially

9. Antoon A. Leenaars and David Lester, "The Changing Suicide Pattern in Canadian Adolescents and Youth, Compared to Their American Counterparts," in *Adolescence* 30, (Fall 1995), 539–47.

males, tend to see suicide as more acceptable and more normal as a solution to problems than do American youth.[10]

Empirical research on adolescent suicide and suicide thought consistently demonstrates marked differences between males and females. Teenage girls are far more likely to think seriously of suicide, make a plan for suicide, or attempt suicide than their male peers. Yet, as noted above, males are more likely to die from suicide. Why are teenage girls more prone to suicide ideation and attempts, yet males are more successful in actually killing themselves? One possible explanation for this pattern is that females respond hastily to an immediate crisis, and because the efforts are so poorly planned the attempts are less likely to succeed.[11] Another suggestion is that females seem to prefer a more passive approach to attempted suicide such as drug overdose, while males tend to employ more violent and unfailing forms such as shooting or hanging themselves.[12]

SUICIDE IDEATION

Suicide *ideation* refers to fantasizing or thinking about killing oneself. While a relatively few number of adolescents actually commit suicide, a large number of teenagers entertain thoughts of taking their own lives. And a large percentage of teenagers who kill themselves begin by thinking about it, threatening it, or attempting to do it. The suicide ideation of yesterday is highly likely to become the suicide attempt of today or the completed suicide of tomorrow.[13]

The United States Department of Health and Human Services examined the prevalence of suicidal ideation and behaviors of 14- to 16-year-olds through the administration of the *Youth Risk Behavior Survey* (YRBS). The research results revealed that for the 12 months preceding the survey 27.3 percent of all youth had seriously considered suicide.

---

10. Ibid.

11. Barbara Newman and Philip Newman, *Adolescent Development* (Columbus, Ohio: Merrill, 1986), 298.

12. Gerald Adams and Thomas Gullotta, *Adolescent Life Experiences* (Pacific Grove, Calif.: Brooks/Cole, 1989); C. Raymond Bingham et al., "An Analysis of Age, Gender and Racial Differences in Recent National Trends of Youth Suicide," in *Journal of Adolescence* 17, (February 1994), 53–71.

13. Magaly Queralt, "Risk Factors Associated With Completed Suicide in Latino Adolescents," in *Adolescence* 28 (Winter 1993), 832–50.

Fewer adolescents (16.3 percent) indicated that they had made specific plans for taking their own lives and about half of those (8.3 percent of all respondents) actually attempted suicide. However, only 2 percent had injured themselves enough to require medical attention.[14]

Roehlkepartain and Benson discovered that 40 percent of the adolescents surveyed had contemplated suicide at least once during the previous 12 months. Suicide ideation was more prevalent for girls (45 percent) than boys (35 percent), especially 14- and 15-year-old girls (54 percent).[15] The results of a research study on 220 secondary school students by Culp, Clyman, and Culp indicated that 33 percent of the respondents had thoughts of suicide.[16]

The Warning Signs of Suicide Ideation

The task of any adult who does religious education with youth is to learn to recognize the warning signs of suicide or suicide ideation. Among the signs that an adolescent might be contemplating taking his or her own life are the following:[17]

• A depressed mood.
• Changes in sleep patterns.
• Changes in appetite patterns.
• A decline in school performance.
• Increased withdrawal.
• A loss of interest and pleasure in previously enjoyable activities.
• Changes in appearance (for example, no longer caring about one's clothing or hair).
• A preoccupation with themes of death (for example, the youth may begin to read books with themes of death and dying).
• An increased irritability and behavior problems.
• Giving away important possessions.
• The abuse of drugs and alcohol.

---

14. Centers for Disease Control, "Attempted Suicide Among High School Students," 633.

15. Eugene C. Roehlkepartain and Peter L. Benson, *Youth In Protestant Churches* (Minneapolis, Minn.: Search Institute, 1993), 104–5.

16. Anne M. Culp, Mary M. Clyman, and Rex E. Culp, "Adolescent Depressed Mood, Reports of Suicide Attempts, and Asking For Help," in *Adolescence* 30, (Winter 1995), 827–37.

17. Adapted from Demetri Papolos and Janice Papolos, *Overcoming Depression* (New York: Harper & Row, 1987), 126.

• A history of previous attempts.
• A history of abuse and neglect.
• A history of learning disabilities and a sense of failure.
• Frequent somatic complaints.
• Verbal expression about self-death (for instance, a teenager who actually says, "I wish I were dead").
• No longer concerned about making plans for the future.

Intervention and Referral

Should a youth religious educator suspect an adolescent is contemplating suicide or an adolescent threatens suicide, the matter should be dealt with immediately. The following actions should be taken.

Assess the Situation: The first step is to discuss the issue of suicide with the teenager and assess the seriousness of the ideation or the lethality of the threat. Often people avoid introducing the subject of suicide because they fear it will plant ideas in the mind of an already fragile or troubled youth. On the contrary, asking a teenager about self destructive ideas can help him or her feel better understood and less trapped.[18] Does the individual have a plan? How lethal is the chosen method? How available is the method?

Contact the Parents or Legal Guardians: The next step is to notify parents of the imminent danger of suicide. Although this contact breaks confidentiality between the youth worker and the teenager, it is a legally and ethically appropriate response to an adolescent's suicide threat or contemplation.[19]

Develop a Written Contract: Many experts have found that developing a contract with the suicidal youth is helpful in deterring a potential suicide. The contract establishes an agreement that the teenager will call and talk to the youth worker before attempting to take his or her life. Most youth will comply with a contract because it ties the troubled individual with a person who really cares.[20]

Refer to a Professional Counselor: When it becomes clear that an adolescent is at risk of suicide, it imperative that he or she is referred to a psychologist or psychiatrist for clinical and legal reasons. The

---

18. Ibid., 26–27.
19. J. Jeffries McWhirter et al., *At-Risk Youth: A Comprehensive Response* (Pacific Grove, Calif.: Brooks/Cole, 1993), 202.
20. Rich Van Pelt, *Intensive Care: Helping Teenagers in Crisis* (Grand Rapids, Mich.: Zondervan, 1988), 131.

professional counselor can then assess the risk of suicide and decide whether hospitalization is necessary, what kind of psychotherapy will be suitable, and whether or not medication is needed.

Maintain Contact With the Suicidal Teenager: Once referral is made to a psychologist or psychiatrist, it is important for the youth religious educator to continue a warm, supportive, and caring relationship with the teenager. Continued supportive contact with the teenager is important so that the individual does not feel abandoned by the youth worker or that the referral was made out of disinterest. A phone call, a brief visit to the youth's home, and/or a meeting over lunch are ways to maintain meaningful contact.

RISK FACTORS RELATED TO
SUICIDE AND SUICIDE IDEATION

Why are teenagers terminating their lives at such an alarming rate? Why do so many adolescents view life and living as so hopeless that suicide appears to be the only realistic alternative? Suicide is a complex subject steeped in myth, erroneous thinking, and misunderstandings. Unless a suicidal adolescent leaves a note of explanation or clearly communicates his or her intention in some other manner, the full circumstances behind the death are not easily understood.

No single cause can adequately explain the dramatic increase in adolescent suicide. It is an understatement to say that the source of the problem is complex as human behavior and contemporary society themselves are. Experts identify five major factors as influencing suicide attempts among adolescents:[21]

• Family problems: including broken families, severe marital conflict, lack of closeness and understanding between fathers and sons, and families where the mother is cold, punitive, and detached.

• Personal loss: including the loss of a loved one or the loss of an important person's love.

• Social isolation: especially feeling alienated from family and peers, being socially withdrawn and self-conscious, and having few or no meaningful relationships.

• Depression: including feelings of worthlessness.

• Substance: the use and abuse of drugs and alcohol.

---

21. Modified from Newman and Newman, *Adolescent Development,* 298.

Dysfunctional Family Life

One of the key factors related to adolescent suicidal behavior is the family and the familial context in which suicide occurs. Suicidal adolescents often come from dysfunctional or disintegrated families where violence, abuse, conflict, and arguments are the norm. The breakup of the traditional family through divorce and separation, the rise of single-parent households, and the lack of skills in parenting, discipline, and communication all combine to augment the risk of teenage suicide.

Shaffi and colleagues found that 55 percent of adolescents who committed suicide experienced physical and emotional abusiveness in the home, compared to 29 percent of a controlled group of nonsuicidal peers.[22] In a Los Angeles Suicide Prevention Center sample of adolescents who committed suicide, nearly two-thirds of them had reported that they were not on good terms with their parents, while 90 percent felt their family did not understand them. Many of the suicidal youth reported physical fights with family members as well as physical and assaultive behavior among family members.[23] According to a Gallup survey on teenage suicide, of those adolescents who attempted suicide or came close to killing themselves, almost one-half (47 percent) cited family problems or problems at home as a factor.[24] A study of Latino adolescents who committed suicide revealed that most did not get along with their parents or were not living with both biological parents. The victims had experienced significantly more family stressors than the non-suicidal teenagers in the control group.[25]

Working with adolescents whose suicide attempts or ideation find their roots at least partially in the family context may be difficult because the situation is often unchangeable or complex. However, the threat of adolescent suicide that comes as a result of family dysfunction and breakups can be reduced through religious education with parents.

---

22. Mohammed Shaffi, "Completed Suicide in Children and Adolescents: Methods of Psychological Autopsy," in Cynthia R. Pfeffer, ed., *Suicide Among Youth: Perspectives on Risk and Prevention* (Washington, D.C.: American Psychiatric Press, 1989), 1–19.

23. Michael Peck, "Suicide in Late Adolescence and Young Adulthood," in Corrine Hatton and Sharon Valente, editors, *Suicide: Assessment and Intervention* (Norwalk, Connecticut: Appleton-Century-Crofts, 1984), 222.

24. *The Gallup Survey on Teenage Suicide* (Princeton, N.J.: The George H. Gallup Institute, 1991), 72.

25. Queralt, "Risk Factors Associated With Completed Suicide in Latino Adolescents," 832–50.

Merton Strommen argues that we can assume that a critical factor in preventing adolescent suicide is helping youth to become affiliated with a caring congregation and helping the parents strengthen their marriages through seminars, counseling, and retreats.[26]

Religious education programs might include marriage-enrichment seminars or Sunday school classes that address issues such as marital conflict and communication skills. James White urges religious educators to take advantage of the variety of audiovisual resources available for instruction and discussion starters in religious education settings.[27] Gary Smalley's highly popular video series *Hidden Keys For a Loving Relationship* is one example of a media resource that a number of churches have found helpful in strengthening marriages and making families stronger.

Jon Harris commends support groups for individuals who are experiencing some degree of family conflict in their lives. The opportunities to see that one is not alone in a particular struggle, to realize the hope presented by those who are more advanced in the healing process, and to be heard and understood by someone else for perhaps the first time are therapeutic and encouraging for many battered, stressed, and hurting people. However, Harris also strongly recommends that religious educators who are going to lead a support group be trained in three areas: small-group dynamics, dysfunctional families, and codependency.[28]

Loss of a Loved One

Another theme related to adolescent suicide or suicide attempts is the loss of a significant person. This may be the dissolution of a love relationship, the death of a parent or sibling, the loss of a parent through divorce or separation, or rejection by one or both parents.

In their study of adolescents, Morano, Cisler, and Lemerond found the experience of the loss of a loved one to be a strong predictor of suicide attempts. Fifty percent of adolescent suicide attempters reported losing a

---

26. Merton Strommen, *Five Cries of Youth,* 2nd. rev. ed. (San Francisco: Harper & Row,1988), 59.

27. James W. White, "Family Ministry Methods," in Blake J. Neff and Donald Ratcliff, eds., *Handbook of Family Religious Education* (Birmingham, Ala.: Religious Education Press, 1995), 207–26.

28. Jon Harris, "Dysfunction, Healing and the Family of Origin," in Blake J. Neff and Donald Ratcliff, eds., *Handbook of Family Religious Education* (Birmingham, Ala.: Religious Education Press, 1995), 202–6.

significant other as compared to only 5 percent of nonattempters.[29] Lucy Davidson and colleagues discovered that a powerful stressor preceding suicide was the loss of a girlfriend or boyfriend, or the fear that a relationship would end.[30] In the aforementioned study of Latino adolescents, 50 percent of the victims had divorced or separated parents, compared to 25 percent of those in the nonsuicidal control group.[31] Francine Klagsbrun suggests that in the case of a parental loss through suicide, children sometimes kill themselves so that they might be reunited with the parent who so abruptly abandoned them.[32]

When an adolescent experiences the loss of a loved one through death, divorce, rejection, or separation, the youth religious educator can reduce the possibility of an attempted suicide by sharing in the individual's grief work. This can be accomplished in at least three ways.

First, encourage the release of emotions, thoughts, and feelings, both positive and negative. Do not be shocked by the intense rage or anguish that is often emitted from the mouth of a grieving adolescent.

Second, provide empathic understanding through expressions of understanding, caring, and support. At these critical junctures in life, adolescents do not need judgment, correction, or even advice. What they do need is a caring person to listen to them. Compassionate listening and attentive caring are the most effective healing activities youth religious educators can provide for a teenager who is experiencing the loss of a significant person.

Third, encourage the adolescent to talk about the loss of the significant person. To talk about the father who has abandoned the family, the sibling who has committed suicide, the boyfriend who has terminated a relationship, or the close friend who was killed in a car accident helps the individual to confront the reality of the devastating experience.[33]

---

29. Christopher D. Morano, Ron A. Cisler, and John Lemerond, "Risk Factors for Adolescent Suicidal Behavior: Loss, Insufficient Familial Support, and Hopelessness," *Adolescence* 28, (Winter 1993), 851–65.

30. Lucy E. Davidson et al., "An Epidemiologic Study of Risk Factors In Two Teenage Suicide Clusters," *Journal of American Medical Association* 262, (November, 1989), 2687–92.

31. Queralt, "Risk Factors Associated With Completed Suicide in Latino Adolescents," 832–50.

32. Klagsbrun, *Too Young To Die,* 107.

33. Adapted from G. Keith Olson, *Counseling Teenagers* (Loveland, Colo.: Group, 1984), 496–500.

Social Isolation and Loneliness

The landmark study of suicide was done at the end of the nineteenth century by French sociologist Émile Durkheim.[34] Durkheim studied the relationship between society and suicide and concluded that there are three types of suicide that grow out of social conditions. When an individual chooses a group identity and values over individual needs, an individual may be willing to sacrifice his or her life for the community and commit an *altruistic* suicide. Examples of altruistic suicides are the Jews at Masada and the Japanese kamikaze pilots of World War II.

There is also the *anomic* suicide. In this case the individual commits suicide because he or she has experienced great societal and personal upheaval in life and is incapable of adjusting to this radical social change. The breakup of the traditional family, changing patterns of family life, economic instability, shifting values, and social problems such as substance abuse, AIDS, poverty, and environmental abuse have all contributed to make contemporary living confusing and stressful.

Most suicides, however, are *egoistic*. Egotistic suicide occurs when an individual has trouble integrating into society and feels lonely and alienated, disengaged from other people.

One of the developmental tasks of adolescence, according to Robert Havighurst, is the achieving of new and more mature relationships with peers of both sexes.[35] Guerney and Arthur suggest that the peer group and relationships that peers offer provide support and emotional security to adolescents who are uncertain of themselves and their position in the grand scheme of life.[36]

For some adolescents, however, the development of friendships and peer relationships is difficult. The social lives of many teenagers are characterized by interpersonal conflict, social isolation, withdrawal, alienation, and loneliness. For example, Peter Benson and colleagues found that 15 percent of the pre- and young adolescents in their study experienced social alienation or estrangement from others.[37] Bibby and

---

34. Émile Durkheim, *A Study in Sociology,* (New York: Free Press, 1951/1897).

35. Robert J. Havighurst, *Developmental Tasks and Education* (New York: Longmans & Green, 1952).

36. Louise Guerney and Joyce Arthur, "Adolescent Social Relationships," in Richard Lerner and Nancy Galambos, eds., *Experiencing Adolescents* (New York: Garland, 1984), 87.

37. Peter Benson, Dorothy Williams, and Arthur Johnson, *The Quicksilver Years* (San Francisco: Harper & Row, 1987), 42.

Posterski discovered that 35 percent of Canadian youth were deeply troubled by severe loneliness.[38] Results of a study of adolescent students in two midwestern schools indicated 66 percent of the youth experienced loneliness. Of sixteen possible survey items, respondents most often identified loneliness as a significant problem in their lives.[39]

It was noted earlier that, according to Émile Durkheim, lonely and antisocial people may be more susceptible to suicide and suicide ideation. His theory was posited a century ago but is still valid today. Shaffi discovered that 65 percent of the suicide victims in his empirical study displayed an *inhibited personality,* further characterized as not sharing problems with others, not having close friends, very quiet, lonely, keeping things inside, and very sensitive. In contrast, only 24 percent of the non-suicidal teenagers in the control group were identified as having an inhibited personality.[40] Benson and associates found that pre- and young adolescents who experienced social alienation were prone to thoughts of suicide.[41] Similarly, 46 percent of the Latino victims of suicide studied by Magaly Queralt were described as inhibited, uncommunicative, excessively sensitive, or withdrawn.[42]

The link between recurrent loneliness and suicide or suicide ideation is a well-documented fact. Youth religious educators are in an ideal position to positively impact the lives of lonely and alienated teenagers who might be experiencing thoughts of suicide. Several suggestions for youth religious education with lonely adolescents are summarized as follows:[43]

• Make special efforts to identify, give special attention to, and spend time with lonely adolescents. For example, give them a phone call, drop them a note, take them out for lunch, or simply talk to them during a youth activity.

---

38. Reginald W. Bibby and Donald C. Posterski, *The Emerging Generation* (Toronto: Irwin, 1985), 60.

39. Anne M. Culp, Mary M. Clyman, and Rex E. Culp, "Adolescent Depressed Mood, Reports of Suicide Attempts, and Asking for Help," in *Adolescence* 30, (Winter 1995), 827–37.

40. Mohammed Shaffi, "Completed Suicide in Children and Adolescents: Methods of Psychological Autopsy," 1–19.

41. Peter Benson et al., *The Quicksilver Years,* 42–43.

42. Queralt, "Risk Factors Associated With Completed Suicide in Latino Adolescents," 832–50.

43. Specific methods and techniques for carrying out these strategies are described in a special section on loneliness in Chapter 4.

• Foster a sense of inclusiveness and acceptance in the youth group. Include recreational activities in the youth program that are cooperative and noncompetitive in nature. For example, the challenge, difficulty, and hardship of outdoor adventure and wilderness activities such as backpacking or canoeing tend to build camaraderie and teamwork within groups of adolescents.

• Equip teenagers with social skills and capacities for building friendships, nurturing relationships, and communicating with others. Skills that will help the withdrawn adolescent in relating better to others include listening and attending, conversation, and self-disclosure.

• Finally, help lonely youth foster or establish a meaningful relationship with God. Often loneliness is spiritual in nature and comes to individuals who are living their lives in separation from the One who created them.

Depression

The most common denominator and hallmark sign of suicide risk for adolescents is depression. Gerald Klerman, a psychiatrist and expert on suicide, reports that there is a complex relationship between depression and suicide. Many depressed patients are suicidal and, conversely, most, but not all, suicidal individuals manifest depressive moods, symptoms, or illnesses.[44] He adds that with the alarming increase in youth suicide, there has been a parallel rise in rates of depression.[45] These findings are given further emphasis by Wade Rowatt, who argues that depression is without a doubt the greatest single factor in pushing a teenager toward self-destruction.[46]

These conclusions are substantiated by research. For example, in an empirical study of 16- to 24-year-olds, Goldberg discovered that the majority of those who reported suicide ideation also reported high levels of depression.[47] Likewise, Michael Peck found the most common diagnostic category in his sample of adolescents who committed suicide

---

44. Gerald Klerman, "Suicide, Depression, and Related Problems Among the Baby Boom Cohort," in Cynthia Pfeffer, ed., *Suicide Among Youth: Perspectives on Risk and Prevention* (Washington, D.C.: American Psychiatric Press, 1989), 63.

45. Ibid.

46. G. Wade Rowatt, *Pastoral Care With Adolescents in Crisis* (Louisville: Westminster/John Knox Press, 1989), 119–20.

47. E. Goldberg, "Depression and Suicide Ideation in the Young Adult," in *American Journal of Psychiatry* 138, (1981), 35–40.

to be depression.[48] Finally, Hoberman and Garfinkle studied suicide victims 25 years and under over a 10-year period. They found 30 percent of the victims to be suffering from depression at the time of the deaths.[49]

What is depression? Why might teenagers be so susceptible to this emotional state? Depression is a state of prolonged melancholia (sadness or unhappiness), arising either for no apparent reason or as an extreme reaction to a trigger event. [50] Most people, including adolescents, experience mild depression in one form or another; nearly everyone has been "down in the dumps" or feels the "blues" at some time. However, more severe forms of depression, what medical experts call clinical depression, are characterized as mood disorders and can be so devastating that the ability to function in a normal manner is impaired. Usually clinical depression is related to a biochemical imbalance and is best treated under a physician's care by the administration of antidepressant medication.

Depressions occur in various types, the two most familiar forms being endogenous and reactive. *Endogenous* depression, sometimes called psychotic depression, arises from within an individual, sometimes for no reason apparent to the sufferer. For example, there is thought to be an inherited tendency toward neurotic types of depression.[51] Endogenous depression can also be brought about in females by the hormonal changes that occur during premenstruation or the early postnatal period.[52]

Reactive depression occurs as a response to events or circumstances in the individual's life. For example, loss of a loved one is a trigger event that sometimes leads to depression exceeding normal mourning in degree or duration.[53] This is the type of depression most often experienced by adolescents, and the usual treatment includes therapeutic counseling. Depression of any type should be distinguished from discouragement, which is a mild, temporary, and normal mood swing that comes in response to failures, losses, or disappointments of life.

---

48. Peck, "Suicide in Late Adolescence and Young Adulthood," 223.
49. Harry M. Hoberman and Barry D. Garfinkle, "Completed Suicide in Youth," in Cynthia R. Pfeffer, ed., *Suicide Among Youth: Perspectives on Risk and Prevention,* (Washington, D.C.: American Psychiatric Press, 1989), 21–40.
50. Caroline M. Shreeve, *Depression* (Wellingborough, Eng.: Thorsons, 1984), 23.
51. Ian H. Gotlib and Catherine A. Colby, *Treatment of Depression* (New York: Pergamon, 1987), 81; Shreeve, *Depression,* 25–28.
52. Shreeve, *Depression,* 25–28.
53. Ibid., 24.

The signs of depression often include the following:[54]
- Feelings of sadness, pessimism, despair, and hopelessness.
- Apathy or lack of interest in things that normally bring interest.
- Loss of energy and fatigue.
- Negative self-esteem.
- Feelings of worthlessness, guilt, and shame.
- Inability to experience pleasure.
- Decreased ability to think or concentrate.
- Sleep disturbance (insomnia, lack of sleep, or too much sleep).
- Withdrawal or spending large amounts of time alone.
- Eating disturbance (loss of appetite or preoccupation with eating).
- Stomach and intestinal disorders (indigestion, constipation, or diarrhea).
- Tension, muscle aches, and headaches.

Depression is a common occurrence among teenagers and is especially prominent in late adolescence. It is generally accepted that girls experience depression two to three times as often as boys.[55] Culp, Clyman, and Culp found that over half (54 percent) of the adolescents in their empirical study had experienced depression in the past year.[56] Roehlkepartain and Benson discovered 40 percent of the adolescents in their study had felt depressed 20 or more times in the previous year.[57] Four developmental factors help explain why teenagers are susceptible to depression.

First, adolescence is a time of life when extreme biological changes occur. The physical changes that take place during puberty are second only to those which occur in infancy. Puberty is popularly thought to be the root of much of the emotional turmoil and moodiness that teenagers experience, although not all young adolescents manifest these difficulties.[58]

---

54. Shreeve, *Depression*, 25–28; Gotlib and Colby, *Treatment of Depression*, 2–4.

55. Anne C. Petersen and W. Edward Craighead, "Emotional and Personality Development in Normal Adolescents and Young Adults," in Gerald Klerman, ed., *Suicide and Depression Among Adolescents and Young Adults* (Washington, D.C.: American Psychiatric Press, 1985), 17–52.

56. Culp, Clyman, and Culp, "Adolescent Depressed Mood, Reports of Suicide Attempts, and Asking For Help," 827–37.

57. Roehlkepartain and Benson, *Youth In Protestant Churches*, 104.

58. Petersen and Craighead, "Emotional and Personality Development in Normal Adolescents and Young Adults," 17–52.

Second, burgeoning cognitive skills facilitate the ability to think about concepts concerning the self and one's identity.[59] For adolescents introspection becomes intensified and they often view themselves supercritically. They may be prone to feel inadequate, deficient, unworthy, or incapable of performing tasks effectively. In some cases parents can intensify negative self-perceptions by placing unrealistic expectations on their teenage children or by demanding perfection in performance areas such as sports, music, and academics.

Third, physiological and hormonal changes dramatically increase the adolescent's awareness of sexuality. Experimentation with masturbation, homosexuality, sex play, and intercourse can create feelings of guilt that in turn may intensify depression.

Finally, adolescence is a stage of the life cycle where the individuation process is intensified. That is, the youth cuts parental ties and becomes a unique, separate individual with his or her own values, personality, interests, and identity. The subconscious may respond to the break with parents as a loss. Coincidentally, to develop a healthy concept of self, the need for acceptance from peers increases with age. Yet many teenagers experience rejection by their age mates and have difficulties nurturing meaningful peer relationships.[60]

It is important for the youth religious educator to remember that discouragement or even temporary depression is a normal part of the adolescent experience. However, for those teenagers who experience severe depression, when the suffering interferes with the ability to cope with normal living, and when the possibility of suicide or suicide attempt becomes a reality, intervention is required.

First, the above information can assist the religious educator in assessing the possibility of depression in the life of a teenager. If the youth worker suspects an adolescent is depressive, referral should be made to a competent psychologist or psychiatrist, especially if the depression appears to be severe enough to warrant medication.

Second, the religious educator must provide a community in which the depressed teenager can find refuge. Experts agree that if teenagers have a family member or reliable friend they can turn to when they feel

---

59. Ibid.

60. Louise Guerney and Joyce Arthur, "Adolescent Social Relationships," in Richard M. Lerner and Nancy L. Galambos, eds., *Experiencing Adolescents* (New York: Garland, 1984), 87–118.

depressed or hopeless, then they are most unlikely to attempt suicide. On the other hand, those without such a relationship are at a much increased risk.[61]

Finally, it is of supreme importance to keep depressed youth from harming themselves. Since depressed people often contemplate killing themselves, the issue of suicide should be addressed directly. The adult youth worker should not hesitate to ask probing question such as "Do you have any thoughts of harming yourself?" or "Have you ever tried to commit suicide?" However, while suicide is the most drastic form of self harm, young people can harm themselves in other ways as well. Quitting school or a job, leaving home, severing relationships, or quitting the church are ways that depressed teenagers can cause hurt to themselves. There is a tendency to make unwise decisions while in depressed states; therefore, the youth religious educator must help the teenagers see the possible consequences of unwise decisions, and encourage them to delay making important decisions to a later time.

Substance Abuse

Experts also identify a close connection between substance abuse and adolescent suicide. It is unknown, however, whether alcohol or drug abuse is a cause of suicide or whether the same factors that lead to suicide also lead to the abuse of drugs and alcohol.

In the Suicide Prevention Center sample of adolescents who had committed suicide, Michael Peck found that 40 to 50 percent of the suicide victims were abusing alcohol or drugs at the time of their death.[62] Hoberman and Garfinkle found the majority of adolescent suicide victims in their empirical study abused both drugs and alcohol.[63] The suicide rate for alcoholics is almost 60 times higher than that of the normal population, and one out of three suicides of the population as a whole is in some way related to alcohol.[64]

What is the connection between substance abuse and suicide? Klagsbrun suggests that severe drinking or drug use may alienate the teenager from family and friends, and this alienation in turn brings on isolation

---

61. Ibid., 200.
62. Peck, "Suicide in Late Adolescence and Young Adulthood," 222.
63. Hoberman and Garfinkle, "Completed Suicide in Youth," 34.
64. Klagsbrun, *Too Young To Die,* 69.

and depression. Overwhelmed by depression, suicide is often the only apparent solution to the troubled teenager.[65]

Adolescents who consume drugs can become suicidal during crash periods or coming-down time, when extreme depression can occur. Youth who take hallucinogens may also become suicidal because they lose touch with reality, imagining themselves all-powerful and immune from any form of danger.[66]

CLUSTER SUICIDES

Recently, experts have focused their attention on a phenomenon they identify as *cluster* suicides. Cluster suicides are defined as three or more suicides that are grouped together in a particular place or geographical area (such as a community or school district) and occur within a relatively short span of time.[67] They are suicides that follow or imitate another. For example, Lucy Davidson and associates investigated two clusters of teenage suicides in Texas between February 1983 and October 1984. Eight of these adolescents' suicides made up the first cluster, while six constituted the second. Both clusters included teenagers who were close personal friends and victims who only knew of the other decedents through the media or by word of mouth.[68] Gould, Wallenstein, and Kleinman estimate that 1 to 2 percent of all teenage suicides occur within a time or space cluster.[69]

While cluster suicides have been known to occur for a number of years, experts do not entirely understand why this imitation pattern sometimes takes place. One possible explanation is the *contagion* theory. Contagion is the notion that suicide may spread among teenagers who are "exposed" to suicide in some manner, either directly (the adolescent actually knew the decedent) or indirectly (the person who committed

---

65. Ibid.

66. Ibid.

67. Mark L. Rosenberg et al.,"Developing Strategies to Prevent Youth Suicide," in Cynthia R. Pfeffer, ed., *Suicide Among Youth: Risk and Prevention* (Washington, D.C.: American Psychiatric Press, 1989), 203–26.

68. Davidson et al., "An Epidemiologic Study of Risk Factors in Two Teenage Suicide Clusters," 2688.

69. Madelyn S. Gould, Sylvan Wallenstein, and Marjorie Kleinman, "Time-space Clustering of Teenage Suicide," in *American Journal of Epidemiology* 131, (1990), 71–78.

suicide was known to the teenager only through news accounts or by word of mouth).[70] Either type of exposure may lead a troubled and susceptible teenager to commit suicide, perhaps imitating or copying the initial suicide by employing a similar method and setting.[71] There is much evidence which suggests that the indirect exposure to suicide through printed media, television news stories, and movies about suicide might lead some vulnerable adolescents to commit suicide.[72]

It is also hypothesized that youth have psychological characteristics consistent with greater susceptibility to imitative suicide. Among these imitative factors might be the false glorification or idealized romanticization associated with suicidal behavior. Mass gatherings, such as memorial assemblies, may nurture the perception that suicide is a powerful act claiming the special attention of one's peers and the public.[73]

Hochkirchen and Jilek eloquently describe the way a community reaction to a teenage suicide can trigger further imitative suicides: "The latest suicide victim may be talked of as a martyred hero. Posthumously he gets attention as never during his lifetime. His entire life is glorified and his 'good old days' are emphasized rather than his more recent, possibly antisocial, behavior. Suicide is seen as the crowning event of his life. His funeral is a big social occasion and the time between death and funeral is filled with memorial services and commemorative gatherings. The attention of the whole community is focused on this particular suicide and on suicide in general, thus making suicidal acts interesting and attractive for predisposed young people."[74]

The incidence of cluster or imitation suicides suggests that one teenager's suicide is a powerful model that influences other youth to also

---

70. Rosenberg et al., "Developing Strategies to Prevent Youth Suicide," 220; Davidson et al., "An Epidemiologic Study of Risk Factors in Two Teenage Suicide Clusters," 2687.

71. Rosenberg et al., "Developing Strategies to Prevent Youth Suicide," 203–25.

72. Davidson et al., "An Epidemiologic Study of Risk Factors in Two Teenage Suicide Clusters," 2687–92; Rosenberg et al., "Developing Strategies to Prevent Youth Suicide," 203–26; David P. Phillips, Lundie L. Carstensen, and Daniel J. Paight, "Effects of Mass Media News Stories on Suicide, With New Evidence on the Role of Story Content," in Cynthia R. Pfeffer, ed., *Suicide Among Youth: Perspectives on Risk and Prevention* (Washington, D.C.: American Psychiatric Press, 1989), 101–16.

73. Davidson et al., "An Epidemiologic Study of Risk Factors in Two Teenage Suicide Clusters," 2691–92.

74. Lucy E. Davidson, "Suicide Clusters and Youth," in Cynthia Pfeffer, ed., *Suicide Among Youth: Perspectives on Risk and Prevention* (Washington, D.C.: American Psychiatric Press, 1989), 83–100.

take their lives.[75] Thus follow-up intervention to a successful suicide is essential. Efforts should be made to deromanticize any suicide. In appropriate cases it might be helpful to acknowledge that the deceased was someone who had serious problems that distinguished him or her from most teenagers. For example, if a teenager struggled with substance abuse or mental illness, it would be important to stress the fact that the problem was related to the death. Furthermore, it should be emphasized that the suicide was an undesirable response and there were, in fact, far better solutions available.[76]

Adult youth workers (both volunteers and paid staff) should be aware of the types of youth who are likely to be at high risk for suicide in a cluster. High-risk adolescents include those in the same social network as the decedent, those who have a history of suicide attempts, and those who are mentally unstable.[77] Once identified, high-risk teenagers should be interviewed by the youth religious educator. If the interviewer senses the youth is a suicidal risk, he or she should be referred to a professional counselor.

CONCLUSION

Suicide behavior can have a devastating effect on the lives of teenagers as well as the lives of those people around them. Thus, it is essential that youth religious educators provide preventive intervention in the early stages of suicide ideation. Since adult youth workers play significant roles in the lives of many adolescents, they must be especially aware of and responsive to the numerous signs of suicide and the steps to take in helping a suicidal youth through the crisis.

---

75. McWhirter et. al., *At-Risk Youth,* 190.
76. Rosenberg et al., "Developing Strategies to Prevent Youth Suicide," 203–25.
77. Davidson, "Suicide Clusters and Youth," 83–100.

Index of Names

Index of Subjects

Printed in the United States
73528LV00005B/79-84